Learning jQuery 3

Fifth Edition

Build interesting, interactive sites using jQuery by automating common tasks and simplifying the complicated ones

Adam Boduch
Jonathan Chaffer
Karl Swedberg

BIRMINGHAM - MUMBAI

Learning jQuery 3

Fifth Edition

First published : July 2007

Second edition: Feburary 2009

Third edition: September 2011

Fourth edition: June 2013

Fifth edition: May 2017

Production reference: 1240517

Published by Packt Publishing Ltd.
Livery Place
35 Livery Street
Birmingham
B3 2PB, UK.
ISBN 978-1-78588-298-2

www.packtpub.com

Credits

Authors
Adam Boduch
Jonathan Chaffer
Karl Swedberg

Reviewer
Andrew Kurz

Commissioning Editor
Amarabha Banerjee

Acquisition Editor
Smeet Thakkar

Content Development Editor
Onkar Wani

Technical Editor
Rashil Shah

Copy Editor
Charlotte Carneiro

Project Coordinator
Devanshi Doshi

Proofreader
Safis Editing

Indexer
Tejal Daruwale Soni

Graphics
Jason Monteiro

Production Coordinator
Nilesh Mohite

About the Authors

Adam Boduch has been involved with large-scale JavaScript development for nearly 10 years. Before moving to the frontend, he worked on several large-scale cloud computing products, using Python and Linux. No stranger to complexity, Adam has practical experience with real-world software systems, and the scaling challenges they pose.

He is the author of several JavaScript books, including React and React Native, and is passionate about innovative user experiences and high performance.

I'd like to thank John Resig for creating jQuery, and I'd like to thank the collective jQuery community for making such a positive impact on web development.

Jonathan Chaffer is a member of Rapid Development Group, a web development firm located in Grand Rapids, Michigan. His work there includes overseeing and implementing projects in a wide variety of technologies, with an emphasis on PHP, MySQL, and JavaScript. In the open source community, he has been very active in the Drupal CMS project, which has adopted jQuery as its JavaScript framework of choice. He is the creator of the Content Construction Kit, now a part of the Drupal core used for managing structured content. He is also responsible for major overhauls of Drupal's menu system and developer API reference. In his spare time, he designs board and card games for the hobby market. He lives in Grand Rapids with his wife, Jennifer.

Karl Swedberg is a web developer at Fusionary Media in Grand Rapids, Michigan, where he spends much of his time writing both client-side and server-side JavaScript. When he isn't coding, he likes to hang out with his family, roast coffee in his garage, and exercise at the local gym.

About the Reviewer

Andrew Kurz is a UI/UX designer and developer with over 12 years of experience designing and building websites and online applications. He has worked for small start-ups, large corporations, and everything in between. He enjoys learning new technology and appreciates attractive, easy-to-use applications. He lives in Atlanta, GA, with his wife and three children. You can view his portfolio and contact him at www.kurzstudio.com.

www.PacktPub.com

For support files and downloads related to your book, please visit www.PacktPub.com.

Did you know that Packt offers eBook versions of every book published, with PDF and ePub files available? You can upgrade to the eBook version at www.PacktPub.comand as a print book customer, you are entitled to a discount on the eBook copy. Get in touch with us at service@packtpub.com for more details.

At www.PacktPub.com, you can also read a collection of free technical articles, sign up for a range of free newsletters and receive exclusive discounts and offers on Packt books and eBooks.

https://www.packtpub.com/mapt

Get the most in-demand software skills with Mapt. Mapt gives you full access to all Packt books and video courses, as well as industry-leading tools to help you plan your personal development and advance your career.

Why subscribe?

- Fully searchable across every book published by Packt
- Copy and paste, print, and bookmark content
- On demand and accessible via a web browser

Customer Feedback

Thanks for purchasing this Packt book. At Packt, quality is at the heart of our editorial process. To help us improve, please leave us an honest review on this book's Amazon page at https://www.amazon.com/dp/1785882988.

If you'd like to join our team of regular reviewers, you can e-mail us at customerreviews@packtpub.com. We award our regular reviewers with free eBooks and videos in exchange for their valuable feedback. Help us be relentless in improving our products!

For Melissa, Jason, Simon, and Kevin. Thanks for all the love and support.

Table of Contents

Preface

I started using jQuery in 2007, and I'm still using it today. Granted, a lot has happened between now and then: new JavaScript libraries, more consistency across browsers, and enhancements to JavaScript itself. The one thing that hasn't changed in 10 years is the expressiveness and conciseness of jQuery. Even with all the new hotness out there today, jQuery remains the go-to tool of choice for getting work done quickly, and efficiently.

This book has a long history behind it, and it remains intact in its fifth edition. It has been a successful book because it is straight to the point and easy to follow. I've done my best to preserve what has worked so well for this book. My goal is to modernize learning jQuery for the current web-development landscape.

What this book covers

Chapter 1, *Getting Started*, gets your feet wet with the jQuery JavaScript library. The chapter begins with a description of jQuery and what it can do for you. It then walks you through downloading and setting up the library as well as writing your first script.

Chapter 2, *Selecting Elements*, teaches you how to use jQuery's selector expressions and DOM-traversal methods to find elements on the page, wherever they may be. You'll use jQuery to apply styling to a diverse set of page elements, sometimes in a way that pure CSS cannot.

Chapter 3, *Handling Events*, walks you through jQuery's event-handling mechanism to fire off behaviors when browser events occur. You'll see how jQuery makes it easy to attach events to elements unobtrusively, even before the page finishes loading. Also, you'll get an overview of deeper topics, such as event bubbling, delegation, and namespacing.

Chapter 4, *Styling and Animating*, introduces you to jQuery's animation techniques and how to hide, show, and move page elements with effects that are both useful and pleasing to the eye.

Chapter 5, *Manipulating the DOM*, teaches you how to change your page on command. This chapter will also teach you how to alter the very structure of an HTML document as well as adding to its content on the fly.

Chapter 6, *Sending Data with Ajax*, walks you through many ways in which jQuery makes it easy to access server-side functionality without resorting to clunky page refreshes. With the basic components of the library well in hand, you will be ready to explore how the library can expand to fit your needs.

Chapter 7, *Using Plugins*, shows you how to find, install, and use plugins, including the powerful jQuery UI and jQuery Mobile plugin libraries.

Chapter 8, *Developing Plugins*, teaches you how to take advantage of jQuery's impressive extension capabilities to develop your own plugins from the ground up. You'll create your own utility functions, add jQuery object methods, and discover the jQuery UI widget factory. Next, you'll take a second tour through jQuery's building blocks, learning more advanced techniques.

Chapter 9, *Advanced Selectors and Traversing*, refines your knowledge of selectors and traversals, gaining the ability to optimize selectors for performance, manipulating the DOM element stack, and writing plugins that expand selecting and traversing capabilities.

Chapter 10, *Advanced Events*, dives further into techniques such as delegation and throttling that can greatly improve event-handling performance. You'll also create custom and special events that add even more capabilities to the jQuery library.

Chapter 11, *Advanced Effects*, shows you how to fine-tune the visual effects of jQuery that can be provided by crafting custom-easing functions and reacting to each step of an animation. You'll gain the ability to manipulate animations as they occur and schedule actions with custom queuing.

Chapter 12, *Advanced DOM Manipulation*, provides you with more practice modifying the DOM with techniques such as attaching arbitrary data to elements. You'll also learn how to extend the way jQuery processes CSS properties on elements.

Chapter 13, *Advanced Ajax*, helps you achieve a greater understanding of Ajax transactions, including the jQuery deferred object system for handling data that may become available at a later time.

Appendix A, *Testing JavaScript with QUnit*, teaches you about the QUnit library, which is used for the unit testing JavaScript programs. This library will be a great addition to your toolkit for developing and maintaining highly sophisticated web applications.

Appendix B, *Quick Reference*, provides a glimpse of the entire jQuery library, including every one of its methods and selector expressions. Its easy-to-scan format is perfect for those moments when you know what you want to do, but you're just unsure about the right method name or selector.

What you need for this book

In order to run the example code demonstrated in this book, you need a modern web browser, such as Google Chrome, Mozilla Firefox, Apple Safari, or Microsoft Edge.

To experiment with the examples and to work on the chapter-ending exercises, you will also need the following:

- A basic text editor
- Web development tools for the browser, such as Chrome Developer Tools or Firebug (as described in the *Using development tools* section of Chapter 1, *Getting Started*)
- The full code package for each chapter, which includes a copy of the jQuery library (seen in the *Downloading the example code* section)

Additionally, to run some of the Ajax examples in Chapter 6, *Sending Data with Ajax* and beyond, you will need Node.js.

Who this book is for

This book is ideal for client-side JavaScript developers. You do not need to have any previous experience with jQuery, although basic JavaScript programming knowledge is necessary.

Conventions

In this book, you will find a number of text styles that distinguish between different kinds of information. Here are some examples of these styles and an explanation of their meaning.

Code words in text, database table names, folder names, filenames, file extensions, pathnames, dummy URLs, user input, and Twitter handles are shown as follows: "When we instruct jQuery to find all elements with the class `collapsible` and hide them, there is no need to loop through each returned element."

A block of code is set as follows:

```
body {
  background-color: #fff;
  color: #000;
  font-family: Helvetica, Arial, sans-serif;
}
h1, h2, h3 {
  margin-bottom: .2em;
}
.poem {
  margin: 0 2em;
}
.highlight {
  background-color: #ccc;
  border: 1px solid #888;
  font-style: italic;
  margin: 0.5em 0;
  padding: 0.5em;
}
```

New terms and **important words** are shown in bold. Words that you see on the screen, for example, in menus or dialog boxes, appear in the text like this: "The **Sources** tab allows us to view the contents of all loaded scripts on the page."

Warnings or important notes appear in a box like this.

Tips and tricks appear like this.

Reader feedback

Feedback from our readers is always welcome. Let us know what you think about this book-what you liked or disliked. Reader feedback is important for us as it helps us develop titles that you will really get the most out of.

To send us general feedback, simply e-mail feedback@packtpub.com, and mention the book's title in the subject of your message.

If there is a topic that you have expertise in and you are interested in either writing or contributing to a book, see our author guide at www.packtpub.com/authors.

Customer support

Now that you are the proud owner of a Packt book, we have a number of things to help you to get the most from your purchase.

Downloading the example code

You can download the example code files for this book from your account at http://www.packtpub.com. If you purchased this book elsewhere, you can visit http://www.packtpub.com/support and register to have the files e-mailed directly to you.

You can download the code files by following these steps:

1. Log in or register to our website using your e-mail address and password.
2. Hover the mouse pointer on the **SUPPORT** tab at the top.
3. Click on **Code Downloads & Errata**.
4. Enter the name of the book in the **Search** box.
5. Select the book for which you're looking to download the code files.
6. Choose from the drop-down menu where you purchased this book from.
7. Click on **Code Download**.

Once the file is downloaded, please make sure that you unzip or extract the folder using the latest version of:

- WinRAR / 7-Zip for Windows
- Zipeg / iZip / UnRarX for Mac
- 7-Zip / PeaZip for Linux

The code bundle for the book is also hosted on GitHub at https://github.com/PacktPublishing/Learning-jQuery-3. We also have other code bundles from our rich catalog of books and videos available at https://github.com/PacktPublishing/. Check them out!

Errata

Although we have taken every care to ensure the accuracy of our content, mistakes do happen. If you find a mistake in one of our books-maybe a mistake in the text or the code-we would be grateful if you could report this to us. By doing so, you can save other readers from frustration and help us improve subsequent versions of this book. If you find any errata, please report them by visiting http://www.packtpub.com/submit-errata, selecting your book, clicking on the **Errata Submission Form** link, and entering the details of your errata. Once your errata are verified, your submission will be accepted and the errata will be uploaded to our website or added to any list of existing errata under the Errata section of that title.

To view the previously submitted errata, go to https://www.packtpub.com/books/content/support and enter the name of the book in the search field. The required information will appear under the **Errata** section.

Piracy

Piracy of copyrighted material on the Internet is an ongoing problem across all media. At Packt, we take the protection of our copyright and licenses very seriously. If you come across any illegal copies of our works in any form on the Internet, please provide us with the location address or website name immediately so that we can pursue a remedy.

Please contact us at copyright@packtpub.com with a link to the suspected pirated material.

We appreciate your help in protecting our authors and our ability to bring you valuable content.

Questions

If you have a problem with any aspect of this book, you can contact us at questions@packtpub.com, and we will do our best to address the problem.

1
Getting Started

Today's **World Wide Web** (**WWW**) is a dynamic environment and its users set a high bar for both the style and function of sites. To build interesting and interactive sites, developers are turning to JavaScript libraries, such as jQuery, to automate common tasks and to simplify complicated ones. One reason the jQuery library is a popular choice is its ability to assist in a wide range of tasks.

It can seem challenging to know where to begin because jQuery performs so many different functions. Yet, there is a coherence and symmetry to the design of the library; many of its concepts are borrowed from the structure of **HTML** and **Cascading Style Sheets** (**CSS**). The library's design lends itself to a quick start for designers with little programming experience, since many have more experience with these technologies than they do with JavaScript. In fact, in this opening chapter, we'll write a functioning jQuery program in just three lines of code. On the other hand, experienced programmers will also appreciate this conceptual consistency.

In this chapter, we will cover:

- The primary features of jQuery
- Setting up a jQuery code environment
- A simple working jQuery script example
- Reasons to choose jQuery over plain JavaScript
- Common JavaScript development tools

What jQuery does?

The jQuery library provides a general-purpose abstraction layer for common web scripting, and it is therefore useful in almost every scripting situation. Its extensible nature means that we could never cover all the possible uses and functions in a single book, as plugins are constantly being developed to add new abilities. The core features, though, assist us in accomplishing the following tasks:

- **Access elements in a document**: Without a JavaScript library, web developers often need to write many lines of code to traverse the **Document Object Model** (**DOM**) tree and locate specific portions of an HTML document's structure. With jQuery, developers have a robust and efficient selector mechanism at their disposal, making it easy to retrieve the exact piece of the document that needs to be inspected or manipulated.

  ```
  $('div.content').find('p');
  ```

- **Modify the appearance of a web page**: CSS offers a powerful method of influencing the way a document is rendered, but it falls short when not all web browsers support the same standards. With jQuery, developers can bridge this gap, relying on the same standards support across all browsers. In addition, jQuery can change the classes or individual style properties applied to a portion of the document even after the page has been rendered.

  ```
  $('ul > li:first').addClass('active');
  ```

- **Alter the content of a document**: Not limited to mere cosmetic changes, jQuery can modify the content of a document itself with a few keystrokes. Text can be changed, images can be inserted or swapped, lists can be reordered, or the entire structure of the HTML can be rewritten and extended--all with a single easy-to-use **Application Programming Interface** (**API**).

  ```
  $('#container').append('<a href="more.html">more</a>');
  ```

- **Respond to a user's interaction**: Even the most elaborate and powerful behaviors are not useful if we can't control when they take place. The jQuery library offers an elegant way to intercept a wide variety of events, such as a user clicking on a link, without the need to clutter the HTML code itself with event handlers.

  ```
  $('button.show-details').click(() => {
    $('div.details').show();
  });
  ```

- **Animate changes being made to a document**: To effectively implement such interactive behaviors, a designer must also provide visual feedback to the user. The jQuery library facilitates this by providing an array of effects such as fades and wipes, as well as a toolkit for crafting new ones.

```
$('div.details').slideDown();
```

- **Retrieve information from a server without refreshing a page**: This pattern is known as **Ajax**, which originally stood for **Asynchronous JavaScript and XML**, but has since come to represent a much greater set of technologies for communicating between the client and the server. The jQuery library removes the browser-specific complexity from this process, allowing developers to focus on the server-side functionality.

```
$('div.details').load('more.html #content');
```

Why jQuery works well?

With the resurgence of interest in dynamic HTML comes a proliferation of JavaScript frameworks. Some are specialized, focusing on just one or two of the tasks previously mentioned. Others attempt to catalog every possible behavior and animation and serves these up prepackaged. To maintain the wide range of features outlined earlier while remaining relatively compact, jQuery employs several strategies:

- **Leverage knowledge of CSS**: By basing the mechanism for locating page elements on CSS selectors, jQuery inherits a terse yet legible way of expressing a document's structure. The jQuery library becomes an entry point for designers who want to add behaviors to their pages because a prerequisite for doing professional web development is knowledge of CSS syntax.
- **Support extensions**: In order to avoid "feature creep", jQuery relegates special-case uses to plugins. The method for creating new plugins is simple and well documented, which has spurred the development of a wide variety of inventive and useful modules. Even most of the features in the basic jQuery download are internally realized through the plugin architecture and can be removed if desired, yielding an even smaller library.

- **Abstract away browser quirks**: An unfortunate reality of web development is that each browser has its own set of deviations from published standards. A significant portion of any web application can be relegated to handling features differently on each platform. While the ever-evolving browser landscape makes a perfectly browser-neutral codebase impossible for some advanced features, jQuery adds an abstraction layer that normalizes the common tasks, reducing the size of code while tremendously simplifying it.

- **Always work with sets**: When we instruct jQuery to find all elements with the class `collapsible` and hide them, there is no need to loop through each returned element. Instead, methods such as `.hide()` are designed to automatically work on sets of objects instead of individual ones. This technique, called *implicit iteration*, means that many looping constructs become unnecessary, shortening code considerably.

- **Allow multiple actions in one line**: To avoid overuse of temporary variables or wasteful repetition, jQuery employs a programming pattern called *chaining* for the majority of its methods. This means that the result of most operations on an object is the object itself, ready for the next action to be applied to it.

These strategies keep the file size of the jQuery package small, while at the same time providing techniques for keeping our custom code that uses the library compact as well.

The elegance of the library comes about partly by design and partly due to the evolutionary process spurred by the vibrant community that has sprung up around the project. Users of jQuery gather to discuss not only the development of plugins but also enhancements to the core library. The users and developers also assist in continually improving the official project documentation, which can be found at `http://api.jquery.com`.

Despite all the efforts required to engineer such a flexible and robust system, the end product is free for all to use. This open source project is licensed under the MIT License to permit free use of jQuery on any site and facilitate its use within proprietary software. If a project requires it, developers can relicense jQuery under the GNU Public License for inclusion in other GNU-licensed open source projects.

What's new in jQuery 3?

The changes introduced in jQuery 3 are quite subtle compared to the changes introduced in jQuery 2. Most of what's changed is under the hood. Let's take a brief look at some changes and how they're likely to impact an existing jQuery project. You can review the fine-grained details (`https://jquery.com/upgrade-guide/3.0`) while reading this book.

Browser support

The biggest change with browser support in jQuery 3 is Internet Explorer. Having to support older versions of this browser is the bane of any web developer's existence. jQuery 3 has taken a big step forward by only supporting IE9+. The support policy for other browsers is the current version and the previous version.

 The days of Internet Explorer are numbered. Microsoft has released the successor to IE called Edge. This browser is a completely separate project from IE and isn't burdened by the issues that have plagued IE. Additionally, recent versions of Microsoft Windows actually push for Edge as the default browser, and updates are regular and predictable. Goodbye and good riddance IE.

Deferred objects

The Deferred object was introduced in jQuery 1.5 as a means to better manage asynchronous behavior. They were kind of like ES2015 promises, but different enough that they weren't interchangeable. Now that the ES2015 version of JavaScript is commonplace in modern browsers, the Deferred object is fully compatible with native Promise objects. This means that quite a lot has changed with the old Deferred implementation.

Asynchronous document-ready

The idea that the document-ready callback function is executed asynchronously might seem counterintuitive at first. There are a couple of reasons this is the case in jQuery 3. First, the $(() => {}) expression returns a Deferred instance, and these now behave like native promises. The second reason is that there's a jQuery.ready promise that resolves when the document is ready. As you'll see later on in this book, you can use this promise alongside other promises to perform other asynchronous tasks before the DOM is ready to render.

All the rest

There are a number of other breaking changes to the API that were introduced in jQuery 3 that we won't dwell on here. The upgrade guide that I mentioned earlier goes into detail about each of these changes and how to deal with them. However, I'll point out functionality that's new or different in jQuery 3 as we make our way through this book.

Making our first jQuery-powered web page

Now that we have covered the range of features available to us with jQuery, we can examine how to put the library into action. To get started, we need to download a copy of jQuery.

Downloading jQuery

No installation is required. To use jQuery, we just need a publicly available copy of the file, no matter whether that copy is on an external site or our own. Since JavaScript is an interpreted language, there is no compilation or build phase to worry about. Whenever we need a page to have jQuery available, we will simply refer to the file's location from a `<script>` element in the HTML document.

The official jQuery website (`http://jquery.com/`) always has the most up-to-date stable version of the library, which can be downloaded right from the home page of the site. Several versions of jQuery may be available at any given moment; the most appropriate for us as site developers will be the latest uncompressed version of the library. This can be replaced with a compressed version in production environments.

As jQuery's popularity has grown, companies have made the file freely available through their **Content Delivery Networks** (**CDNs**). Most notably, Google (`https://developers.go ogle.com/speed/libraries/devguide`), Microsoft (`http://www.asp.net/ajaxlibrary/cd n.ashx`), and the jQuery project itself (`http://code.jquery.com`) offer the file on powerful, low-latency servers distributed around the world for fast download, regardless of the user's location. While a CDN-hosted copy of jQuery has speed advantages due to server distribution and caching, using a local copy can be convenient during development. Throughout this book, we'll use a copy of the file stored on our own system, which will allow us to run our code whether we're connected to the Internet or not.

To avoid unexpected bugs, always use a specific version of jQuery. For example, 3.1.1. Some CDNs allow you to link to the latest version of the library. Similarly, if you're using `npm` to install jQuery, always make sure that your `package.json` requires a specific version.

Setting up jQuery in an HTML document

There are three pieces to most examples of jQuery usage: the HTML document, CSS files to
style it, and JavaScript files to act on it. For our first example, we'll use a page with a book
excerpt that has a number of classes applied to portions of it. This page includes a reference
to the latest version of the jQuery library, which we have downloaded, renamed
jquery.js, and placed in our local project directory:

```
<!DOCTYPE html>

<html lang="en">
  <head>
    <meta charset="utf-8">
    <title>Through the Looking-Glass</title>

    <link rel="stylesheet" href="01.css">

    <script src="jquery.js"></script>
    <script src="01.js"></script>
  </head>

  <body>
    <h1>Through the Looking-Glass</h1>
    <div class="author">by Lewis Carroll</div>

    <div class="chapter" id="chapter-1">
      <h2 class="chapter-title">1. Looking-Glass House</h2>
      <p>There was a book lying near Alice on the table,
        and while she sat watching the White King (for she
        was still a little anxious about him, and had the
        ink all ready to throw over him, in case he fainted
        again), she turned over the leaves, to find some
        part that she could read, <span class="spoken">
        "&mdash;for it's all in some language I don't know,"
        </span> she said to herself.</p>
      <p>It was like this.</p>
      <div class="poem">
        <h3 class="poem-title">YKCOWREBBAJ</h3>
        <div class="poem-stanza">
          <div>sevot yhtils eht dna ,gillirb sawT'</div>
          <div>;ebaw eht ni elbmig dna eryg diD</div>
          <div>,sevogorob eht erew ysmim llA</div>
          <div>.ebargtuo shtar emom eht dnA</div>
        </div>
      </div>
      <p>She puzzled over this for some time, but at last
        a bright thought struck her. <span class="spoken">
```

```
          "Why, it's a Looking-glass book, of course! And if
          I hold it up to a glass, the words will all go the
          right way again."</span></p>
        <p>This was the poem that Alice read.</p>
        <div class="poem">
          <h3 class="poem-title">JABBERWOCKY</h3>
          <div class="poem-stanza">
            <div>'Twas brillig, and the slithy toves</div>
            <div>Did gyre and gimble in the wabe;</div>
            <div>All mimsy were the borogoves,</div>
            <div>And the mome raths outgrabe.</div>
          </div>
        </div>
      </div>
    </div>
  </body>
</html>
```

Immediately following the normal HTML preamble, the stylesheet is loaded. For this example, we'll use a simple one:

```
body {
  background-color: #fff;
  color: #000;
  font-family: Helvetica, Arial, sans-serif;
}
h1, h2, h3 {
  margin-bottom: .2em;
}
.poem {
  margin: 0 2em;
}
.highlight {
  background-color: #ccc;
  border: 1px solid #888;
  font-style: italic;
  margin: 0.5em 0;
  padding: 0.5em;
}
```

Getting the example code

You can access the example code from the following GitHub repository: https://github.com/PacktPublishing/Learning-jQuery-3.

After the stylesheet is referenced, the JavaScript files are included. It is important that the `script` tag for the jQuery library be placed before the tag for our custom scripts; otherwise, the jQuery framework will not be available when our code attempts to reference it.

 Throughout the rest of this book, only the relevant portions of HTML and CSS files will be printed. The files in their entirety are available from the book's companion code examples: `https://github.com/PacktPublishin g/Learning-jQuery-3`.

Now, we have a page that looks like this:

Through the Looking-Glass

by Lewis Carroll

1. Looking-Glass House

There was a book lying near Alice on the table, and while she sat watching the White King (for she was still a little anxious about him, and had the ink all ready to throw over him, in case he fainted again), she turned over the leaves, to find some part that she could read, "—for it's all in some language I don't know," she said to herself.

It was like this.

YKCOWREBBAJ
sevot yhtils eht dna ,gillirb sawT'
;ebaw eht ni elbmig dna eryg diD
,sevogorob eht erew ysmim llA
.ebargtuo shtar emom eht dnA

She puzzled over this for some time, but at last a bright thought struck her. "Why, it's a Looking-glass book, of course! And if I hold it up to a glass, the words will all go the right way again."

This was the poem that Alice read.

JABBERWOCKY
'Twas brillig, and the slithy toves
Did gyre and gimble in the wabe;
All mimsy were the borogoves,
And the mome raths outgrabe.

We will use jQuery to apply a new style to the poem text.

> This example is to demonstrate a simple use of jQuery. In real-world situations, this type of styling could be performed purely with CSS.

Adding our jQuery code

Our custom code will go in the second, currently empty, JavaScript file, which we included from the HTML using `<script src="01.js"></script>`. For this example, we only need three lines of code:

```
$(() => {
  $('div.poem-stanza').addClass('highlight')
});
```

> I'll be using newer ES2015 **arrow function** syntax for most callback functions throughout the book. The only reason is that it's more concise than having the `function` keyword all over the place. However, if you're more comfortable with the `function() {}` syntax, by all means, use it.

Now let's step through this script piece by piece to see how it works.

Finding the poem text

The fundamental operation in jQuery is selecting a part of the document. This is done with the `$()` function. Typically, it takes a string as a parameter, which can contain any CSS selector expression. In this case, we wish to find all of the `<div>` elements in the document that have the `poem-stanza` class applied to them, so the selector is very simple. However, we will cover much more sophisticated options through the course of the book. We will walk through many ways of locating parts of a document in Chapter 2, *Selecting Elements*.

When called, the `$()` function returns a new jQuery object instance, which is the basic building block we will be working with from now on. This object encapsulates zero or more DOM elements and allows us to interact with them in many different ways. In this case, we wish to modify the appearance of these parts of the page and we will accomplish this by changing the classes applied to the poem text.

Injecting the new class

The .addClass() method, like most jQuery methods, is named self descriptively; it applies a CSS class to the part of the page that we have selected. Its only parameter is the name of the class to add. This method, and its counterpart, .removeClass(), will allow us to easily observe jQuery in action as we explore the different selector expressions available to us. For now, our example simply adds the highlight class, which our stylesheet has defined as italicized text with a gray background and a border.

 Note that no iteration is necessary to add the class to all the poem stanzas. As we discussed, jQuery uses implicit iteration within methods such as .addClass(), so a single function call is all it takes to alter all the selected parts of the document.

Executing the code

Taken together, $() and .addClass() are enough for us to accomplish our goal of changing the appearance of the poem text. However, if this line of code is inserted alone in the document header, it will have no effect. JavaScript code is run as soon as it is encountered in the browser, and at the time the header is being processed, no HTML is yet present to style. We need to delay the execution of the code until after the DOM is available for our use.

With the $(() => {}) construct (passing a function instead of a selector expression), jQuery allows us to schedule function calls for firing once the DOM is loaded, without necessarily waiting for images to fully render. While this event scheduling is possible without the aid of jQuery, $(() => {}) provides an especially elegant cross-browser solution that includes the following features:

- It uses the browser's native DOM-ready implementations when available and adds a window.onload event handler as a safety net
- It executes functions passed to $() even if it is called after the browser event has already occurred
- It handles the event scheduling asynchronously to allow scripts to delay if necessary

The $() function's parameter can accept a reference to an already defined function, as shown in the following code snippet:

```
function addHighlightClass()  {
  $('div.poem-stanza').addClass('highlight');
}

$(addHighlightClass);
```

Listing 1.1

However, as demonstrated in the original version of the script and repeated in *Listing 1.2*, the method can also accept an anonymous function:

```
$(() =>
  $('div.poem-stanza').addClass('highlight')
);
```

Listing 1.2

This anonymous function idiom is convenient in jQuery code for methods that take a function as an argument when that function isn't reusable. Moreover, the closure it creates can be an advanced and powerful tool. If you're using arrow functions, you also get lexically bound this as a context, which avoids having to bind functions. It may also have unintended consequences and ramifications of memory use, however, if not dealt with carefully.

The finished product

Now that our JavaScript is in place, the page looks like this:

Through the Looking-Glass

by Lewis Carroll

1. Looking-Glass House

There was a book lying near Alice on the table, and while she sat watching the White King (for she was still a little anxious about him, and had the ink all ready to throw over him, in case he fainted again), she turned over the leaves, to find some part that she could read, "—for it's all in some language I don't know," she said to herself.

It was like this.

YKCOWREBBAJ

sevot yhtils eht dna ,gillirb sawT'
;ebaw eht ni elbmig dna eryg diD
,sevogorob eht erew ysmim llA
.ebargtuo shtar emom eht dnA

She puzzled over this for some time, but at last a bright thought struck her. "Why, it's a Looking-glass book, of course! And if I hold it up to a glass, the words will all go the right way again."

This was the poem that Alice read.

JABBERWOCKY

'Twas brillig, and the slithy toves
Did gyre and gimble in the wabe;
All mimsy were the borogoves,
And the mome raths outgrabe.

The poem stanzas are now italicized and enclosed in boxes, as specified by the `01.css` stylesheet, due to the insertion of the `highlight` class by the JavaScript code.

Plain JavaScript versus jQuery

Even a task as simple as this can be complicated without jQuery at our disposal. In plain JavaScript, we could add the highlight class this way:

```
window.onload = function() {
  const divs = document.getElementsByTagName('div');
  const hasClass = (elem, cls) =>
    new RegExp(` ${cls} `).test(` ${elem.className} `);

  for (let div of divs) {
    if (hasClass(div, 'poem-stanza') && !hasClass(div, 'highlight')) {
      div.className += ' highlight';
    }
  }
};
```

Listing 1.3

Despite its length, this solution does not handle many of the situations that jQuery takes care of for us in *Listing 1.2*, such as:

- Properly respecting other window.onload event handlers
- Acting as soon as the DOM is ready
- Optimizing element retrieval and other tasks with modern DOM methods

We can see that our jQuery-driven code is easier to write, simpler to read, and faster to execute than its plain JavaScript equivalent.

Using development tools

As this code comparison has shown, jQuery code is typically shorter and clearer than its basic JavaScript equivalent. However, this doesn't mean we will always write code that is free from bugs or that we will intuitively understand what is happening on our pages at all times. Our jQuery coding experience will be much smoother with the assistance of standard development tools.

High-quality development tools are available in all modern browsers. We can feel free to use the environment that is most comfortable to us. Options include the following:

- Microsoft Edge (`https://developer.microsoft.com/en-us/microsoft-edge/platform/documentation/f12-devtools-guide/`)
- Internet Explorer Developer Tools (`http://msdn.microsoft.com/en-us/library/dd565628.aspx`)
- Safari Web Development Tools (`https://developer.apple.com/safari/tools/`)
- Chrome Developer Tools (`https://developer.chrome.com/devtools`)
- Firefox Developer Tools (`https://developer.mozilla.org/en-US/docs/Tools`)

Each of these toolkits offers similar development features, including:

- Exploring and modifying aspects of the DOM
- Investigating the relationship between CSS and its effect on page presentation
- Convenient tracing of script execution through special methods
- Pausing execution of running scripts and inspecting variable values

While the details of these features vary from one tool to the next, the general concepts remain the same. In this book, some examples will require the use of one of these toolkits; we will use Chrome Developer Tools for these demonstrations, but development tools for other browsers are fine alternatives.

Chrome Developer Tools

Up-to-date instructions for accessing and using Chrome Developer Tools can be found on the project's documentation pages at `https://developer.chrome.com/devtools`. The tools are too involved to explore in great detail here, but a survey of some of the most relevant features will be useful to us.

Understanding these screenshots
Chrome Developer Tools is a quickly evolving project, so the following screenshots may not exactly match your environment.

When Chrome Developer Tools is activated, a new panel appears offering information about the current page. In the default **Elements** tab of this panel, we can see a representation of the page structure on the left-hand side and details of the selected element (such as the CSS rules that apply to it) on the right-hand side. This tab is especially useful for investigating the structure of the page and debugging CSS issues:

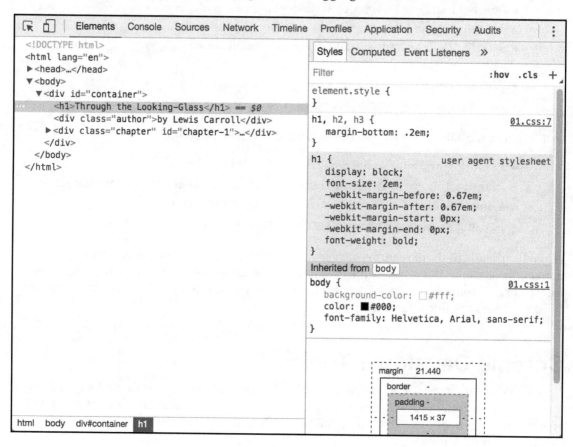

The **Sources** tab allows us to view the contents of all loaded scripts on the page. By right-clicking on a line number, we can set a breakpoint, set a conditional breakpoint, or have the script continue to that line after another breakpoint is reached. Breakpoints are effective ways to pause the execution of a script and examine what occurs in a step-by-step fashion. On the right-hand side of the page, we can enter a list of variables and expressions we wish to know the value of at any time:

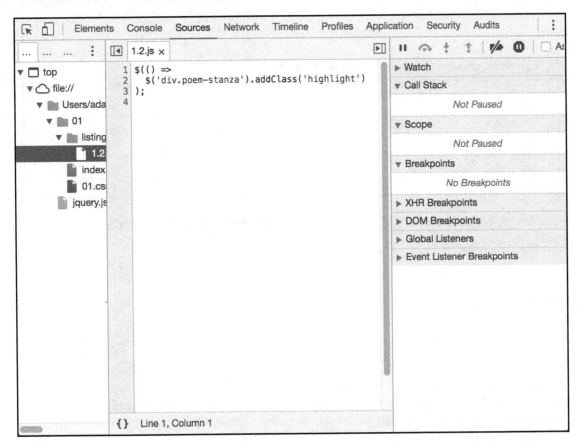

The **Console** tab will be of most frequent use to us while learning jQuery. A field at the bottom of the panel allows us to enter any JavaScript statement, and the result of the statement is then presented in the panel.

In this example, we perform the same jQuery selector as in *Listing 1.2*, but we are not performing any action on the selected elements. Even so, the statement gives us interesting information: we see that the result of the selector is a jQuery object pointing to the two `.poem-stanza` elements on the page. We can use this console feature to quickly try out jQuery code at any time, right from within the browser:

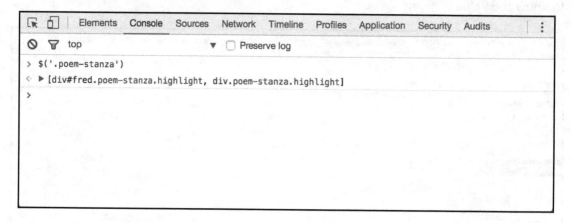

In addition, we can interact with this console directly from our code using the `console.log()` method:

```
$(() => {
  console.log('hello');
  console.log(52);
  console.log($('div.poem-stanza'));
});
```

Listing 1.4

This code illustrates that we can pass any kind of expression into the `console.log()` method. Simple values such as strings and numbers are printed directly, and more complicated values such as jQuery objects are nicely formatted for our inspection:

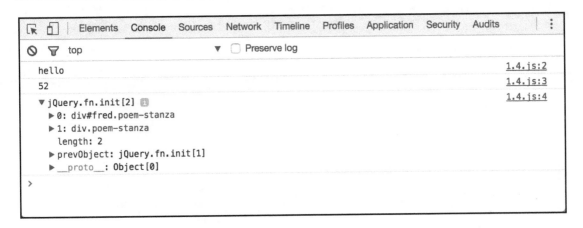

This `console.log()` function (which works in each of the browser developer tools we mentioned earlier) is a convenient alternative to the JavaScript `alert()` function, and will be very useful as we test our jQuery code.

Summary

In this chapter, we learned how to make jQuery available to JavaScript code on our web page, use the `$()` function to locate a part of the page that has a given class, call `.addClass()` to apply additional styling to this part of the page, and invoke `$(() => {})` to cause this function to execute upon loading the page. We have also explored the development tools we will be relying on when writing, testing, and debugging our jQuery code.

We now have an idea of why a developer would choose to use a JavaScript framework rather than writing all code from scratch, even for the most basic tasks. We have also seen some of the ways in which jQuery excels as a framework, why we might choose it over other options, and in general, which tasks jQuery makes easier.

The simple example we have been using demonstrates how jQuery works, but is not very useful in real-world situations. In the next chapter, we will expand on this code by exploring jQuery's sophisticated selector language, finding practical uses for this technique.

2
Selecting Elements

The jQuery library harnesses the power of **Cascading Style Sheets** (**CSS**) selectors to let us quickly and easily access elements or groups of elements in the **Document Object Model** (**DOM**).

In this chapter, we will cover:

- The structure of the elements on a web page
- How to use CSS selectors to find elements on the page
- What happens when the specificity of a CSS selector changes
- Custom jQuery extensions to the standard set of CSS selectors
- The DOM traversal methods, which provide greater flexibility for accessing elements on the page
- Using modern JavaScript language features to iterate over jQuery objects efficiently

Understanding the DOM

One of the most powerful aspects of jQuery is its ability to make selecting elements in the DOM easy. The DOM serves as the interface between JavaScript and a web page; it provides a representation of the source HTML as a network of objects rather than as plain text.

This network takes the form of a family tree of elements on the page. When we refer to the relationships that elements have with one another, we use the same terminology that we use when referring to family relationships: parents, children, siblings, and so on. A simple example can help us understand how the family tree metaphor applies to a document:

```
<html>
  <head>
    <title>the title</title>
  </head>
  <body>
    <div>
      <p>This is a paragraph.</p>
      <p>This is another paragraph.</p>
      <p>This is yet another paragraph.</p>
    </div>
  </body>
</html>
```

Here, <html> is the ancestor of all the other elements; in other words, all the other elements are descendants of <html>. The <head> and <body> elements are not only descendants, but children of <html> as well. Likewise, in addition to being the ancestor of <head> and <body>, <html> is also their parent. The <p> elements are children (and descendants) of <div>, descendants of <body> and <html>, and siblings of each other.

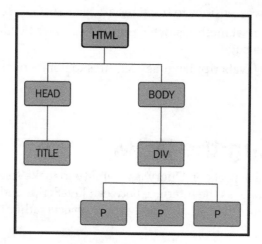

To help visualize the family tree structure of the DOM, we can use the browser's developer tools to inspect the DOM structure of any page. This is especially helpful when you're curious about how some other application works, and you want to implement something similar.

With this tree of elements at our disposal, we'll be able to use jQuery to efficiently locate any set of elements on the page. Our tools to achieve this are jQuery **selectors** and **traversal methods**.

Using the $() function

The resulting set of elements from jQuery's selectors and methods is always represented by a jQuery object. These objects are very easy to work with when we want to actually do something with the things that we find on a page. We can easily bind events to these objects and add visual effects to them, as well as chain multiple modifications or effects together.

Note that jQuery objects are different from regular DOM elements or node lists, and as such do not necessarily provide the same methods and properties for some tasks. In the final part of this chapter, we will look at ways to directly access the DOM elements that are collected within a jQuery object.

In order to create a new jQuery object, we use the $() function. This function typically accepts a CSS selector as its sole parameter and serves as a factory, returning a new jQuery object pointing to the corresponding elements on the page. Just about anything that can be used in a stylesheet can also be passed as a string to this function, allowing us to apply jQuery methods to the matched set of elements.

Making jQuery play well with other JavaScript libraries

In jQuery, the dollar sign ($) is simply an alias for jQuery. Because a $() function is very common in JavaScript libraries, conflicts could arise if more than one of these libraries were being used in a given page. We can avoid such conflicts by replacing every instance of $ with jQuery in our custom jQuery code. Additional solutions to this problem are addressed in Chapter 10, *Advanced Events*. On the other hand, jQuery is so prominent in frontend development, that libraries tend to leave the $ symbol alone.

The three primary building blocks of selectors are **tag name**, **ID**, and **class**. They can be used either on their own or in combination with others. The following simple examples illustrate how these three selectors appear in code:

Selector type	CSS	jQuery	What it does
Tag name	`p { }`	`$('p')`	This selects all paragraphs in the document.
ID	`#some-id { }`	`$('#some-id')`	This selects the single element in the document that has an ID of `some-id`.
Class	`.some-class { }`	`$('.some-class')`	This selects all elements in the document that have a class of `some-class`.

As mentioned in `Chapter 1`, *Getting Started*, when we call methods of a jQuery object, the elements referred by the selector we passed to `$()` are looped through automatically and implicitly. Therefore, we can usually avoid explicit iteration, such as a `for` loop, that is so often required in DOM scripting.

Now that we covered the basics, we're ready to start exploring some more powerful uses of selectors.

CSS selectors

The jQuery library supports nearly all the selectors included in CSS specifications 1 through 3, as outlined on the World Wide Web Consortium's site:
`http://www.w3.org/Style/CSS/specs`. This support allows developers to enhance their websites without worrying about which browsers might not understand more advanced selectors, as long as the browsers have JavaScript enabled.

Progressive Enhancement

Responsible jQuery developers should always apply the concepts of progressive enhancement and graceful degradation to their code, ensuring that a page will render as accurately, even if not as beautifully, with JavaScript disabled as it does with JavaScript turned on. We will continue to explore these concepts throughout the book. More information on progressive enhancement can be found at http://en.wikipedia.org/wik i/Progressive_enhancement. Having said this, it's not very often that you'll encounter users with JavaScript disabled these days--even on mobile browsers.

To begin learning how jQuery works with CSS selectors, we'll use a structure that appears on many websites, often for navigation--the nested unordered list:

```
<ul id="selected-plays">
  <li>Comedies
    <ul>
      <li><a href="/asyoulikeit/">As You Like It</a></li>
      <li>All's Well That Ends Well</li>
      <li>A Midsummer Night's Dream</li>
      <li>Twelfth Night</li>
    </ul>
  </li>
  <li>Tragedies
    <ul>
      <li><a href="hamlet.pdf">Hamlet</a></li>
      <li>Macbeth</li>
      <li>Romeo and Juliet</li>
    </ul>
  </li>
  <li>Histories
    <ul>
      <li>Henry IV (<a href="mailto:henryiv@king.co.uk">email</a>)
        <ul>
          <li>Part I</li>
          <li>Part II</li>
        </ul>
        <li><a href="http://www.shakespeare.co.uk/henryv.htm">Henry
V</a></li>
        <li>Richard II</li>
    </ul>
  </li>
</ul>
```

Note that the first `<ul>` has an ID of `selecting-plays`, but none of the `<li>` tags have a class associated with them. Without any styles applied, the list looks like this:

> **Selected Shakespeare Plays**
> - Comedies
>   - As You Like It
>   - All's Well That Ends Well
>   - A Midsummer Night's Dream
>   - Twelfth Night
> - Tragedies
>   - Hamlet
>   - Macbeth
>   - Romeo and Juliet
> - Histories
>   - Henry IV (email)
>   - Part I
>   - Part II
>   - Henry V
>   - Richard II

The nested list appears as we would expect it to--a set of bulleted items arranged vertically and indented according to their level.

Styling list-item levels

Let's suppose that we want the top-level items, and only the top-level items--**Comedies**, **Tragedies**, and **Histories**--to be arranged horizontally. We can start by defining a `horizontal` class in the stylesheet:

```
.horizontal {
  float: left;
  list-style: none;
  margin: 10px;
}
```

The `horizontal` class floats the element to the left-hand side of the one following it, removes the bullet from it if it's a list item, and adds a 10-pixel margin on all sides of it.

Rather than attaching the `horizontal` class directly in our HTML, we'll add it dynamically to the top-level list items only, to demonstrate jQuery's use of selectors:

```
$(() => {
  $('#selected-plays > li')
    .addClass('horizontal');
});
```

Listing 2.1

As discussed in `Chapter 1`, *Getting Started*, we begin jQuery code by calling `$(() => {})`, which runs the function passed to it once the DOM has been loaded, but not before.

The second line uses the child combinator (>) to add the `horizontal` class to all the top-level items only. In effect, the selector inside the `$()` function is saying, "Find each list item (`li`) that is a child (>) of the element with an ID of `selected-plays` (`#selected-plays`)".

With the class now applied, the rules defined for that class in the stylesheet take effect, which in this case means that the list items are arranged horizontally rather than vertically. Now, our nested list looks like this:

Selected Shakespeare Plays

Comedies
- o As You Like It
- o All's Well That Ends Well
- o A Midsummer Night's Dream
- o Twelfth Night

Tragedies
- o Hamlet
- o Macbeth
- o Romeo and Juliet

Histories
- o Henry IV (email)
  - Part I
  - Part II
- o Henry V
- o Richard II

Styling all the other items--those that are not in the top level--can be done in a number of ways. Since we have already applied the `horizontal` class to the top-level items, one way to select all sub-level items is to use a negation pseudo-class to identify all list items that do not have a class of `horizontal`:

```
$(() => {
  $('#selected-plays > li')
    .addClass('horizontal');
  $('#selected-plays li:not(.horizontal)')
    .addClass('sub-level');
});
```

Listing 2.2

This time we are selecting every list item (`<li>`) that:

- Is a descendant of the element with an ID of `selected-plays` (`#selected-plays`)
- Does not have a class of `horizontal` (`:not(.horizontal)`)

When we add the `sub-level` class to these items, they receive the shaded background defined in the stylesheet:

```
.sub-level {
  background: #ccc;
}
```

Now the nested list looks like this:

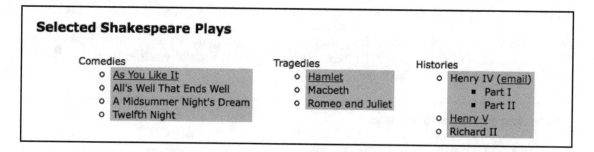

Selector specificity

Selectors in jQuery have a spectrum of specificity, from very general selectors, to very targeted selectors. The goal is to select the correct elements, otherwise your selector is broken. The tendency for jQuery beginners is to implement very specific selectors for everything. Perhaps through trial and error, they've fixed selector bugs by adding more specificity to a given selector. However, this isn't always the best solution.

Let's look at an example that increases the size of the first letter for top-level `<li>` text. Here's the style we want to apply:

```
.big-letter::first-letter {
  font-size: 1.4em;
}
```

And here's what the list item text looks like:

Selected Shakespeare Plays

Comedies
- As You Like It
- All's Well That Ends Well
- A Midsummer Night's Dream
- Twelfth Night

Tragedies
- Hamlet
- Macbeth
- Romeo and Juliet

Histories
- Henry IV (email)
  - Part I
  - Part II
- Henry V
- Richard II

Shakespeare's Plays

As You Like It	Comedy	
All's Well that Ends Well	Comedy	1601
Hamlet	Tragedy	1604
Macbeth	Tragedy	1606
Romeo and Juliet	Tragedy	1595
Henry IV, Part I	History	1596
Henry V	History	1599

Shakespeare's Sonnets

The Fair Youth	1–126
The Dark Lady	127–152
The Rival Poet	78–86

As you see, **Comedies**, **Tragedies**, and **Histories** have the `big-letter` style applied to them as expected. In order to do this, we need a selector that's more specific than just `$('#selected-plays li')`, which would apply the style to every `<li>`, even the sub-elements. We can use change the specificity of the jQuery selector to make sure we're only getting what we expect:

```
$(() => {
  $('#selected-plays > li')
    .addClass('big-letter');

  $('#selected-plays li.horizontal')
    .addClass('big-letter');

  $('#selected-plays li:not(.sub-level)')
    .addClass('big-letter');
});
```

Listing 2.3

All three of these selectors do the same thing--apply the `big-letter` style to the top-level `<li>` elements in `#selected-plays`. The specificity is different in each of these selectors. Let's review how each of these work, and what their strengths are:

- `#selected-plays > li`: This finds `<li>` elements that are direct children of `#selected-plays`. This is easy to read, and semantically relevant to the DOM structure.
- `#selected-plays li.horizontal`: This finds `<li>` elements or sub-elements of `#selected-plays` with the `horizontal` class. This is also easy to read and enforces a particular DOM schema (applying the `horizontal` class).
- `#selected-plays li:not(.sub-level)`: This is difficult to read, inefficient, and doesn't reflect the actual DOM structure.

There are endless examples where selector-selector specificity comes up. Every application is unique, and as we just saw, there's no one correct way to implement selector specificity. What's important is that we exercise good judgement by considering the ramifications of selectors on the DOM structure, and consequently, the maintainability of our application or website.

Attribute selectors

Attribute selectors are a particularly helpful subset of CSS selectors. They allow us to specify an element by one of its HTML attributes, such as a link's `title` attribute or an image's `alt` attribute. For example, to select all images that have an `alt` attribute, we write the following:

```
$('img[alt]')
```

Styling links

Attribute selectors accept a wildcard syntax inspired by regular expressions for identifying the value at the beginning (^) or end ($) of a string. They can also take an asterisk (*) to indicate the value at an arbitrary position within a string or an exclamation mark (!) to indicate a negated value.

Let's say we want to have different styles for different types of links. We first define the styles in our stylesheet:

```
a {
  color: #00c;
}
a.mailto {
  background: url(images/email.png) no-repeat right top;
  padding-right: 18px;
}
a.pdflink {
  background: url(images/pdf.png) no-repeat right top;
  padding-right: 18px;
}
a.henrylink {
  background-color: #fff;
  padding: 2px;
  border: 1px solid #000;
}
```

Then, we add the three classes--`mailto`, `pdflink`, and `henrylink`--to the appropriate links using jQuery.

To add a class for all e-mail links, we construct a selector that looks for all anchor elements (`a`) with an `href` attribute (`[href]`) that begins with `mailto:` (`^="mailto:"`), as follows:

```
$(() => {
  $('a[href^="mailto:"]')
    .addClass('mailto');
});
```

Listing 2.4

Because of the rules defined in the page's stylesheet, an envelope image appears after the **mailto:** link on the page.

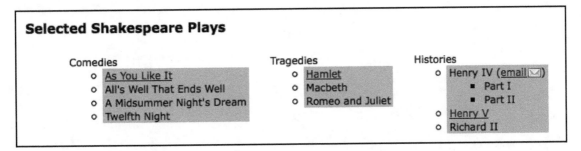

To add a class for all the links to PDF files, we use the dollar sign rather than the caret symbol. This is because we're selecting links with an `href` attribute that ends with `.pdf`:

```
$(() => {
  $('a[href^="mailto:"]')
    .addClass('mailto');
  $('a[href$=".pdf"]')
    .addClass('pdflink');
});
```

Listing 2.5

The stylesheet rule for the newly added `pdflink` class causes an Adobe Acrobat icon to appear after each link to a PDF document, as shown in the following screenshot:

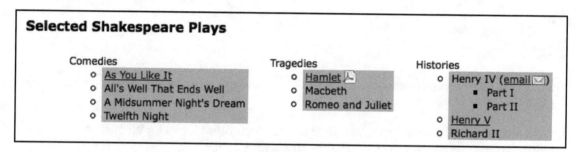

Attribute selectors can be combined as well. We can, for example, add the class `henrylink` to all links with an `href` value that both starts with `http` and contains `henry` anywhere:

```
$(() => {
  $('a[href^="mailto:"]')
    .addClass('mailto');
  $('a[href$=".pdf"]')
    .addClass('pdflink');
  $('a[href^="http"][href*="henry"]')
    .addClass('henrylink');
});
```

Listing 2.6

With the three classes applied to the three types of links, we should see the following:

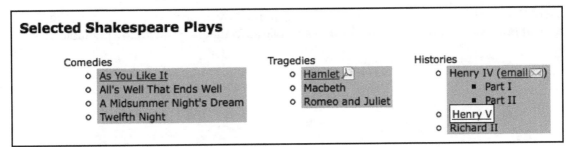

Note the PDF icon to the right-hand side of the **Hamlet** link, the envelope icon next to the **email** link, and the white background and black border around the **Henry V** link.

Custom selectors

To the wide variety of CSS selectors, jQuery adds its own custom selectors. These custom selectors enhance the capabilities of CSS selectors to locate page elements in new ways.

Performance note

When possible, jQuery uses the native DOM selector engine of the browser to find elements. This extremely fast approach is not possible when custom jQuery selectors are used. For this reason, it is recommended to avoid frequent use of custom selectors when a native option is available.

Most of the custom selectors allow us to choose one or more elements from a collection of elements that we have already found. The custom selector syntax is the same as the CSS pseudo-class syntax, where the selector starts with a colon (:). For example, to select the second item from a set of <div> elements with a class of horizontal, we write this:

```
$('div.horizontal:eq(1)')
```

Note that :eq(1) selects the second item in the set because JavaScript array numbering is zero-based, meaning that it starts with zero. In contrast, CSS is one-based, so a CSS selector such as $('div:nth-child(1)') would select all div selectors that are the first child of their parent. Because it can be difficult to remember which selectors are zero based and which are one based, we should consult the jQuery API documentation at http://api.jque ry.com/category/selectors/ when in doubt.

Styling alternate rows

Two very useful custom selectors in the jQuery library are :odd and :even. Let's take a look at how we can use one of them for basic table striping given the following tables:

```
<h2>Shakespeare's Plays</h2>
<table>
  <tr>
    <td>As You Like It</td>
    <td>Comedy</td>
    <td></td>
  </tr>
  <tr>
    <td>All's Well that Ends Well</td>
    <td>Comedy</td>
    <td>1601</td>
  </tr>
  <tr>
    <td>Hamlet</td>
    <td>Tragedy</td>
    <td>1604</td>
  </tr>
  <tr>
    <td>Macbeth</td>
    <td>Tragedy</td>
    <td>1606</td>
  </tr>
  <tr>
    <td>Romeo and Juliet</td>
    <td>Tragedy</td>
    <td>1595</td>
  </tr>
  <tr>
    <td>Henry IV, Part I</td>
    <td>History</td>
    <td>1596</td>
  </tr>
  <tr>
    <td>Henry V</td>
    <td>History</td>
    <td>1599</td>
  </tr>
</table>
<h2>Shakespeare's Sonnets</h2>
<table>
  <tr>
    <td>The Fair Youth</td>
    <td>1-126</td>
```

```
    </tr>
    <tr>
      <td>The Dark Lady</td>
      <td>127-152</td>
    </tr>
    <tr>
      <td>The Rival Poet</td>
      <td>78-86</td>
    </tr>
  </table>
```

With minimal styles applied from our stylesheet, these headings and tables appear quite plain. The table has a solid white background, with no styling separating one row from the next, as shown in the following screenshot:

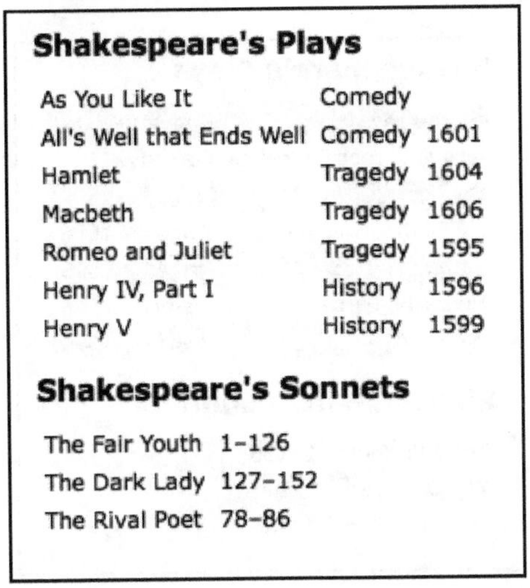

Now, we can add a style to the stylesheet for all the table rows and use an alt class for the odd rows:

```
tr {
  background-color: #fff;
}
.alt {
  background-color: #ccc;
}
```

Finally, we write our jQuery code, attaching the class to the odd-numbered table rows (`<tr>` tags):

```
$(() => {
  $('tr:even').addClass('alt');
});
```

Listing 2.7

But wait! Why use the `:even` selector for odd-numbered rows? Well, just as with the `:eq()` selector, the `:even` and `:odd` selectors use JavaScript's native zero-based numbering. Therefore, the first row counts as zero (even) and the second row counts as one (odd), and so on. With this in mind, we can expect our simple bit of code to produce tables that look like this:

Shakespeare's Plays

As You Like It	Comedy	
All's Well that Ends Well	Comedy	1601
Hamlet	Tragedy	1604
Macbeth	Tragedy	1606
Romeo and Juliet	Tragedy	1595
Henry IV, Part I	History	1596
Henry V	History	1599

Shakespeare's Sonnets

The Fair Youth	1–126
The Dark Lady	127–152
The Rival Poet	78–86

Note that for the second table, this result may not be what we intend. Since the last row in the **Plays** table has the alternate gray background, the first row in the **Sonnets** table has the plain white background. One way to avoid this type of problem is to use the `:nth-child()` selector instead, which counts an element's position relative to its parent element rather than relative to all the elements selected so far. This selector can take a number, `odd` or `even` as its argument:

```
$(() => {
  $('tr:nth-child(odd)').addClass('alt');
});
```

Listing 2.8

As before, note that `:nth-child()` is the only jQuery selector that is one based. To achieve the same row striping as we did earlier--except with consistent behavior for the second table--we need to use `odd` rather than `even` as the argument. With this selector in place, both tables are now striped nicely, as shown in the following screenshot:

Shakespeare's Plays

As You Like It	Comedy	
All's Well that Ends Well	Comedy	1601
Hamlet	Tragedy	1604
Macbeth	Tragedy	1606
Romeo and Juliet	Tragedy	1595
Henry IV, Part I	History	1596
Henry V	History	1599

Shakespeare's Sonnets

The Fair Youth	1–126
The Dark Lady	127–152
The Rival Poet	78–86

The `:nth-child()` selector is a native CSS selector in modern browsers.

Finding elements based on textual content

For one final custom selector, let's suppose for some reason we want to highlight any table cell that referred to one of the **Henry** plays. All we have to do--after adding a class to the stylesheet to make the text bold and italicized (`.highlight {font-weight:bold; font-style: italic;}`)--is add a line to our jQuery code using the `:contains()` selector:

```
$(() => {
  $('tr:nth-child(odd)')
    .addClass('alt');
  $('td:contains(Henry)')
    .addClass('highlight');
});
```

Listing 2.9

So, now we can see our lovely striped table with the **Henry** plays prominently featured:

Shakespeare's Plays

As You Like It	Comedy	
All's Well that Ends Well	Comedy	1601
Hamlet	Tragedy	1604
Macbeth	Tragedy	1606
Romeo and Juliet	Tragedy	1595
Henry IV, Part I	History	1596
Henry V	History	1599

Shakespeare's Sonnets

The Fair Youth	1–126
The Dark Lady	127–152
The Rival Poet	78–86

It's important to note that the :contains() selector is case sensitive. Using $('td:contains(henry)') instead, without the uppercase "H", would select no cells. It's also important to note that :contains() can cause catastrophically bad performance, since the text of every element that matches the first part of the selector needs to be loaded and compared to our supplied argument. When :contains() has the potential to search hundreds of nodes for content, it's time to rethink our approach.

Admittedly, there are ways to achieve the row striping and text highlighting without jQuery--or any client-side programming, for that matter. Nevertheless, jQuery, along with CSS, is a great alternative for this type of styling in cases where the content is generated dynamically and we don't have access to either the HTML or server-side code.

Form selectors

The capabilities of custom selectors are not limited to locating elements based on their position. For example, when working with forms, jQuery's custom selectors and complementary CSS3 selectors can make short work of selecting just the elements we need. The following table describes a handful of these form selectors:

Selector	Match
:input	**Input, text area, select, and button elements**
:button	Button elements and input elements with a `type` attribute equal to `button`
:enabled	Form elements that are enabled
:disabled	Form elements that are disabled
:checked	Radio buttons or checkboxes that are checked
:selected	Option elements that are selected

As with the other selectors, form selectors can be combined for greater specificity. We can, for example, select all checked radio buttons (but not checkboxes) with `$('input[type="radio"]:checked')` or select all password inputs and disabled text inputs with `$('input[type="password"], input[type="text"]:disabled')`. Even with custom selectors, we can use the same basic principles of CSS to build the list of matched elements.

> We have only scratched the surface of available selector expressions here. We will dive further into the topic in `Chapter 9`, *Advanced Selectors and Traversing*.

DOM traversal methods

The jQuery selectors that we have explored so far allow us to select a set of elements as we navigate across and down the DOM tree and filter the results. If this were the only way to select elements, our options would be somewhat limited. There are many occasions when selecting a parent or ancestor element is essential; that is where jQuery's DOM traversal methods come into play. With these methods, we can go up, down, and all around the DOM tree with ease.

Some of the methods have a nearly identical counterpart among the selector expressions. For example, the line we first used to add the `alt` class, `$('tr:even').addClass('alt')`, could be rewritten with the `.filter()` method as follows:

```
$('tr')
  .filter(':even')
  .addClass('alt');
```

For the most part, however, the two ways of selecting elements complement each other. Also, the `.filter()` method in particular has enormous power because it can take a function as its argument. The function allows us to create complex tests for whether elements should be included in the matched set. Let's suppose, for example, that we want to add a class to all external links:

```
a.external {
  background: #fff url(images/external.png) no-repeat 100% 2px;
  padding-right: 16px;
}
```

jQuery has no selector for this sort of thing. Without a filter function, we'd be forced to explicitly loop through each element, testing each one separately. With the following filter function, however, we can still rely on jQuery's implicit iteration and keep our code compact:

```
$('a')
  .filter((i, a) =>
    a.hostname && a.hostname !== location.hostname
  )
  .addClass('external');
```

Listing 2.10

The supplied function filters the set of `<a>` elements by two criteria:

- They must have an `href` attribute with a domain name (`a.hostname`). We use this test to exclude mailto links, for instance.
- The domain name that they link to (again, `a.hostname`) must not match (`!==`) the domain name of the current page (`location.hostname`).

More precisely, the `.filter()` method iterates through the matched set of elements, calling the function once for each and testing the return value. If the function returns `false`, the element is removed from the matched set. If it returns `true`, the element is kept.

With the `.filter()` method in place, the **Henry V** link is styled to indicate it is external:

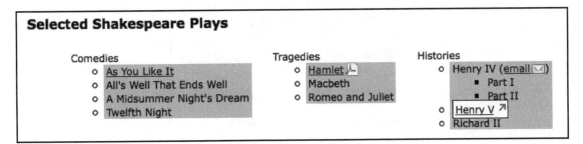

In the next section, we'll take another look at our striped table example to see what else is possible with traversal methods.

Styling specific cells

Earlier, we added a `highlight` class to all cells containing the text **Henry**. To instead style the cell next to each cell containing **Henry**, we can begin with the selector that we have already written and simply call the `.next()` method on the result:

```
$(() => {
  $('td:contains(Henry)')
    .next()
    .addClass('highlight');
});
```

Listing 2.11

The tables should now look like this:

Shakespeare's Plays

As You Like It	Comedy	
All's Well that Ends Well	Comedy	1601
Hamlet	Tragedy	1604
Macbeth	Tragedy	1606
Romeo and Juliet	Tragedy	1595
Henry IV, Part I	*History*	1596
Henry V	*History*	1599

Shakespeare's Sonnets

The Fair Youth	1–126
The Dark Lady	127–152
The Rival Poet	78–86

The `.next()` method selects only the very next sibling element. To highlight all of the cells following the one containing **Henry**, we could use the `.nextAll()` method instead:

```
$(() => {
  $('td:contains(Henry)')
    .nextAll()
    .addClass('highlight');
});
```

Listing 2.12

Since the cells containing **Henry** are in the first column of the table, this code causes the rest of the cells in these rows to be highlighted:

As we might expect, the .next() and .nextAll() methods have counterparts: .prev() and .prevAll(). Additionally, .siblings() selects all other elements at the same DOM level, regardless of whether they come before or after the previously selected element.

To include the original cell (the one that contains **Henry**) along with the cells that follow, we can add the .addBack() method:

```
$(() => {
  $('td:contains(Henry)')
    .nextAll()
    .addBack()
    .addClass('highlight');
});
```

Listing 2.13

With this modification in place, all of the cells in the row get their styles from the `highlight` class:

Shakespeare's Plays

As You Like It	Comedy	
All's Well that Ends Well	Comedy	1601
Hamlet	Tragedy	1604
Macbeth	Tragedy	1606
Romeo and Juliet	Tragedy	1595
Henry IV, Part I	*History*	*1596*
Henry V	*History*	*1599*

Shakespeare's Sonnets

The Fair Youth	1–126
The Dark Lady	127–152
The Rival Poet	78–86

There are a multitude of selector and traversal-method combinations by which we can select the same set of elements. Here, for example, is another way to select every cell in each row where at least one of the cells contains **Henry**:

```
$(() => {
  $('td:contains(Henry)')
    .parent()
    .children()
    .addClass('highlight');
});
```

Listing 2.14

Rather than traversing across to sibling elements, we travel up one level in the DOM to the `<tr>` tag with `.parent()` and then select all of the row's cells with `.children()`.

Chaining

The traversal method combinations that we have just explored illustrate jQuery's chaining capability. With jQuery, it is possible to select multiple sets of elements and do multiple things with them, all within a single line of code. This chaining not only helps keep jQuery code concise, but it can also improve a script's performance when the alternative is to respecify a selector.

How chaining works
Almost all jQuery methods return a jQuery object and so can have more jQuery methods applied to the result. We will explore the inner workings of chaining in Chapter 8, *Developing Plugins*.

It is also possible to break a single line of code into multiple lines for greater readability, as we've been doing throughout this chapter so far. For example, a single chained sequence of methods could be written in one line:

```
$('td:contains(Henry)').parent().find('td:eq(1)')
    .addClass('highlight').end().find('td:eq(2)')
                        .addClass('highlight');
```

Listing 2.15

This same sequence of methods could also be written in seven lines:

```
$('td:contains(Henry)') // Find every cell containing "Henry"
  .parent() // Select its parent
  .find('td:eq(1)') // Find the 2nd descendant cell
  .addClass('highlight') // Add the "highlight" class
  .end() // Return to the parent of the cell containing "Henry"
  .find('td:eq(2)') // Find the 3rd descendant cell
  .addClass('highlight'); // Add the "highlight" class
```

Listing 2.16

The DOM traversal in this example is contrived and not recommended. There are clearly simpler, more direct methods at our disposal. The point of the example is simply to demonstrate the tremendous flexibility that chaining affords us, especially when many calls need to be made.

Chaining can be like speaking a whole paragraph's worth of words in a single breath--it gets the job done quickly, but it can be hard for someone else to understand. Breaking it up into multiple lines and adding judicious comments can save more time in the long run.

Iterating over jQuery objects

New in jQuery 3 is the ability to iterate over jQuery objects using a `for...of` loop. This by itself isn't a big deal. For one thing, it's rare that we need to explicitly iterate over jQuery objects, especially when the same result is possible by using implicit iteration in jQuery functions. But sometimes, explicit iteration can't be avoided. For example, imaging you need to reduce an array of elements (a jQuery object) to an array of string values. The `each()` function is a tool of choice here:

```
const eachText = [];

$('td')
  .each((i, td) => {
    if (td.textContent.startsWith('H')) {
      eachText.push(td.textContent);
    }
  });

console.log('each', eachText);
// ["Hamlet", "Henry IV, Part I", "History", "Henry V", "History"]
```

Listing 2.17

We start off with an array of `<td>` elements, the result of our `$('td')` selector. We then reduce it to an array of strings by passing the `each()` function a callback that pushes each string that starts with "H" onto the `eachText` array. There's nothing wrong with this approach, but having callback functions for such a straightforward task seems like a bit much. Here's the same functionality using `for...of` syntax:

```
const forText = [];

for (let td of $('td')) {
  if (td.textContent.startsWith('H')) {
    forText.push(td.textContent);
  }
}

console.log('for', forText);
// ["Hamlet", "Henry IV, Part I", "History", "Henry V", "History"]
```

Listing 2.18

We can now reduce jQuery objects using simple for loops and if statements. We'll revisit this `for...of` approach later on in the book for more advanced usage scenarios involving generators.

Accessing DOM elements

Every selector expression and most jQuery methods return a jQuery object. This is almost always what we want because of the implicit iteration and chaining capabilities that it affords.

Still, there may be points in our code when we need to access a DOM element directly. For example, we may need to make a resulting set of elements available to another JavaScript library, or we might need to access an element's tag name, which is available as a property of the DOM element. For these admittedly rare situations, jQuery provides the `.get()` method. To access the first DOM element referred to by a jQuery object, for example, we would use `.get(0)`. So, if we want to know the tag name of an element with an ID of `my-element`, we would write:

```
$('#my-element').get(0).tagName;
```

For even greater convenience, jQuery provides a shorthand for `.get()`. Instead of writing the previous line, we can use square brackets immediately following the selector:

```
$('#my-element')[0].tagName;
```

It's no accident that this syntax appears to treat the jQuery object as an array of DOM elements; using the square brackets is like peeling away the jQuery layer to get at the node list, and including the index (in this case, 0) is like plucking out the DOM element itself.

Summary

With the techniques that we covered in this chapter, we should now be able to locate sets of elements on the page in a variety of ways. In particular, we learned how to style top-level and sub-level items in a nested list using basic CSS selectors, how to apply different styles to different types of links using attribute selectors, add rudimentary striping to a table using either the custom jQuery selectors :odd and :even or the advanced CSS selector :nth-child(), and highlight text within certain table cells by chaining jQuery methods.

So far, we have been using the $(() => {}) document ready handler to add a class to a matched set of elements. In the next chapter, we'll explore ways in which to add a class in response to a variety of user-initiated events.

Further reading

The topic of selectors and traversal methods will be explored in more detail in Chapter 9, *Advanced Selectors and Traversing*. A complete list of jQuery's selectors and traversal methods is available in Appendix B of this book and in the official jQuery documentation at http://api.jquery.com/.

Exercises

Challenge exercises may require the use of the official jQuery documentation at http://api.jquery.com/:

1. Add a class of special to all of the <li> elements at the second level of the nested list.
2. Add a class of year to all the table cells in the third column of a table.
3. Add the class special to the first table row that has the word **Tragedy** in it.
4. Here's a challenge for you. Select all the list items (<li>s) containing a link (<a>). Add the class afterlink to the sibling list items that follow the ones selected.
5. Here's another challenge for you. Add the class tragedy to the closest ancestor <ul> of any .pdf link.

3
Handling Events

JavaScript has several built-in ways of reacting to user interaction and other events. To make a page dynamic and responsive, we need to harness this capability so that we can, at the appropriate times, use the jQuery techniques you learned so far and the other tricks you'll learn later. While we could do this with vanilla JavaScript, jQuery enhances and extends the basic event-handling mechanisms to give them a more elegant syntax while making them more powerful at the same time.

In this chapter, we will cover:

- Executing JavaScript code when the page is ready
- Handling user events, such as mouse clicks and keystrokes
- The flow of events through the document, and how to manipulate that flow
- Simulating events as if the user initiated them

Performing tasks on page load

We have already seen how to make jQuery react to the loading of a web page. The $(() => {}) event handler can be used to run code that depends on HTML elements, but there's a bit more to be said about it.

Timing of code execution

In Chapter 1, *Getting Started*, we noted that `$(() => {})` was jQuery's primary way to perform tasks on page load. It is not, however, the only method at our disposal. The native `window.onload` event can do the same thing. While the two methods are similar, it is important to recognize their difference in timing, even though it can be quite subtle depending on the number of resources being loaded.

The `window.onload` event fires when a document is completely downloaded to the browser. This means that every element on the page is ready to be manipulated by JavaScript, which is a boon for writing feature-rich code without worrying about load order.

On the other hand, a handler registered using `$(() => {})` is invoked when the DOM is completely ready for use. This also means that all elements are accessible by our scripts, but does not mean that every associated file has been downloaded. As soon as the HTML file has been downloaded and parsed into a DOM tree, the code can run.

Style loading and code execution

To ensure that the page has also been styled before the JavaScript code executes, it is good practice to place the `<link rel="stylesheet">` and `<style>` tags prior to any `<script>` tags within the document's `<head>` element.

Consider, for example, a page that presents an image gallery; such a page may have many large images on it, which we can hide, show, move, and otherwise manipulate with jQuery. If we set up our interface using the `onload` event, users will have to wait until each and every image is completely downloaded before they can use those features. Even worse, if behaviors are not yet attached to elements that have default behaviors (such as links), user interactions could produce unintended outcomes. However, when we use `$(() => {})` for the setup, the interface is ready to be used earlier with the correct behavior.

What is loaded and what is not?

Using `$(() => {})` is almost always preferred over using an `onload` handler, but we need to keep in mind that, because supporting files may not have loaded, attributes such as image height and width are not necessarily available at this time. If these are needed, we may at times also choose to implement an `onload` handler; the two mechanisms can coexist peacefully.

Handling multiple scripts on one page

The traditional mechanism for registering event handlers through JavaScript (rather than adding handler attributes right in the HTML content) is to assign a function to the DOM element's corresponding property. For example, suppose we had defined the following function:

```
function doStuff() {
  // Perform a task...
}
```

We could then either assign it within our HTML markup:

```
<body onload="doStuff();">
```

Or, we could assign it from within JavaScript code:

```
window.onload = doStuff;
```

Both of these approaches will cause the function to execute when the page is loaded. The advantage of the second is that the behavior is cleanly separated from the markup.

Referencing versus calling functions

When we assign a function as a handler, we use the function name but omit the trailing parentheses. With the parentheses, the function is called immediately; without the parantheses, the name simply identifies, or *references*, the function, and can be used to call it later.

With one function, this strategy works quite well. However, suppose we have a second function as follows:

```
function doOtherStuff() {
  // Perform another task...
}
```

We could then attempt to assign this function to run on page load:

```
window.onload = doOtherStuff;
```

However, this assignment trumps the first one. The .onload attribute can only store one function reference at a time, so we can't add to the existing behavior.

The $(() => {}) mechanism handles this situation gracefully. Each call adds the new function to an internal queue of behaviors; when the page is loaded, all of the functions will execute. The functions will run in the order in which they were registered.

To be fair, jQuery doesn't have a monopoly on workarounds to this issue. We can write a JavaScript function that calls the existing `onload` handler, then calls a passed-in handler. This approach avoids conflicts between rival handlers like `$(() => {})` does, but lacks some of the other benefits we have discussed. In modern browsers, the `DOMContentLoaded` event can be triggered with the W3C standard `document.addEventListener()` method. However, the `$(() => {})` is more concise and elegant.

Passing an argument to the document ready callback

In some cases, it may prove useful to use more than one JavaScript library on the same page. Since many libraries make use of the `$` identifier (since it is short and convenient), we need a way to prevent collisions between libraries.

Fortunately, jQuery provides a method called `jQuery.noConflict()` to return control of the `$` identifier back to other libraries. Typical usage of `jQuery.noConflict()` follows the following pattern:

```
<script src="prototype.js"></script>
<script src="jquery.js"></script>
<script>
  jQuery.noConflict();
</script>
<script src="myscript.js"></script>
```

First, the other library (`prototype.js` in this example) is included. Then, `jquery.js` itself is included, taking over `$` for its own use. Next, a call to `.noConflict()` frees up `$`, so that control of it reverts to the first included library (`prototype.js`). Now in our custom script, we can use both libraries, but whenever we want to use a jQuery method, we need to write `jQuery` instead of `$` as an identifier.

The `$(() => {})` document ready handler has one more trick up its sleeve to help us in this situation. The callback function we pass to it can take a single parameter--the `jQuery` object itself. This allows us to effectively rename it without fear of conflicts using the following syntax:

```
jQuery(($) => {
  // In here, we can use $ like normal!
});
```

Handling simple events

There are other times, apart from the loading of the page, at which we might want to perform a task. Just as JavaScript allows us to intercept the page load event with `<body onload="">` or `window.onload`, it provides similar hooks for user-initiated events such as mouse clicks (`onclick`), form fields being modified (`onchange`), and windows changing size (`onresize`). When assigned directly to elements in the DOM, these hooks have similar drawbacks to the ones we outlined for `onload`. Therefore, jQuery offers an improved way of handling these events as well.

A simple style switcher

To illustrate some event handling techniques, suppose we wish to have a single page rendered in several different styles based on user input; we will present buttons that allow the user to toggle between a normal view, a view in which the text is constrained to a narrow column, and a view with large print for the content area.

Progressive enhancement

In a real-world example, a good web citizen will employ the principle of progressive enhancement here. In `Chapter 5`, *Manipulating the DOM*, you will learn how we can inject content like this style switcher right from our jQuery code, so that users without JavaScript available will not see nonfunctional controls.

The HTML markup for the style switcher is as follows:

```
<div id="switcher" class="switcher">
  <h3>Style Switcher</h3>
  <button id="switcher-default">
    Default
  </button>
  <button id="switcher-narrow">
    Narrow Column
  </button>
  <button id="switcher-large">
    Large Print
  </button>
</div>
```

Getting the example code
You can access the example code from the following GitHub repository: ht tps://github.com/PacktPublishing/Learning-jQuery-3.

Combined with the rest of the page's HTML markup and some basic CSS, we get a page that looks like the following:

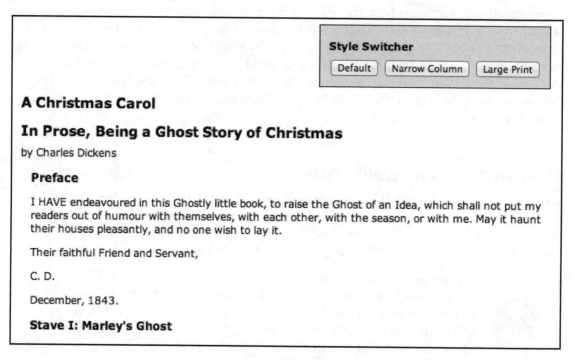

To begin with, we'll make the **Large Print** button operate. We need a bit of CSS to implement our alternative view of the page as follows:

```
body.large .chapter {
    font-size: 1.5em;
}
```

Our goal, then, is to apply the `large` class to the `<body>` tag. This will allow the stylesheet to reformat the page appropriately. Using what you learned in Chapter 2, *Selecting Elements*, we already know the statement needed to accomplish this:

```
$('body').addClass('large');
```

However, we want this to occur when the button is clicked, not when the page is loaded as we have seen so far. To do this, we'll introduce the `.on()` method. This method allows us to specify any DOM event and to attach a behavior to it. In this case, the event is called `click`, and the behavior is a function consisting of our previous one liner:

```
$(() => {
    $('#switcher-large')
```

```
    .on('click', () => {
      $('body').addClass('large');
    });
});
```

Listing 3.1

Now when the button gets clicked on, our code runs and the text is enlarged:

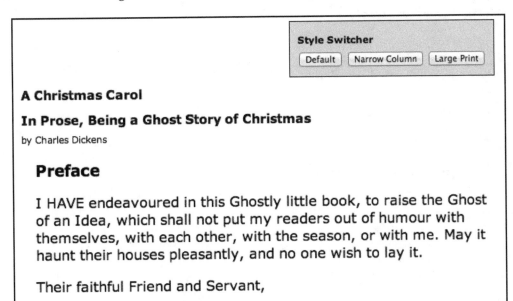

That's all there is to binding a behavior to an event. The advantages we discussed with the $(() => {}) document ready handler apply here as well. Multiple calls to .on() coexist nicely, appending additional behaviors to the same event as necessary.

This isn't necessarily the most elegant or efficient way to accomplish this task. As we proceed through this chapter, we will extend and refine this code into something we can be proud of.

Enabling the other buttons

We now have a **Large Print** button that works as advertised, but we need to apply similar handling to the other two buttons (**Default** and **Narrow Column**) to make them perform their tasks. This is straightforward: we use .on() to add a click handler to each of them, removing and adding classes as necessary. The new code reads as follows:

```
$(() => {
  $('#switcher-default')
    .on('click', () => {
      $('body')
        .removeClass('narrow')
        .removeClass('large');
    });

  $('#switcher-narrow')
    .on('click', () => {
      $('body')
        .addClass('narrow')
        .removeClass('large');
    });

  $('#switcher-large')
    .on('click', () => {
      $('body')
        .removeClass('narrow')
        .addClass('large');
    });
});
```

Listing 3.2

This is combined with a CSS rule for the narrow class:

```
body.narrow .chapter {
  width: 250px;
}
```

Now, after clicking the **Narrow Column** button, its corresponding CSS is applied and the text gets laid out differently:

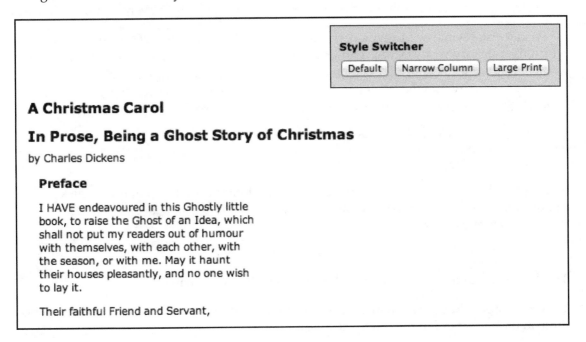

Clicking on **Default** removes both class names from the <body> tag, returning the page to its initial rendering.

Making use of event handler context

Our switcher is behaving correctly, but we are not giving the user any feedback about which button is currently active. Our approach for handling this will be to apply the selected class to the button when it is clicked, and to remove this class from the other buttons. The selected class simply makes the button's text bold:

```
.selected {
   font-weight: bold;
}
```

We could accomplish this class modification as we did previously by referring to each button by ID and applying or removing classes as necessary, but, instead, we'll explore a more elegant and scalable solution that exploits the context in which event handlers run.

When any event handler is triggered, the keyword `this` refers to the DOM element to which the behavior was attached. Earlier we noted that the `$()` function could take a DOM element as its argument; this is one of the key reasons why that facility is available. By writing `$(this)` within the event handler, we create a jQuery object corresponding to the element, and we can act on it just as if we had located it with a CSS selector.

With this in mind, we can write the following:

```
$(this).addClass('selected');
```

Placing this line in each of the three handlers will add the class when a button is clicked. To remove the class from the other buttons, we can take advantage of jQuery's implicit iteration feature, and write:

```
$('#switcher button').removeClass('selected');
```

This line removes the class from every button inside the style switcher.

We should also add the class to the **Default** button when the document is ready. So, placing these in the correct order, the code is as follows:

```
$(() => {
  $('#switcher-default')
    .addClass('selected')
    .on('click', function() {
      $('body')
        .removeClass('narrow');
        .removeClass('large');
      $('#switcher button')
        .removeClass('selected');
      $(this)
        .addClass('selected');
    });

  $('#switcher-narrow')
    .on('click', function() {
      $('body')
        .addClass('narrow')
        .removeClass('large');
      $('#switcher button')
        .removeClass('selected');
      $(this)
        .addClass('selected');
```

```
});

$('#switcher-large')
  .on('click', function() {
    $('body')
      .removeClass('narrow')
      .addClass('large');
    $('#switcher button')
      .removeClass('selected');
    $(this)
      .addClass('selected');
  });
});
```

Listing 3.3

Now the style switcher gives appropriate feedback.

Generalizing the statements by using the handler context allows us to be yet more efficient. We can factor the highlighting routine out into a separate handler, as shown in *Listing 3.4*, because it is the same for all three buttons:

```
$(() => {
  $('#switcher-default')
    .addClass('selected')
    .on('click', function() {
      $('body')
        .removeClass('narrow')
        .removeClass('large');
    });
  $('#switcher-narrow')
    .on('click', () => {
      $('body')
        .addClass('narrow')
        .removeClass('large');
    });

  $('#switcher-large')
    .on('click', () => {
      $('body')
        .removeClass('narrow')
        .addClass('large');
    });

  $('#switcher button')
    .on('click', function() {
      $('#switcher button')
        .removeClass('selected');
```

```
    $(this)
      .addClass('selected');
  });
});
```

Listing 3.4

This optimization takes advantage of three jQuery features we have already discussed. First, **implicit iteration** is once again useful when we bind the same `click` handler to each button with a single call to `.on()`. Second, **behavior queuing** allows us to bind two functions to the same click event without the second overwriting the first.

When an event handler function references its context using `this`, you can't use an arrow function (`() => {}`). These functions have a **lexical context**. This means that when jQuery attempts to set the context as the element that triggered the event, it doesn't work.

Consolidating code using event context

The code optimization we've just completed is an example of **refactoring**--modifying existing code to perform the same task in a more efficient or elegant way. To explore further refactoring opportunities, let's look at the behaviors we have bound to each button. The `.removeClass()` method's parameter is optional; when omitted, it removes all classes from the element. We can streamline our code a bit by exploiting this as follows:

```
$(() => {
  $('#switcher-default')
    .addClass('selected')
    .on('click', () => {
      $('body').removeClass();
    });
  $('#switcher-narrow')
    .on('click', () => {
      $('body')
        .removeClass()
        .addClass('narrow');
    });

  $('#switcher-large')
    .on('click', () => {
      $('body')
        .removeClass()
        .addClass('large');
    });
```

```
$('#switcher button')
  .on('click', function() {
    $('#switcher button')
      .removeClass('selected');
    $(this)
      .addClass('selected');
  });
});
```

Listing 3.5

Note that the order of operations has changed a bit to accommodate our more general class removal; we need to execute `.removeClass()` first so that it doesn't undo the call to `.addClass()`, which we perform in the same breath.

 We can only safely remove all classes because we are in charge of the HTML in this case. When we are writing code for reuse (such as for a plugin), we need to respect any classes that might be present and leave them intact.

Now we are executing some of the same code in each of the button's handlers. This can be easily factored out into our general button `click` handler:

```
$(() => {
  $('#switcher-default')
    .addClass('selected');
  $('#switcher button')
    .on('click', function() {
      $('body')
        .removeClass();
      $('#switcher button')
        .removeClass('selected');
      $(this)
        .addClass('selected');
    });

  $('#switcher-narrow')
    .on('click', () => {
      $('body')
        .addClass('narrow');
    });

  $('#switcher-large')
    .on('click', () => {
      $('body')
        .addClass('large');
    });
```

```
});
```

Listing 3.6

Note that we need to move the general handler above the specific ones now. The
`.removeClass()` call needs to happen before `.addClass()` executes, and we can count on
this because jQuery always triggers event handlers in the order in which they were
registered.

Finally, we can get rid of the specific handlers entirely by, once again, exploiting **event
context**. Since the context keyword `this` gives us a DOM element rather than a jQuery
object, we can use native DOM properties to determine the ID of the element that was
clicked. We can thus bind the same handler to all the buttons, and within the handler
perform different actions for each button:

```
$(() => {
  $('#switcher-default')
    .addClass('selected');
  $('#switcher button')
    .on('click', function() {
      const bodyClass = this.id.split('-')[1];
      $('body')
        .removeClass()
        .addClass(bodyClass);
      $('#switcher button')
        .removeClass('selected');
      $(this)
        .addClass('selected');
    });
});
```

Listing 3.7

The value of the `bodyClass` variable will be `default`, `narrow`, or `large`, depending on
which button is clicked. Here, we are departing somewhat from our previous code; in that
we are adding a `default` class to `<body>` when the user clicks on `<button
id="switcher-default">`. While we do not need this class applied, it isn't causing any
harm either, and the reduction of code complexity more than makes up for an unused class
name.

Shorthand events

Binding a handler for an event (such as a simple `click` event) is such a common task that jQuery provides an even terser way to accomplish it; shorthand event methods work in the same way as their `.on()` counterparts with fewer keystrokes.

For example, our style switcher could be written using `.click()` instead of `.on()` as follows:

```
$(() => {
  $('#switcher-default')
    .addClass('selected');

  $('#switcher button')
    .click(function() {
      const bodyClass = this.id.split('-')[1];
      $('body')
        .removeClass()
        .addClass(bodyClass);
      $('#switcher button')
        .removeClass('selected');
      $(this)
        .addClass('selected');
    });
});
```

Listing 3.8

Shorthand event methods such as the previous one exist for the other standard DOM events such as `blur`, `keydown`, and `scroll` as well. Each shortcut method binds a handler to the event with the corresponding name.

Showing and hiding page elements

Suppose that we wanted to be able to hide our style switcher when it is not needed. One convenient way to hide page elements is to make them collapsible. We will allow one click on the label to hide the buttons, leaving the label alone. Another click on the label will restore the buttons. We need another class that will hide buttons:

```
.hidden {
  display: none;
}
```

We could implement this feature by storing the current state of the buttons in a variable and checking its value each time the label is clicked to know whether to add or remove the hidden class on the buttons. However, jQuery provides an easy way for us to add or remove a class depending on whether that class is already present--the `.toggleClass()` method:

```
$(() => {
  $('#switcher h3')
    .click(function() {
      $(this)
        .siblings('button')
        .toggleClass('hidden');
    });
});
```

Listing 3.9

After the first click, the buttons are all hidden:

A second click then returns them to visibility:

Once again, we rely on implicit iteration, this time to hide all the buttons - siblings of the <h3> - in one fell swoop.

Event propagation

In illustrating the ability of the click event to operate on normally non-clickable page elements, we have crafted an interface that doesn't indicate that the style switcher label--just an <h3> element-is actually a *live* part of the page awaiting user interaction. To remedy this, we can give it a rollover state, making it clear that it interacts in some way with the mouse:

```
.hover {
  cursor: pointer;
  background-color: #afa;
}
```

The CSS specification includes a pseudo-class called :hover, which allows a stylesheet to affect an element's appearance when the user's mouse cursor hovers over it. This would certainly solve our problem in this instance, but instead, we will take this opportunity to introduce jQuery's .hover() method, which allows us to use JavaScript to change an element's styling--and indeed, perform any arbitrary action--both when the mouse cursor enters the element and when it leaves the element.

The .hover() method takes two function arguments, unlike the simple event methods we have so far encountered. The first function will be executed when the mouse cursor enters the selected element, and the second is fired when the cursor leaves. We can modify the classes applied to the buttons at these times to achieve a rollover effect:

```
$(() => {
  $('#switcher h3')
    .hover(function() {
      $(this).addClass('hover');
    }, function() {
      $(this).removeClass('hover');
    });
});
```

Listing 3.10

We once again use implicit iteration and event context for short and simple code. Now when hovering over the <h3> element, we see our class applied:

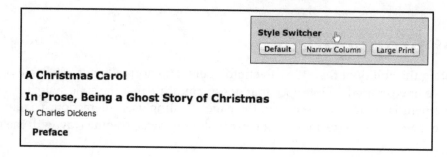

The use of .hover() also means we avoid headaches caused by event propagation in JavaScript. To understand this, we need to take a look at how JavaScript decides which element gets to handle a given event.

The journey of an event

When an event occurs on a page, an entire hierarchy of DOM elements gets a chance to handle the event. Consider a page model like the following:

```
<div class="foo">
  <span class="bar">
    <a href="http://www.example.com/">
      The quick brown fox jumps over the lazy dog.
    </a>
  </span>
  <p>
    How razorback-jumping frogs can level six piqued gymnasts!
  </p>
</div>
```

We then visualize the code as a set of nested elements:

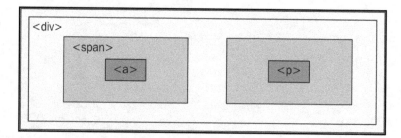

For any event, there are multiple elements that could logically be responsible for reacting. When the link on this page is clicked, for example, the `<div>`, `<span>`, and `<a>` elements should all get the opportunity to respond to the click. After all, these three elements are all under the user's mouse cursor at the time. The `<p>` element, on the other hand, is not part of this interaction at all.

One strategy for allowing multiple elements to respond to a user interaction is called **event capturing**. With event capturing, the event is first given to the most all-encompassing element, and then to progressively more specific ones. In our example, this means that first the `<div>` element gets passed the event, then the `<span>` element, and finally the `<a>` element, as shown in the following figure:

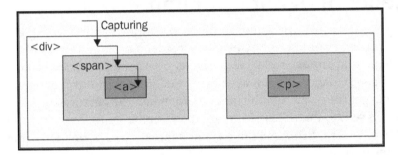

The opposite strategy is called **event bubbling**. The event gets sent to the most specific element, and after this element has an opportunity to react, the event **bubbles up** to more general elements. In our example, the `<a>` element would be handed the event first, and then the `<span>` and `<div>` elements in that order, as shown in the following figure:

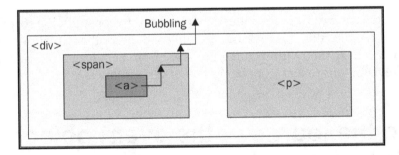

Unsurprisingly, different browser developers originally decided on different models for event propagation. The DOM standard that was eventually developed thus specified that both strategies should be used: first the event is captured from general elements to specific ones, and then the event bubbles back up to the top of the DOM tree. Event handlers can be registered for either part of the process.

To provide consistent and easy-to-understand behavior, jQuery always registers event handlers for the bubbling phase of the model. We can always assume that the most specific element will get the first opportunity to respond to any event.

Side effects of event bubbling

Event bubbling can cause unexpected behavior, especially when the wrong element responds to a mouseover or mouseout event. Consider a mouseout event handler attached to the <div> element in our example. When the user's mouse cursor exits the <div> element, the mouseout handler is run as anticipated. Since this is at the top of the hierarchy, no other elements get the event. On the other hand, when the cursor exits the <a> element, a mouseout event is sent to that. This event will then bubble up to the <span> element and then to the <div> element, firing the same event handler. This bubbling sequence is unlikely to be desired.

The mouseenter and mouseleave events, either bound individually or combined in the .hover() method, are aware of these bubbling issues and, when we use them to attach events, we can ignore the problems caused by the wrong element getting a mouseover or mouseout event.

The mouseout scenario just described illustrates the need to constrain the scope of an event. While .hover() handles this specific case, we will encounter other situations in which we need to limit an event spatially (preventing the event from being sent to certain elements) or temporally (preventing the event from being sent at certain times).

Altering the journey - the event object

We have already seen one situation in which event bubbling can cause problems. To show a case in which .hover() does not help our cause, we'll alter the collapsing behavior that we implemented earlier.

Suppose we wish to expand the clickable area that triggers the collapsing or expanding of the style switcher. One way to do this is to move the event handler from the label, `<h3>`, to its containing `<div>` element. In *Listing 3.9*, we added a `click` handler to `#switcher h3`; we will attempt this change by attaching the handler to `#switcher` instead:

```
$(() => {
  $('#switcher')
    .click(() => {
      $('#switcher button').toggleClass('hidden');
    });
});
```

Listing 3.11

This alteration makes the entire area of the style switcher clickable to toggle its visibility. The downside is that clicking on a button also collapses the style switcher after the style on the content has been altered. This is due to event bubbling; the event is first handled by the buttons, then passed up through the DOM tree until it reaches the `<div id="switcher">` element, where our new handler is activated and hides the buttons.

To solve this problem, we need access to the `event` object. This is a DOM construct that is passed to each element's event handler when it is invoked. It provides information about the event, such as where the mouse cursor was at the time of the event. It also provides some methods that can be used to affect the progress of the event through the DOM.

Event object reference
For detailed information about jQuery's implementation of the event object and its properties, see
`http://api.jquery.com/category/events/event-object/`.

To use the event object in our handlers, we only need to add a parameter to the function:

```
$(() => {
  $('#switcher')
    .click(function(event) {
      $('#switcher button').toggleClass('hidden');
    });
});
```

Note that we have named this parameter `event` because it is descriptive, not because we need to. Naming it `flapjacks` or anything else for that matter would work just as well.

Event targets

Now we have the event object available to us as `event` within our handler. The property `event.target` can be helpful in controlling *where* an event takes effect. This property is a part of the DOM API, but is not implemented in some older browser versions; jQuery extends the event object as necessary to provide the property in every browser. With `.target`, we can determine which element in the DOM was the first to receive the event. In the case of a `click` event, this will be the actual item clicked on. Remembering that `this` gives us the DOM element handling the event, we can write the following code:

```
$(() => {
  $('#switcher')
    .click(function(event) {
      if (event.target == this) {
        $(this)
          .children('button')
          .toggleClass('hidden');
      }
    });
});
```

Listing 3.12

This code ensures that the item clicked on was `<div id="switcher">`, not one of its sub-elements. Now, clicking on buttons will not collapse the style switcher, but clicking on the switcher's background *will*. However, clicking on the label, `<h3>`, now does nothing, because it, too, is a sub-element. Instead of placing this check here, we can modify the behavior of the buttons to achieve our goals.

Stopping event propagation

The event object provides the `.stopPropagation()` method, which can halt the bubbling process completely for the event. Like `.target`, this method is a basic DOM feature, but using the jQuery implementation will hide any browser inconsistencies from our code.

We'll remove the `event.target == this` check we just added, and instead add some code in our buttons' `click` handlers:

```
$(() => {
  $('#switcher')
    .click((e) => {
      $(e.currentTarget)
        .children('button')
```

```
        .toggleClass('hidden');
    });
});
$(() => {
  $('#switcher-default')
    .addClass('selected');
  $('#switcher button')
    .click((e) => {
      const bodyClass = e.target.id.split('-')[1];

      $('body')
        .removeClass()
        .addClass(bodyClass);
      $(e.target)
        .addClass('selected')
        .removeClass('selected');

      e.stopPropagation();
    });
});
```

Listing 3.13

As before, we need to add an event parameter to the function we're using as the click handler: e. Then, we simply call e.stopPropagation() to prevent any other DOM element from responding to the event. Now our click is handled by the buttons, and only the buttons; clicks anywhere else on the style switcher will collapse or expand it.

Preventing default actions

If our click event handler was registered on a link element (<a>) rather than a generic <button> element outside of a form, we would face another problem. When a user clicks on a link, the browser loads a new page. This behavior is not an event handler in the same sense as the ones we have been discussing; instead, this is the default action for a click on a link element. Similarly, when the *Enter* key is pressed while the user is editing a form, the submit event may be triggered on the form, but then the form submission actually occurs after this.

If these default actions are undesired, calling .stopPropagation() on the event will not help. These actions don't occur in the normal flow of event propagation. Instead, the .preventDefault() method serves to stop the event in its tracks before the default action is triggered.

Calling .preventDefault() is often useful after we have done some tests on the environment of the event. For example, during a form submission, we might wish to check that required fields are filled in and prevent the default action only if they are not. With links, we can check if some precondition has been met before allowing the href to be followed, in essence, disabling the link under some circumstances.

Event propagation and default actions are independent mechanisms; either of them can be stopped while the other still occurs. If we wish to halt both, we can return false at the end of our event handler, which is a shortcut for calling both .stopPropagation() and .preventDefault() on the event.

Delegating events

Event bubbling isn't always a hindrance; we can often use it to great benefit. One great technique that exploits bubbling is called **event delegation**. With it, we can use an event handler on a single element to do the work of many.

In our example, there are just three <button> elements that have attached click handlers. But what if there were many more than three? This is more common than you might think. Consider, for example, a large table of information in which each row has an interactive item requiring a click handler. Implicit iteration makes assigning all of these click handlers easy, but performance can suffer because of the looping being done internally to jQuery, and because of the memory footprint of maintaining all the handlers.

Instead, we can assign a single click handler to an ancestor element in the DOM. An uninterrupted click event will eventually reach the ancestor due to event bubbling, and we can do our work there.

As an example, let's apply this technique to our style switcher (even though the number of items does not demand the approach). As seen in *Listing 3.12* previously, we can use the e.target property to check which element is under the mouse cursor when the click event occurs.

```
$(() => {
  $('#switcher')
    .click((e) => {
      if ($(event.target).is('button')) {
        const bodyClass = e.target.id.split('-')[1];

        $('body')
          .removeClass()
```

```
           .addClass(bodyClass);
        $(e.target)
          .addClass('selected')
          .removeClass('selected');

        e.stopPropagation();
      }
    });
  });
```

Listing 3.14

We've used a new method here called `.is()`. This method accepts the selector expressions we investigated in the previous chapter and tests the current jQuery object against the selector. If at least one element in the set is matched by the selector, `.is()` returns `true`. In this case, `$(e.target).is('button')` asks whether the element clicked is a `<button>` element. If so, we proceed with the previous code, with one significant alteration: the keyword `this` now refers to `<div id="switcher">`, so every time we are interested in the clicked button, we must now refer to it with `e.target`.

.is() and .hasClass()
We can test for the presence of a class on an element with `.hasClass()`. The `.is()` method is more flexible, however, and can test any selector expression.

We have an unintentional side-effect from this code, however. When a button is clicked now, the switcher collapses, as it did before we added the call to `.stopPropagation()`. The handler for the switcher visibility toggle is now bound to the same element as the handler for the buttons, so halting the event bubbling does not stop the toggle from being triggered. To sidestep this issue, we can remove the `.stopPropagation()` call and instead add another `.is()` test. Also, since we're making the entire switcher `<div>` element clickable, we ought to toggle the `hover` class while the user's mouse is over any part of it:

```
$(() => {
  const toggleHover = (e) => {
    $(e.target).toggleClass('hover');
  };

  $('#switcher')
    .hover(toggleHover, toggleHover);
});

$(() => {
  $('#switcher')
    .click((e) => {
```

```
            if (!$(e.target).is('button')) {
              $(e.currentTarget)
                .children('button')
                .toggleClass('hidden');
            }
          });
        });

        $(() => {
          $('#switcher-default')
            .addClass('selected');
          $('#switcher')
            .click((e) => {
              if ($(e.target).is('button')) {
                const bodyClass = e.target.id.split('-')[1];

                $('body')
                  .removeClass()
                  .addClass(bodyClass);
                $(e.target)
                  .addClass('selected')
                  .siblings('button')
                  .removeClass('selected');
              }
            });
        });
```

Listing 3.15

This example is a bit over complicated for its size, but as the number of elements with event handlers increases, so does event delegation's benefit. Also, we can avoid some of the code repetition by combining the two `click` handlers and using a single `if-else` statement for the `.is()` test:

```
$(() => {
  $('#switcher-default')
    .addClass('selected');
  $('#switcher')
    .click((e) => {
      if ($(e.target).is('button')) {
        const bodyClass = e.target.id.split('-')[1];
        $('body')
          .removeClass()
          .addClass(bodyClass);
        $(e.target)
          .addClass('selected')
          .removeClass('selected');
```

```
      } else {
        $(e.currentTarget)
          .children('button')
          .toggleClass('hidden');
      }
    });
  });
```

Listing 3.16

While our code could still use some fine tuning, it is approaching a state at which we can feel comfortable using it for what we set out to do. Nevertheless, for the sake of learning more about jQuery's event handling, we'll back up to *Listing 3.15* and continue to modify that version of the code.

 Event delegation is also useful in other situations we'll see later, such as when new elements are added by DOM manipulation methods (Chapter 5, *Manipulating the DOM*) or Ajax routines (Chapter 6, *Sending Data with Ajax*).

Using built-in event delegation capabilities

Because event delegation can be helpful in so many situations, jQuery includes a set of tools to aid developers in using this technique. The .on() method we have already discussed can perform event delegation when provided with appropriate parameters:

```
$(() => {
  $('#switcher-default')
    .addClass('selected');
  $('#switcher')
    .on('click', 'button', (e) => {
      const bodyClass = e.target.id.split('-')[1];

      $('body')
        .removeClass()
        .addClass(bodyClass);
      $(e.target)
        .addClass('selected')
        .siblings('button')
        .removeClass('selected');

      e.stopPropagation();
    })
    .on('click', (e) => {
      $(e.currentTarget)
```

```
        .children('button')
        .toggleClass('hidden');
    });
});
```

Listing 3.17

This is looking pretty good now. We have two really simple handlers for all click events in switcher feature. We added a selector expression to the `.on()` method as the second argument. Specifically, we want to make sure that any elements that bubble click events up to `#switch` are in fact button elements. This is better than writing a bunch of logic in the event handler to determine how to handle the event based on the element that generated it.

We did have to add a call to `e.stopPropagation()`. The reason is so that the second click handler, the one that handles toggling the button visibility, doesn't have to worry about checking where the event came from. It's often easier to prevent propagation than it is to introduce edge case handling into event handler code.

With a few minor trade offs, we now have a single button click handler function that works with 3 buttons, or with 300 buttons. It's the little things like this that make jQuery code scale well.

 We'll fully examine this use of `.on()`, in `Chapter 10`, *Advanced Events*.

Removing an event handler

There are times when we will be done with an event handler we previously registered. Perhaps the state of the page has changed such that the action no longer makes sense. It is possible to handle this situation with conditional statements inside our event handlers, but it is more elegant to unbind the handler entirely.

Suppose that we want our collapsible style switcher to remain expanded whenever the page is not using the normal style. While the **Narrow Column** or **Large Print** button is selected, clicking on the background of the style switcher should do nothing. We can accomplish this by calling the `.off()` method to remove the collapsing handler when one of the non-default style switcher buttons is clicked:

```
$(() => {
  $('#switcher')
```

```
      .click((e) => {
        if (!$(e.target).is('button')) {
          $(e.currentTarget)
            .children('button')
            .toggleClass('hidden');
        }
      });
    $('#switcher-narrow, #switcher-large')
      .click(() => {
        $('#switcher').off('click');
      });
  });
```

Listing 3.18

Now when a button such as **Narrow Column** is clicked, the `click` handler on the style switcher `<div>` is removed, and clicking on the background of the box no longer collapses it. However, the buttons don't work anymore! They are affected by the `click` event of the style switcher `<div>` as well, because we rewrote the button-handling code to use event delegation. This means that when we call `$('#switcher').off('click')`, both behaviors are removed.

Giving namespaces to event handlers

We need to make our `.off()` call more specific so that it does not remove both of the click handlers we have registered. One way of doing this is to use **event namespacing**. We can introduce additional information when an event is bound that allows us to identify that particular handler later. To use namespaces, we need to return to the non-shorthand method of binding event handlers, the `.on()` method itself.

The first parameter we pass to `.on()` is the name of the event we want to watch for. We can use a special syntax here, though, that allows us to subcategorize the event:

```
$(() => {
  $('#switcher')
    .on('click.collapse', (e) => {
      if (!$(e.target).is('button')) {
        $(e.currentTarget)
          .children('button')
          .toggleClass('hidden');
      }
    });
  $('#switcher-narrow, #switcher-large')
    .click(() => {
```

```
    $('#switcher').off('click.collapse');
  });
});
```

Listing 3.19

The `.collapse` suffix is invisible to the event handling system; `click` events are handled by this function, just as if we wrote `.on('click')`. However, the addition of the namespace means that we can unbind just this handler without affecting the separate `click` handler we wrote for the buttons.

> There are other ways of making our `.off()` call more specific, as we will see in a moment. However, event namespacing is a useful tool in our arsenal. It is especially handy in the creation of plugins, as we'll see in later chapters.

Rebinding events

Now clicking on the **Narrow Column** or **Large Print** button causes the style switcher collapsing functionality to be disabled. However, we want the behavior to return when the **Default** button is pressed. To do this, we will need to **rebind** the handler whenever **Default** is clicked.

First, we should give our handler function a name so that we can use it more than once without repeating ourselves:

```
$(() => {
  const toggleSwitcher = (e) => {
    if (!$(e.target).is('button')) {
      $(e.currentTarget)
        .children('button')
        .toggleClass('hidden');
    }
  };

  $('#switcher')
    .on('click.collapse', toggleSwitcher);
  $('#switcher-narrow, #switcher-large')
    .click((e) => {
      $('#switcher').off('click.collapse');
    });
});
```

Listing 3.20

Recall that we are passing .on() a **function reference** as its second argument. It is important to remember when referring to a function that we must omit parentheses after the function name; parentheses would cause the function to be *called* rather than *referenced*.

Now that the toggleSwitcher() function can be referenced, we can bind it again later, without repeating the function definition:

```
$(() => {
  const toggleSwitcher = (e) => {
    if (!$(e.target).is('button')) {
      $(e.currentTarget)
        .children('button')
        .toggleClass('hidden');
    }
  };

  $('#switcher').on('click.collapse', toggleSwitcher);
  $('#switcher-narrow, #switcher-large')
    .click(() => {
      $('#switcher').off('click.collapse');
    });
  $('#switcher-default')
    .click(() => {
      $('#switcher').on('click.collapse', toggleSwitcher);
    });
});
```

Listing 3.21

Now the toggle behavior is bound when the document is loaded, unbound when **Narrow Column** or **Large Print** is clicked, and rebound when **Default** is clicked after that.

Since we have named the function, we no longer need to use namespacing. The .off() method can take a function as a second argument; in this case, it unbinds only that specific handler. However, we have run into another problem. Remember that when a handler is bound to an event in jQuery, previous handlers remain in effect. In this case, each time **Default** is clicked, another copy of the toggleSwitcher handler is bound to the style switcher. In other words, the function is called an extra time for each additional click until the user clicks **Narrow** or **Large Print**, which unbinds all of the toggleSwitcher handlers at once.

When an even number of `toggleSwitcher` handlers are bound, clicks on the style switcher (but not on a button) appear to have no effect. In fact, the `hidden` class is being toggled multiple times, ending up in the same state it was when it began. To remedy this problem, we can unbind the handler when a user clicks on *any* button, and rebind only after ensuring that the clicked button's ID is `switcher-default`:

```
$(() => {
  const toggleSwitcher = (e) => {
    if (!$(e.target).is('button')) {
      $(e.currentTarget)
        .children('button')
        .toggleClass('hidden');
    }
  };

  $('#switcher')
    .on('click', toggleSwitcher);
  $('#switcher button')
    .click((e) => {
      $('#switcher').off('click', toggleSwitcher);

      if (e.target.id == 'switcher-default') {
        $('#switcher').on('click', toggleSwitcher);
      }
    });
});
```

Listing 3.22

A shortcut is also available for the situation in which we want to unbind an event handler immediately after the first time it is triggered. This shortcut, called `.one()`, is used as follows:

```
$('#switcher').one('click', toggleSwitcher);
```

This would cause the toggle action to occur only once.

Simulating user interaction

At times, it is convenient to execute code that we have bound to an event, even if the event isn't triggered directly by user input. For example, suppose we wanted our style switcher to begin in its collapsed state. We could accomplish this by hiding buttons from within the stylesheet, or by adding our `hidden` class or calling the `.hide()` method from a `$(() =>` `{})` handler. Another way would be to simulate a click on the style switcher so that the toggling mechanism we've already established is triggered.

The `.trigger()` method allows us to do just this:

```
$(() => {
  $('#switcher').trigger('click');
});
```

Listing 3.23

Now when the page loads, the switcher is collapsed just as if it had been clicked, as shown in the following screenshot:

If we were hiding content that we wanted people without JavaScript enabled to see, this would be a reasonable way to implement **graceful degradation**. Although, this is very uncommon these days.

The `.trigger()` method provides the same set of shortcut methods that `.on()` does. When these shortcuts are used with no arguments, the behavior is to trigger the action rather than bind it:

```
$(() => {
  $('#switcher').click();
});
```

Listing 3.24

Reacting to keyboard events

As another example, we can add keyboard shortcuts to our style switcher. When the user types the first letter of one of the display styles, we will have the page behave as if the corresponding button was clicked. To implement this feature, we will need to explore **keyboard events**, which behave a bit differently from **mouse events**.

There are two types of keyboard events: those that react to the keyboard directly (keyup and keydown) and those that react to text input (keypress). A single character entry event could correspond to several keys, for example, when the *Shift* key in combination with the *X* key creates the capital letter **X**. While the specifics of implementation differ from one browser to the next (unsurprisingly), a safe rule of thumb is: if you want to know what key the user pushed, you should observe the keyup or keydown event; if you want to know what character ended up on the screen as a result, you should observe the keypress event. For this feature, we just want to know when the user presses the *D*, *N*, or *L* key, so we will use keyup.

Next, we need to determine which element should watch for the event. This is a little less obvious than with mouse events, where we have a visible mouse cursor to tell us about the event's target. Instead, the target of a keyboard event is the element that currently has the **keyboard focus**. The element with focus can be changed in several ways, including using mouse clicks and pressing the *Tab* key. Not every element can get the focus, either; only items that have default keyboard-driven behaviors such as form fields, links, and elements with a .tabIndex property are candidates.

In this case, we don't really care what element has the focus; we want our switcher to work whenever the user presses one of the keys. Event bubbling will once again come in handy, as we can bind our keyup event to the document element and have assurance that eventually any key event will bubble up to us.

Finally, we will need to know which key was pressed when our keyup handler gets triggered. We can inspect the event object for this. The .which property of the event contains an identifier for the key that was pressed, and for alphabetic keys, this identifier is the ASCII value of the uppercase letter. With this information, we can now create an **object literal** of letters and their corresponding buttons to click. When the user presses a key, we'll see if its identifier is in the map, and if so, trigger the click:

```
$(() => {
  const triggers = {
    D: 'default',
    N: 'narrow',
    L: 'large'
  };
```

```
$(document)
  .keyup((e) => {
    const key = String.fromCharCode(e.which);

    if (key in triggers) {
      $(`#switcher-${triggers[key]}`).click();
    }
  });
});
```

Listing 3.25

Presses of these three keys now simulate mouse clicks on the buttons--provided that the key event is not interrupted by features such as Firefox's **search for text when I start typing**.

As an alternative to using .trigger() to simulate this click, let's explore how to factor out code into a function so that more than one handler can call it--in this case, both click and keyup handlers. While not necessary in this case, this technique can be useful in eliminating code redundancy:

```
$(() => {
  // Enable hover effect on the style switcher
  const toggleHover = (e) => {
    $(e.target).toggleClass('hover');
  };

  $('#switcher').hover(toggleHover, toggleHover);

  // Allow the style switcher to expand and collapse.
  const toggleSwitcher = (e) => {
    if (!$(e.target).is('button')) {
      $(e.currentTarget)
        .children('button')
        .toggleClass('hidden');
    }
  };

  $('#switcher')
    .on('click', toggleSwitcher)
    // Simulate a click so we start in a collaped state.
    .click();

  // The setBodyClass() function changes the page style.
  // The style switcher state is also updated.
  const setBodyClass = (className) => {
    $('body')
      .removeClass()
```

```
        .addClass(className);

    $('#switcher button').removeClass('selected');
    $(`#switcher-${className}`).addClass('selected');
    $('#switcher').off('click', toggleSwitcher);

    if (className == 'default') {
      $('#switcher').on('click', toggleSwitcher);
    }
  };

  // Begin with the switcher-default button "selected"
  $('#switcher-default').addClass('selected');

  // Map key codes to their corresponding buttons to click
  const triggers = {
    D: 'default',
    N: 'narrow',
    L: 'large'
  };

  // Call setBodyClass() when a button is clicked.
  $('#switcher')
    .click((e) => {
      if ($(e.target).is('button')) {
        setBodyClass(e.target.id.split('-')[1]);
      }
    });

  // Call setBodyClass() when a key is pressed.
  $(document)
    .keyup((e) => {
      const key = String.fromCharCode(e.which);

      if (key in triggers) {
        setBodyClass(triggers[key]);
      }
    });
});
```

Listing 3.26

This final revision consolidates all the previous code examples of this chapter. We have moved the entire block of code into a single $(() => {}) handler and made our code less redundant.

Summary

The abilities we've discussed in this chapter allow us to react to various user-driven and browser-initiated events. We have learned how to safely perform actions when the page loads, how to handle mouse events such as clicking on links or hovering over buttons, and how to interpret keystrokes.

In addition, we have delved into some of the inner workings of the event system, and can use this knowledge to perform event delegation and to change the default behavior of an event. We can even simulate the effects of an event as if the user initiated it.

We can use these capabilities to build interactive pages. In the next chapter, we'll learn how to provide visual feedback to the user during these interactions.

Further reading

The topic of event handling will be explored in more detail in `Chapter 10`, *Advanced Events*. A complete list of jQuery's event methods is available in *Appendix C* of this book, or in the official jQuery documentation at `http://api.jquery.com/`.

Exercises

Challenge exercises may require the use of the official jQuery documentation at `http://api.jquery.com/`.

1. When **Charles Dickens** is clicked, apply the `selected` style to it.
2. When a chapter title (`<h3 class="chapter-title">`) is double-clicked, toggle the visibility of the chapter text.
3. When the user presses the right arrow key, cycle to the next `body` class. The key code for the right arrow key is `39`.
4. **Challenge**: Use the `console.log()` function to log the coordinates of the mouse as it moves across any paragraph. (Note: `console.log()` displays its results via the Firebug extension for Firefox, Safari's Web Inspector, or the Developer Tools in Chrome or Internet Explorer).
5. **Challenge**: Use `.mousedown()` and `.mouseup()` to track mouse events anywhere on the page. If the mouse button is released *above* where it was pressed, add the `hidden` class to all paragraphs. If it is released *below* where it was pressed, remove the `hidden` class from all paragraphs.

4
Styling and Animating

If actions speak louder than words, then in the JavaScript world, effects make actions speak louder still. With jQuery, we can easily add impact to our actions through a set of simple visual effects and even craft our own sophisticated animations.

The effects offered by jQuery supply simple visual flourishes that grant a sense of movement and modernity to any page. However, apart from being mere decoration, they can also provide important usability enhancements that help orient the user when something happens on a page (especially common in Ajax applications).

In this chapter, we will cover:

- Changing the styling of elements on the fly
- Hiding and showing elements with various built-in effects
- Creating custom animations of elements
- Sequencing effects to happen one after another

Modifying CSS with inline properties

Before we jump into jQuery effects, a quick look at CSS is in order. In previous chapters, we have been modifying a document's appearance by defining styles for classes in a separate stylesheet and then adding or removing those classes with jQuery. Typically, this is the preferred process for injecting CSS into HTML because it respects the stylesheet's role in dealing with the presentation of a page. However, there may be times when we need to apply styles that haven't been or can't easily be defined in a stylesheet. Fortunately, jQuery offers the .css() method for such occasions.

This method acts as both a **getter** and a **setter**. To get the value of a single style property, we simply pass the name of the property as a string and get a string in return. To get the value of multiple style properties, we can pass the property names as an array of strings to get an object of property-value pairs in return. Multiword property names, such as `backgroundColor` can be interpreted by jQuery when in hyphenated CSS notation (`background-color`) or camel-cased DOM notation (`backgroundColor`):

```
// Get a single property's value
.css('property')
// "value"

// Get multiple properties' values
.css(['property1', 'property-2'])
// {"property1": "value1", "property-2": "value2"}
```

For setting style properties, the `.css()` method comes in two flavors. One flavor takes a single style property and its value, and the other takes an object of property-value pairs:

```
// Single property and its value
.css('property', 'value')

// Object of property-value pairs
.css({
  property1: 'value1',
  'property-2': 'value2'
})
```

These simple key-value collections, called **object literals**, are real JavaScript objects that are created directly in code.

Object literal notation

In a property value, strings are enclosed in quotes as usual, but other data types such as numbers do not require them. Since property names are strings, they would typically be contained in quotes. However, quotation marks are not required for property names if they are valid JavaScript identifiers, such as when they are written in camel-cased DOM notation.

We use the `.css()` method the same way we've been using `.addClass()`; we apply it to a jQuery object, which in turn points to a collection of DOM elements. To demonstrate this, we'll play with a style switcher similar to the one from Chapter 3, *Handling Events*:

```
<div id="switcher">
  <div class="label">Text Size</div>
  <button id="switcher-default">Default</button>
  <button id="switcher-large">Bigger</button>
  <button id="switcher-small">Smaller</button>
```

```
    </div>
    <div class="speech">
      <p>Fourscore and seven years ago our fathers brought forth
          on this continent a new nation, conceived in liberty,
          and dedicated to the proposition that all men are created
          equal.</p>
    ...
    </div>
```

Getting the example code

You can access the example code from the GitHub repository: `https://gi` `thub.com/PacktPublishing/Learning-jQuery-3`.

By linking to a stylesheet with a few basic style rules, the page will initially look like this:

Abraham Lincoln's Gettysburg Address

Text Size
(Default) (Bigger) (Smaller)

Fourscore and seven years ago our fathers brought forth on this continent a new nation, conceived in liberty, and dedicated to the proposition that all men are created equal.

Once we're done with our code, clicking on the **Bigger** and **Smaller** buttons will increase or decrease the text size of `<div class="speech">`, while clicking on the **Default** button will reset `<div class="speech">` to its original text size.

Setting computed style property values

If all we wanted was to change the font size a single time to a predetermined value, we could still use the `.addClass()` method. But, let's suppose now that we want the text to continue increasing or decreasing incrementally each time the respective button is clicked. Although it might be possible to define a separate class for each click and iterate through them, a more straightforward approach would be to compute the new text size each time by getting the current size and increasing it by a set factor (for example, 40 percent).

Our code will start with the `$(() => {})` and `$('#switcher-large').click()` event handlers:

```
$(() => {
```

```
$('#switcher-large')
  .click((e) => {

  });
});
```

Listing 4.1

Next, the font size can be easily discovered using the `.css()` method: `$('div.speech').css('fontSize')`. However, the returned value is a string, containing both the numeric font size value and the units of that value (px). We'll need to strip the unit label off in order to perform calculations with the numeric value. Also, when we plan to use a jQuery object more than once, it's generally a good idea to cache the selector by storing the resulting jQuery object in a constant:

```
$(() => {
  const $speech = $('div.speech');
  $('#switcher-large')
    .click(() => {
      const num = parseFloat($speech.css('fontSize'));
    });
});
```

Listing 4.2

The first line inside `$(() => {})` creates a **constant** containing a jQuery object pointing to `<div class="speech">`. Note the use of a dollar ($) sign in the name, `$speech`. Since the dollar sign is a legal character in JavaScript identifiers, we can use it as a reminder that the constant is a jQuery object. Unlike in other programming languages such as PHP, the dollar symbol holds no special significance in JavaScript.

 There's a good reason to use constants (`const`) instead of variables (`var`). Constants were introduced in the ES2015 version of JavaScript, and they can help reduce certain types of bugs. Take our `$speech` constant for instance. Is it ever going to hold a value other than `<div class="speech">`? No, it isn't. Since we've declared this as a constant, trying to assign another value to `$speech` results in an error. These errors are easy to fix. If `$speech` were declared as a variable and we mistakenly assigned it a new value, the failures would be subtle and difficult to diagnose. Of course, sometimes we *need* the ability to assign new values, in which case, you would use a variable.

Inside the .click() handler, we use parseFloat() to get the font size property's numeric value only. The parseFloat() function looks at a string from the left-hand side to the right-hand side until it encounters a non-numeric character. The string of digits is converted into a floating-point (decimal) number. For example, it would convert the string '12' to the number 12. In addition, it strips non-numeric trailing characters from the string, so '12px' becomes 12. If the string begins with a non-numeric character, parseFloat() returns NaN, which stands for *Not a Number*.

All that's left to do is to modify the parsed numeric value and to reset the font size based on the new value. For our example, we'll increase the font size by 40 percent each time the button is clicked. To achieve this, we'll multiply num by 1.4 and then set the font size by concatenating the result and 'px':

```
$(() => {
  const $speech = $('div.speech');

  $('#switcher-large')
    .click(() => {
      const num = parseFloat($speech.css('fontSize'));
      $speech.css('fontSize', `${num * 1.4}px`);
    });
});
```

Listing 4.3

Now when a user clicks on the **Bigger** button, the text becomes larger. Another click and the text becomes larger:

Abraham Lincoln's Gettysburg Address

Text Size

Fourscore and seven years ago our fathers brought forth on this continent a new nation, conceived in liberty, and dedicated to the proposition that all men are created equal.

To get the **Smaller** button to decrease the font size, we will divide rather than multiply: -num / 1.4. Better still, we'll combine the two into a single .click() handler on all the <button> elements within <div id="switcher">. Then, after finding the numeric value, we can either multiply or divide depending on the ID of the button that was clicked. *Listing 4.4* illustrates this.

```
$(() => {
  const sizeMap = {
    'switcher-small': n => n / 1.4,
    'switcher-large': n => n * 1.4
  };

  const $speech = $('div.speech');

  $('#switcher button')
    .click((e) => {
      const num = parseFloat($speech.css('fontSize'));
      $speech.css(
        'fontSize',
        `${sizeMap[e.target.id](num)}px`
      );
    });
});
```

Listing 4.4

The e.target.id value is used to determine the behavior of the click event. The sizeMap is where these behaviors are stored. This is a simple object that maps the element ID to a function. This function is passed the current fontSize value. The reason we want to use a map like this is that it's a lot easier to add or remove behavior than if it were coded as something like an if statement. For example, let's say the current font size was "10px" and the user clicked the **Bigger** button. Then, the template string `${sizeMap[e.target.id](num)}px` would result in "14px".

It would also be nice to have a way to return the font size to its initial value. To allow the user to do so, we can simply store the font size in a variable as soon as the DOM is ready. We can then restore this value whenever the **Default** button is clicked. All we have to do is add another function to the sizeMap:

```
$(() => {
  const sizeMap = {
    'switcher-small': n => n / 1.4,
    'switcher-large': n => n * 1.4,
    'switcher-default': () => defaultSize
  };
```

```
const $speech = $('div.speech');
const defaultSize = parseFloat($speech.css('fontSize'));

$('#switcher button')
  .click((e) => {
    const num = parseFloat($speech.css('fontSize'));
    $speech.css(
      'fontSize',
      `${sizeMap[e.target.id](num)}px`
    );
  });
});
```

Listing 4.5

Notice how we didn't have to touch the click handler at all to accommodate this new behavior? We created a new constant called `defaultSize`, which will always hold the original font size. Then, we just needed to add a new function for the `switcher-default` ID to `sizeMap`, which returns the `defaultSize` value.

With a map like this one, it's much easier to change our click handler behavior than it would be if we had to maintain `if` or `switch` statements in the handler.

Using vendor-specific style properties

When browser vendors introduce experimental style properties, they often prefix the property name until the browser's implementation aligns with the CSS specification. When both the implementation and the specification are stable enough, vendors will shed that prefix and allow the standard name to be used. In a stylesheet, therefore, it is not uncommon to see a set of CSS declarations like the following:

```
-webkit-property-name: value;
-moz-property-name: value;
-ms-property-name: value;
-o-property-name: value;
property-name: value;
```

If we wanted to apply the same in JavaScript, we would need to test for the existence of the DOM equivalent of these variations: `propertyName`, `WebkitPropertyName`, `msPropertyName`, and so on. With jQuery, however, we can simply apply the standard property name, such as `.css('propertyName', 'value')`. If that name is not found as a property of the style object, jQuery loops through the vendor prefixes behind the scenes-- `Webkit`, `O`, `Moz`, and `ms`--and uses the first one it does find as a property, if any.

Hiding and showing elements

The basic `.hide()` and `.show()` methods, without any parameters, can be thought of as smart shorthand methods for `.css('display', 'string')`, where `'string'` is the appropriate display value. The effect, as might be expected, is that the matched set of elements will be immediately hidden or shown with no animation.

The `.hide()` method sets the inline style attribute of the matched set of elements to `display: none`. The smart part here is that it remembers the value of the display property--typically `block`, `inline`, or `inline-block`--before it was changed to `none`. Conversely, the `.show()` method restores the display properties of the matched set of elements to whatever they initially were before `display: none` was applied.

The display property

For more information about the `display` property and how its values are visually represented in a web page, visit the Mozilla Developer Center at `https://developer.mozilla.org/en-US/docs/CSS/display` and view examples at `https://developer.mozilla.org/samples/cssref/display.html`.

This feature of `.show()` and `.hide()` is especially helpful when hiding elements that have had their default `display` property overridden in a stylesheet. For example, the `<li>` element has the property `display: list-item` by default, but we might want to change it to `display: inline` for a horizontal menu. Fortunately, using the `.show()` method on a hidden element such as one of the `<li>` tags would not merely reset it to its default `display: list-item`, because that would put the `<li>` tag on its own line. Instead, the element is restored to its previous `display: inline` state, thus preserving the horizontal design.

We can set up a quick demonstration of these two methods by working with a second paragraph and adding a **read more** link after the first paragraph in the example HTML:

```
<div class="speech">
    <p>Fourscore and seven years ago our fathers brought forth
        on this continent a new nation, conceived in liberty,
        and dedicated to the proposition that all men are
        created equal.
    </p>
    <p>Now we are engaged in a great civil war, testing whether
        that nation, or any nation so conceived and so dedicated,
        can long endure. We are met on a great battlefield of
        that war. We have come to dedicate a portion of that
        field as a final resting-place for those who here gave
```

```
      their lives that the nation might live. It is altogether
      fitting and proper that we should do this. But, in a
      larger sense, we cannot dedicate, we cannot consecrate,
      we cannot hallow, this ground.
    </p>
    <a href="#" class="more">read more</a>
      ...
  </div>
```

When the DOM is ready, we select an element and call `.hide()` on it:

```
$(() => {
  $('p')
    .eq(1)
    .hide();
});
```

Listing 4.6

The `.eq()` method is similar to the `:eq()` pseudo-class discussed in `Chapter 2`, *Selecting Elements*. It returns a jQuery object pointing to a single element at the provided zero-based index. In this case, the method selects the second paragraph and hides it so that the **read more** link appears immediately following the first paragraph:

Abraham Lincoln's Gettysburg Address

Fourscore and seven years ago our fathers brought forth on this continent a new nation, conceived in liberty, and dedicated to the proposition that all men are created equal.

read more

The brave men, living and dead, who struggled here have consecrated it, far above our poor power

When the user clicks on **read more** at the end of the first paragraph, we call .show() to display the second paragraph and .hide() to hide the clicked link:

```
$(() => {
  $('p')
    .eq(1)
    .hide();

  $('a.more')
    .click((e) => {
      e.preventDefault();
      $('p')
        .eq(1)
        .show();
      $(e.target)
        .hide();
    });
});
```

Listing 4.7

Note the use of .preventDefault() to keep the link from activating its default action. Now the speech looks like this:

Abraham Lincoln's Gettysburg Address

Text Size

(Default) (Bigger) (Smaller)

Fourscore and seven years ago our fathers brought forth on this continent a new nation, conceived in liberty, and dedicated to the proposition that all men are created equal.

Now we are engaged in a great civil war, testing whether that nation, or any nation so conceived and so dedicated, can long endure. We are met on a great battlefield of that war. We have come to dedicate a portion of that field as a final resting-place for those who here gave their lives that the nation might live. It is altogether fitting and proper that we should do this. But, in a larger sense, we cannot dedicate, we cannot consecrate, we cannot hallow, this ground.

The brave men, living and dead, who struggled here have consecrated it, far above our poor power

The .hide() and .show() methods are quick and useful, but they aren't very flashy. To add some flair, we can give them a duration.

Effects and duration

When we include a duration (sometimes also referred to as a speed) with `.show()` or `.hide()`, it becomes animated--occurring over a specified period of time. The `.hide(duration)` method, for example, decreases an element's height, width, and opacity simultaneously until all three reach zero, at which point the CSS rule `display: none` is applied. The `.show(duration)` method will increase the element's height from top to bottom, width from the left-hand side to the right-hand side, and opacity from 0 to 1 until its contents are completely visible.

Speeding in

With any jQuery effect, we can use one of the two preset speeds, `'slow'` or `'fast'`. Using `.show('slow')` makes the show effect complete in 600 milliseconds (0.6 seconds), `.show('fast')` in 200 milliseconds. If any other string is supplied, jQuery's default animation duration of 400 milliseconds will be used. For even greater precision, we can specify a number of milliseconds, for example, `.show(850)`.

Let's include a speed in our example when showing the second paragraph of **Abraham Lincoln's Gettysburg Address**:

```
$(() => {
  $('p')
    .eq(1)
    .hide();

  $('a.more')
    .click((e) => {
      e.preventDefault();
      $('p')
        .eq(1)
        .show('slow');
      $(e.target)
        .hide();
    });
});
```

Listing 4.8

When we capture the paragraph's appearance at roughly halfway through the effect, we see the following:

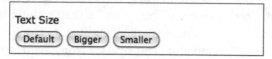

Abraham Lincoln's Gettysburg Address

Text Size
(Default) (Bigger) (Smaller)

Fourscore and seven years ago our fathers brought forth on this continent a new nation, conceived in liberty, and dedicated to the proposition that all men are created equal.

Now we are engaged in a great civil war, testing whether that nation, or any nation so conceived and so dedicated, can long endure. We are met on a great battlefield of that

The brave men, living and dead, who struggled here have consecrated it, far above our poor power to add or detract. The world will little note, nor long remember, what we say here, but it can never forget what they did here. It is for us the living, rather, to be dedicated here to the unfinished work which they who fought here have thus far so nobly advanced.

Fading in and fading out

While the animated `.show()` and `.hide()` methods are certainly flashy, in practice, they animate more properties than are useful. Fortunately, jQuery offers a couple of other prebuilt animations for a more subtle effect. For example, to have the whole paragraph appear just by gradually increasing the opacity, we can use `fadeIn('slow')` instead:

```
$(() => {
  $('p')
    .eq(1)
    .hide();

  $('a.more')
    .click((e) => {
      e.preventDefault();
      $('p')
        .eq(1)
        .fadeIn('slow');
      $(e.target)
        .hide();
    });
});
```

Listing 4.9

Now when we look at the paragraph during the effect, it looks like this:

Abraham Lincoln's Gettysburg Address

Text Size
(Default) (Bigger) (Smaller)

Fourscore and seven years ago our fathers brought forth on this continent a new nation, conceived in liberty, and dedicated to the proposition that all men are created equal.

Now we are engaged in a great civil war, testing whether that nation, or any nation so conceived and so dedicated, can long endure. We are met on a great battlefield of that war. We have come to dedicate a portion of that field as a final resting-place for those who here gave their lives that the nation might live. It is altogether fitting and proper that we should do this. But, in a larger sense, we cannot dedicate, we cannot consecrate, we cannot hallow, this ground.

The brave men, living and dead, who struggled here have consecrated it, far above our poor power

The difference here is that the `.fadeIn()` effect starts by setting the dimensions of the paragraph so that the contents can simply fade into it. To gradually decrease the opacity we can use `.fadeOut()`.

Sliding up and sliding down

The fading animations are very useful for items that are outside the flow of the document. For example, these are typical effects to apply to *lightbox* elements that are overlaid on the page. However, when an element is part of the document flow, calling `.fadeIn()` on it causes the document to jump to provide the real estate needed for the new element, which is not aesthetically pleasing.

In these cases, jQuery's `.slideDown()` and `.slideUp()` methods are the right choice. These effects animate only the height of the selected elements. To have our paragraph appear using a vertical slide effect, we can call `.slideDown('slow')`:

```
$(() => {
  $('p')
    .eq(1)
    .hide();

  $('a.more')
    .click((e) => {
      e.preventDefault();
      $('p')
```

```
        .eq(1)
        .slideDown('slow');
    $(e.target)
        .hide();
    });
});
```

Listing 4.10

This time when we examine the paragraph at the animation's midpoint, we see the following:

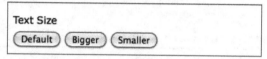

Abraham Lincoln's Gettysburg Address

Text Size

(Default) (Bigger) (Smaller)

Fourscore and seven years ago our fathers brought forth on this continent a new nation, conceived in liberty, and dedicated to the proposition that all men are created equal.

Now we are engaged in a great civil war, testing whether that nation, or any nation so conceived and so dedicated, can long endure. We are met on a great battlefield of that war. We have come to

The brave men, living and dead, who struggled here have consecrated it, far above our poor power

To reverse the effect, we would instead call `.slideUp()`.

Toggling visibility

Sometimes we have a need to toggle the visibility of elements, rather than displaying them once as we have done in the previous examples. This toggling can be achieved by first checking the visibility of the matched elements and then calling the appropriate method. Using the fade effects again, we can modify the example script to look like this:

```
$(() => {
  const $firstPara = $('p')
    .eq(1)
    .hide();

  $('a.more')
    .click((e) => {
      e.preventDefault();

      if ($firstPara.is(':hidden')) {
```

```
        $firstPara.fadeIn('slow');
        $(e.target).text('read less');
      } else {
        $firstPara.fadeOut('slow');
        $(e.target).text('read more');
      }
    });
  });
```

Listing 4.11

As we did earlier in the chapter, we're caching our selector here to avoid repeated DOM traversal. Notice too that we're no longer hiding the clicked link; instead, we're changing its text.

> To examine the text contained by an element and to change that text, we're using the `.text()` method. We will delve into this method more fully in `Chapter 5`, *Manipulating the DOM*.

Using an `if-else` statement is a perfectly reasonable way to toggle an element's visibility. But with jQuery's compound effect methods, we can remove some conditional logic from our code. jQuery provides compound methods `.fadeToggle()` and `.slideToggle()`, which show or hide elements using the corresponding effects. Here is what the script looks like when we use the `.slideToggle()` method:

```
$(() => {
  const $firstPara = $('p')
    .eq(1)
    .hide();

  $('a.more')
    .click((e) => {
      e.preventDefault();

      $firstPara.slideToggle('slow');
      $(e.target)
        .text(
          $(e.target).text() === 'read more' ?
            'read less' : 'read more'
        );
    });
});
```

Listing 4.12

The **ternary expression** (`$(e.target).text() === 'read more' ?`) checks for the text of the link rather than the visibility of the second paragraph, since we're only using it to change the text. We can use ternary expressions as a shorter alternative to full-blown `if` statements when we need a value based on some condition. Think of ternary expressions as calling a function that returns a different value based on the arguments supplied.

Creating custom animations

In addition to the prebuilt effect methods, jQuery provides a powerful `.animate()` method that allows us to create our own custom animations with fine-grained control. The `.animate()` method comes in two forms. The first takes up to four arguments:

- An object of style properties and values, which is similar to the `.css()` argument discussed earlier in this chapter
- An optional duration, which can be one of the preset strings or a number of milliseconds
- An optional easing type, which is an option that we will not use now, but which we will discuss in Chapter 11, *Advanced Effects*
- An optional callback function, which will be discussed later in this chapter

All together, the four arguments look like this:

```
.animate(
  { property1: 'value1', property2: 'value2'},
  duration,
  easing,
  () => {
    console.log('The animation is finished.');
  }
);
```

The second form takes two arguments: an object of properties and an object of options:

```
.animate({properties}, {options})
```

In this form, the second argument wraps up the second through fourth arguments of the first form into another object and adds some more advanced options to the mix. Here's what the second form looks like with actual arguments passed:

```
.animate(
  {
    property1: 'value1',
    property2: 'value2'
```

```
  },
  {
    duration: 'value',
    easing: 'value',
    specialEasing: {
      property1: 'easing1',
      property2: 'easing2'
    },
    complete: () => {
      console.log('The animation is finished.');
    },
    queue: true,
    step: callback
  }
);
```

For now, we'll use the first form of the `.animate()` method, but we'll return to the second form later in the chapter when we discuss queuing effects.

Building effects by hand

We have already seen several prepackaged effects for showing and hiding elements. To begin our discussion of the `.animate()` method, it will be useful to see how we could achieve the same results by calling `.slideToggle()` using this lower-level interface. Replacing the `.slideToggle()` line of the previous example with our custom animation turns out to be quite simple:

```
$(() => {
  const $firstPara = $('p')
    .eq(1)
    .hide();

  $('a.more')
    .click((e) => {
      e.preventDefault();

      $firstPara.animate({ height: 'toggle' }, 'slow');
      $(e.target)
        .text(
          $(e.target).text() === 'read more' ?
            'read less' : 'read more'
        );
    });
});
```

Listing 4.13

This is not a perfect replacement for `.slideToggle()`; the actual implementation also animates the margin and padding of elements.

As the example illustrates, the `.animate()` method provides convenient shorthand values for CSS properties, such as `'show'`, `'hide'`, and `'toggle'`, to ease the process when we want to emulate the behavior of prepackaged effect methods such as `.slideToggle()`.

Animating multiple properties at once

With the `.animate()` method, we can modify any combination of properties simultaneously. For example, to create a simultaneous sliding and fading effect when toggling the second paragraph, we simply add `opacity` to the properties that are passed to `.animate()`:

```
$(() => {
  const $firstPara = $('p')
    .eq(1)
    .hide();

  $('a.more')
    .click((e) => {
      e.preventDefault();

      $firstPara.animate({
        opacity: 'toggle',
        height: 'toggle'
      }, 'slow');
      $(e.target)
        .text(
          $(e.target).text() === 'read more' ?
            'read less' : 'read more'
        );
    });
});
```

Listing 4.14

Additionally, we have not only the style properties used for the shorthand effect methods at our disposal, but also numeric CSS properties such as `left`, `top`, `fontSize`, `margin`, `padding`, and `borderWidth`. In *Listing 4.5*, we changed the text size of the speech paragraphs. We could animate this increase or decrease in size by simply substituting the `.animate()` method for the `.css()` method:

```
$(() => {
  const sizeMap = {
    'switcher-small': n => n / 1.4,
    'switcher-large': n => n * 1.4,
    'switcher-default': () => defaultSize
  };

  const $speech = $('div.speech');
  const defaultSize = parseFloat($speech.css('fontSize'));

  $('#switcher button')
    .click((e) => {
      const num = parseFloat($speech.css('fontSize'));
      $speech.animate({
        fontSize: `${sizeMap[e.target.id](num)}px`
      });
    });
});
```

Listing 4.15

The extra animation properties allow us to create much more complex effects, too. We can, for example, move an item from the left-hand side of the page to the right-hand side while increasing its height by 20 pixels and changing its border width to 5 pixels. We will illustrate this complicated set of property animations with the `<div id="switcher">` box. Here is what it looks like before we animate it:

Abraham Lincoln's Gettysburg Address

Fourscore and seven years ago our fathers brought forth on this continent a new nation, conceived in liberty, and dedicated to the proposition that all men are created equal.

With a flexible-width layout, we need to compute the distance that the box needs to travel before it lines up at the right-hand side of the page. Assuming that the paragraph's width is 100 percent, we can subtract the **Text Size** box's width from the paragraph's width. We have the `jQuery.outerWidth()` method at our disposal to calculate these widths, including padding and border. We'll use this method to compute the new `left` property of the switcher. For the sake of this example, we'll trigger the animation by clicking on the **Text Size** label just above the buttons. Here is what the code should look like:

```
$(() => {
  $('div.label')
    .click((e) => {
      const $switcher = $(e.target).parent();
      const paraWidth = $('div.speech p').outerWidth();
      const switcherWidth = $switcher.outerWidth();

      $switcher.animate({
        borderWidth: '5px',
        left: paraWidth - switcherWidth,
        height: '+=20px'
      }, 'slow');
    });
});
```

Listing 4.16

It is worth examining these animated properties in detail. The `borderWidth` property is straightforward, as we are specifying a constant value with units, just as we would in a stylesheet. The `left` property is a computed numeric value. The unit suffix is optional on these properties; since we omit it here, `px` is assumed. Finally, the `height` property uses a syntax we have not seen before. The `+=` prefix on a property value indicates a relative value. So, instead of animating the height to 20 pixels, the height is animated to 20 pixels greater than the current height. Because of the special characters involved, relative values must be specified as a string.

Although this code successfully increases the height of the `<div>` tag and widens its border, at the moment, the `left` position appears unchanged:

Abraham Lincoln's Gettysburg Address

Text Size
(Default) (Bigger) (Smaller)

Fourscore and seven years ago our fathers brought forth on this continent a new nation, conceived in liberty, and dedicated to the proposition that all men are created equal.

We still need to enable changing this box's position in the CSS.

Positioning with CSS

When working with .animate(), it's important to keep in mind the limitations that CSS imposes on the elements that we wish to change. For example, adjusting the left property will have no effect on the matching elements unless those elements have their CSS position set to relative or absolute. The default CSS position for all block-level elements is static, which accurately describes how those elements will remain if we try to move them without first changing their position value.

 For more information on absolute and relative positioning, see CSS Tricks: https://css-tricks.com/almanac/properties/p/position/.

In our stylesheet, we could set <div id="switcher"> to be relatively positioned:

```
#switcher {
  position: relative;
}
```

Instead, though, let's practice our jQuery skills by altering this property through JavaScript when needed:

```
$(() =>
  $('div.label')
    .click((e) => {
      const $switcher = $(e.target).parent();
      const paraWidth = $('div.speech p').outerWidth();
      const switcherWidth = $switcher.outerWidth();

      $switcher
```

```
        .css('position', 'relative')
        .animate({
          borderWidth: '5px',
          left: paraWidth - switcherWidth,
          height: '+=20px'
        }, 'slow');
    });
});
```

Listing 4.17

With the CSS taken into account, the result of clicking on **Text Size** after the animation has completed will look like this:

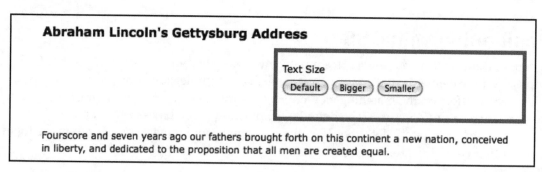

Simultaneous versus queued effects

The `.animate()` method, as we've just discovered, is very useful for creating **simultaneous** effects affecting a particular set of elements. There may be times, however, when we want to **queue** our effects to have them occur one after the other.

Working with a single set of elements

When applying multiple effects to the same set of elements, queuing is easily achieved by chaining those effects. To demonstrate this queuing, we'll revisit *Listing 4.17* by moving the **Text Size** box to the right-hand side, increasing its height and border width. This time, however, we perform the three effects sequentially simply by placing each in its own `.animate()` method and chaining the three together:

```
$(() => {
  $('div.label')
    .click((e) => {
```

```
    const $switcher = $(e.target).parent();
    const paraWidth = $('div.speech p').outerWidth();
    const switcherWidth = $switcher.outerWidth();

    $switcher
      .css('position', 'relative')
      .animate({ borderWidth: '5px' }, 'slow')
      .animate({ left: paraWidth - switcherWidth }, 'slow')
      .animate({ height: '+=20px' }, 'slow');
  });
});
```

<div align="center">Listing 4.18</div>

Recall that chaining permits us to keep all three .animate() methods on the same line, but here we have indented them and put each on its own line for greater readability.

We can queue any of the jQuery effect methods by chaining them, not just .animate(). We could, for example, queue effects on <div id="switcher"> in the following order:

1. Fade its opacity to 0.5 with .fadeTo().
2. Move it to the right-hand side with .animate().
3. Fade it back in to full opacity with .fadeTo().
4. Hide it with .slideUp().
5. Show it once more with .slideDown().

All we need to do is chain the effects in the same order in our code:

```
$(() => {
  $('div.label')
    .click((e) => {
      const $switcher = $(e.target).parent();
      const paraWidth = $('div.speech p').outerWidth();
      const switcherWidth = $switcher.outerWidth();

      $switcher
        .css('position', 'relative')
        .fadeTo('fast', 0.5)
        .animate({ left: paraWidth - switcherWidth }, 'slow')
        .fadeTo('slow', 1.0)
        .slideUp('slow')
        .slideDown('slow');
    });
});
```

<div align="center">Listing 4.19</div>

Bypassing the queue

But what if we want to move the `<div>` tag to the right-hand side at the same time as it fades to half opacity? If the two animations were occurring at the same speed, we could simply combine them into a single `.animate()` method. But, in this example, the fade is using the `'fast'` speed while the move to the right-hand side is using the `'slow'` speed. Here is where the second form of the `.animate()` method comes in handy:

```
$(() => {
  $('div.label')
    .click((e) => {
      const $switcher = $(e.target).parent();
      const paraWidth = $('div.speech p').outerWidth();
      const switcherWidth = $switcher.outerWidth();

      $switcher
        .css('position', 'relative')
        .fadeTo('fast', 0.5)
        .animate(
          { left: paraWidth - switcherWidth },
          { duration: 'slow', queue: false }
        )
        .fadeTo('slow', 1.0)
        .slideUp('slow')
        .slideDown('slow');
    });
});
```

Listing 4.20

The second argument, an options object, provides the `queue` option, which when set to `false` makes the animation start simultaneously with the previous one. Which makes sense if you think about it, because anything that sits in a queue, has to wait for anything that's already in the queue.

Queuing effects manually

One final observation about queuing effects on a single set of elements is that queuing does not automatically apply to other non-effect methods such as `.css()`. So, let's suppose we wanted to change the background color of `<div id="switcher">` to red after the `.slideUp()` method, but before the `slideDown()` method.

We could try doing it like this:

```
$(() => {
  $('div.label')
    .click((e) => {
      const $switcher = $(e.target).parent();
      const paraWidth = $('div.speech p').outerWidth();
      const switcherWidth = $switcher.outerWidth();

      $switcher
        .css('position', 'relative')
        .fadeTo('fast', 0.5)
        .animate(
          { left: paraWidth - switcherWidth },
          { duration: 'slow', queue: false }
        )
        .fadeTo('slow', 1.0)
        .slideUp('slow')
        .css('backgroundColor', '#f00')
        .slideDown('slow');
    });
});
```

Listing 4.21

However, even though the code that changes the background color is placed at the correct position in the chain, it occurs immediately upon the click.

One way we can add non-effect methods to the queue is to use the appropriately named `.queue()` method. Here is what it would look like in our example:

```
$(() => {
  $('div.label')
    .click((e) => {
      const $switcher = $(e.target).parent();
      const paraWidth = $('div.speech p').outerWidth();
      const switcherWidth = $switcher.outerWidth();

      $switcher
        .css('position', 'relative')
        .fadeTo('fast', 0.5)
        .animate(
          { left: paraWidth - switcherWidth },
          { duration: 'slow', queue: false }
        )
        .fadeTo('slow', 1.0)
        .slideUp('slow')
        .queue((next) => {
```

```
        $switcher.css('backgroundColor', '#f00');
        next();
      })
      .slideDown('slow');
    });
  });
```

Listing 4.22

When given a callback function, as it is here, the `.queue()` method adds the function to the queue of effects to perform on the matched elements. Within the function, we set the background color to red and then call `next()`, a function that is passed as a parameter to our callback. Including this `next()` function call allows the animation queue to pick up where it left off and complete the chain with the following `.slideDown('slow')` line. If we hadn't called `next()`, the animation would have stopped.

 For more information and examples of `.queue()`, visit `http://api.jquery.com/category/effects/`.

We'll discover another way to queue non-effect methods as we examine effects with multiple sets of elements.

Working with multiple sets of elements

Unlike with a single set of elements, when we apply effects to different sets, they occur at virtually the same time. To see these simultaneous effects in action, we'll slide one paragraph down while sliding another paragraph up. We'll be working with paragraphs three and four of our sample document:

```
<p>Fourscore and seven years ago our fathers brought forth
   on this continent a new nation, conceived in liberty,
   and dedicated to the proposition that all men are
   created equal.</p>
<p>Now we are engaged in a great civil war, testing whether
   that nation, or any nation so conceived and so
   dedicated, can long endure. We are met on a great
   battlefield of that war. We have come to dedicate a
   portion of that field as a final resting-place for those
   who here gave their lives that the nation might live. It
   is altogether fitting and proper that we should do this.
   But, in a larger sense, we cannot dedicate, we cannot
   consecrate, we cannot hallow, this ground.</p>
```

```
<a href="#" class="more">read more</a>
<p>The brave men, living and dead, who struggled here have
   consecrated it, far above our poor power to add or
   detract. The world will little note, nor long remember,
   what we say here, but it can never forget what they did
   here. It is for us the living, rather, to be dedicated
   here to the unfinished work which they who fought here
   have thus far so nobly advanced.</p>
<p>It is rather for us to be here dedicated to the great
   task remaining before us&mdash;that from these honored
   dead we take increased devotion to that cause for which
   they gave the last full measure of devotion&mdash;that
   we here highly resolve that these dead shall not have
   died in vain&mdash;that this nation, under God, shall
   have a new birth of freedom and that government of the
   people, by the people, for the people, shall not perish
   from the earth.</p>
```

To help us see what's happening during the effect, we'll give the third paragraph a 1-pixel border and the fourth paragraph a gray background. We'll also hide the fourth paragraph when the DOM is ready:

```
$(() => {
  $('p')
    .eq(2)
    .css('border', '1px solid #333');
  $('p')
    .eq(3)
    .css('backgroundColor', '#ccc')
    .hide();
});
```

Listing 4.23

Our sample document now displays the opening paragraph followed by the **read more** link and the bordered paragraph:

Fourscore and seven years ago our fathers brought forth on this continent a new nation, conceived in liberty, and dedicated to the proposition that all men are created equal.

read more

The brave men, living and dead, who struggled here have consecrated it, far above our poor power to add or detract. The world will little note, nor long remember, what we say here, but it can never forget what they did here. It is for us the living, rather, to be dedicated here to the unfinished work which they who fought here have thus far so nobly advanced.

Finally, we'll apply a `click` handler to the third paragraph so that when it is clicked, the third paragraph will slide up (and eventually out of view) while the fourth paragraph slides down (and into view):

```
$(() => {
  $('p')
    .eq(2)
    .css('border', '1px solid #333')
    .click((e) => {
      $(e.target)
        .slideUp('slow')
        .next()
        .slideDown('slow');
    });
  $('p')
    .eq(3)
    .css('backgroundColor', '#ccc')
    .hide();
});
```

Listing 4.24

A screenshot of these two effects in mid-slide confirms that they do, indeed, occur simultaneously:

Fourscore and seven years ago our fathers brought forth on this continent a new nation, conceived in liberty, and dedicated to the proposition that all men are created equal.

read more

The brave men, living and dead, who struggled here have consecrated it, far above our poor power

It is rather for us to be here dedicated to the great task remaining before us—that from these honored dead we take increased devotion to that cause for which they gave the last full measure of devotion—that we here highly resolve that these dead shall not have died in vain—that this nation,

The third paragraph, which started visible, is halfway through sliding up at the same time as the fourth paragraph, which started hidden, is halfway through sliding down.

Queuing with callbacks

In order to allow queuing effects on different elements, jQuery provides a callback function for each effect method. As we have seen with event handlers and with the `.queue()` method, callbacks are simply functions passed as method arguments. In the case of effects, they appear as the last argument of the method.

If we use a callback to queue the two slide effects, we can have the fourth paragraph slide down before the third paragraph slides up. Let's first try moving the `.slideUp()` call into the `.slideDown()` method's completion callback:

```
$(() => {
  $('p')
    .eq(2)
    .css('border', '1px solid #333')
    .click((e) => {
      $(e.target)
        .next()
        .slideDown('slow', () => {
          $(e.target).slideUp('slow');
        });
    });
  $('p')
    .eq(3)
    .css('backgroundColor', '#ccc')
    .hide();
});
```

Listing 4.25

Had we decided to use `$(this)` in both the `click()` callback function and in the `slideDown()` callback function, things wouldn't have worked as expected. That's because `this` is contextual. Instead, we can avoid it all together and reference `$(e.target)` to get the <p> element that we need.

This time, a snapshot halfway through the effects reveals that both the third and the fourth paragraphs are visible; the fourth has finished sliding down and the third is about to begin sliding up:

Fourscore and seven years ago our fathers brought forth on this continent a new nation, conceived in liberty, and dedicated to the proposition that all men are created equal.

read more

The brave men, living and dead, who struggled here have consecrated it, far above our poor power to add or detract. The world will little note, nor long remember, what we say here, but it can never forget what they did here. It is for us the living, rather, to be dedicated here to the unfinished work which they who fought here have thus far so nobly advanced.

It is rather for us to be here dedicated to the great task remaining before us—that from these honored dead we take increased devotion to that cause for which they gave the last full measure of devotion—that we here highly resolve that these dead shall not have died in vain—that this nation, under God, shall have a new birth of freedom and that government of the people, by the people, for

---

Now that we've discussed callbacks, we can return to the code from *Listing 4.22*, in which we queued a background-color change near the end of a series of effects. Instead of using the .queue() method, as we did then, we can simply use a callback function:

```
$(() => {
  $('div.label')
    .click((e) => {
      const $switcher = $(e.target).parent();
      const paraWidth = $('div.speech p').outerWidth();
      const switcherWidth = $switcher.outerWidth();

      $switcher
        .css('position', 'relative')
        .fadeTo('fast', 0.5)
        .animate(
          { left: paraWidth - switcherWidth },
          { duration: 'slow', queue: false }
        )
        .fadeTo('slow', 1.0)
        .slideUp('slow', () => {
          $switcher.css('backgroundColor', '#f00');
        })
        .slideDown('slow');
    });
});
```

Listing 4.26

Here again, the background color of `<div id="switcher">` changes to red after it slides up and before it slides back down. Note that when using an effect's completion callback rather than `.queue()`, we don't need to worry about calling `next()` from within the callback.

In a nutshell

With all the variations to consider when applying effects, it can become difficult to remember whether the effects will occur simultaneously or sequentially. A brief outline might help.

Effects on a single set of elements are:

- Simultaneous when applied as multiple properties in a single `.animate()` method
- Queued when applied in a chain of methods, unless the `queue` option is set to `false`

Effects on multiple sets of elements are:

- Simultaneous by default
- Queued when applied within the callback of another effect or within the callback of the `.queue()` method

Summary

Using the effect methods that we have explored in this chapter, we should now be able to modify inline style attributes from JavaScript, apply prepackaged jQuery effects to elements, and create our own custom animations. In particular, you learned how to incrementally increase and decrease text size using either the `.css()` or `.animate()` methods, gradually hide and show page elements by modifying several attributes, and how to animate elements (simultaneously or sequentially) in a number of ways.

In the first four chapters of this book, all of our examples have involved manipulating elements that have been hardcoded into the page's HTML. In Chapter 5, *Manipulating the DOM*, we will explore ways to manipulate the DOM directly, including using jQuery to create new elements and insert them into the DOM wherever we choose.

Further reading

The topic of animation will be explored in more detail in Chapter 11, *Advanced Effects*. A complete list of effect and styling methods is available in Appendix B of this book, or in the official jQuery documentation at http://api.jquery.com/.

Exercises

The challenge exercise may require the use of the official jQuery documentation at http://api.jquery.com/:

1. Alter the stylesheet to hide the contents of the page initially. When the page is loaded, fade in the contents slowly.
2. Give each paragraph a yellow background only when the mouse is over it.
3. Make a click on the title (<h2>) and simultaneously fade it to 25 percent opacity and grow its left-hand margin to 20px. Then, when this animation is complete, fade the speech text to 50 percent opacity.
4. Here's a challenge for you. React to presses of the arrow keys by smoothly moving the switcher box 20 pixels in the corresponding direction. The key codes for the arrow keys are: 37 (left), 38 (up), 39 (right), and 40 (down).

5

Manipulating the DOM

The Web experience is a partnership between web servers and web browsers. Traditionally, it has been the domain of the server to produce an HTML document that is ready for consumption by the browser. The techniques we have seen in this book have shifted this arrangement slightly, using CSS techniques to alter the appearance of the HTML document on the fly. To really flex our JavaScript muscles, though, you'll need to learn to alter the document itself.

In this chapter, we will cover:

- Modifying the document using the interface provided by the **Document Object Model (DOM)**
- Creating elements and text on a page
- Moving or deleting elements
- Transforming a document by adding, removing, or modifying attributes and properties

Manipulating attributes and properties

Throughout the first four chapters of this book, we have been using the `.addClass()` and `.removeClass()` methods to demonstrate how we can change the appearance of elements on a page. Although we discussed these methods informally in terms of manipulating the `class` attribute, jQuery actually modifies a DOM property called `className`. The `.addClass()` method creates or adds to the property, while `.removeClass()` deletes or shortens it. Add to these the `.toggleClass()` method, which alternates between adding and removing class names, and we have an efficient and robust way of handling classes. These methods are particularly helpful in that they avoid adding a class if it already exists on an element (so we don't end up with `<div class="first first">`, for example), and correctly handle cases where multiple classes are applied to a single element, such as `<div class="first second">`.

Non-class attributes

We may need to access or change several other attributes or properties from time to time. For manipulating attributes such as `id`, `rel`, and `href`, jQuery provides the `.attr()` and `.removeAttr()` methods. These methods make changing an attribute a simple matter. In addition, jQuery lets us modify more than one attribute at a time, similar to the way we worked with multiple CSS properties using the `.css()` method in Chapter 4, *Styling and Animating*.

For example, we can easily set the `id`, `rel`, and `title` attributes for links all at once. Let's start with some sample HTML:

```
<h1 id="f-title">Flatland: A Romance of Many Dimensions</h1>
<div id="f-author">by Edwin A. Abbott</div>
<h2>Part 1, Section 3</h2>
<h3 id="f-subtitle">
   Concerning the Inhabitants of Flatland
</h3>
<div id="excerpt">an excerpt</div>
<div class="chapter">
  <p class="square">Our Professional Men and Gentlemen are
    Squares (to which class I myself belong) and Five-Sided
    Figures or <a
    href="http://en.wikipedia.org/wiki/Pentagon">Pentagons
    </a>.
  </p>
  <p class="nobility hexagon">Next above these come the
    Nobility, of whom there are several degrees, beginning at
```

```
        Six-Sided Figures, or <a
        href="http://en.wikipedia.org/wiki/Hexagon">Hexagons</a>,
        and from thence rising in the number of their sides till
        they receive the honourable title of <a
        href="http://en.wikipedia.org/wiki/Polygon">Polygonal</a>,
        or many-Sided. Finally when the number of the sides
        becomes so numerous, and the sides themselves so small,
        that the figure cannot be distinguished from a <a
        href="http://en.wikipedia.org/wiki/Circle">circle</a>, he
        is included in the Circular or Priestly order; and this is
        the highest class of all.
    </p>
    <p><span class="pull-quote">It is a <span class="drop">Law
        of Nature</span> with us that a male child shall have
        <strong>one more side</strong> than his father</span>, so
        that each generation shall rise (as a rule) one step in
        the scale of development and nobility. Thus the son of a
        Square is a Pentagon; the son of a Pentagon, a Hexagon;
        and so on.
    </p>
<!-- . . . code continues . . . -->
</div>
```

Getting the example code

You can access the example code from the following GitHub repository: ht
tps://github.com/PacktPublishing/Learning-jQuery-3.

Now, we can iterate through each of the links inside `<div class="chapter">` and apply
attributes to them one by one. If we need to set a single attribute value for all of the links,
we can do so with a single line of code within our `$(() => {})` handler:

```
$(() => {
  $('div.chapter a').attr({ rel: 'external' });
});
```

Listing 5.1

Much like the `.css()` method, `.attr()` can accept a pair of parameters, the first specifying
the attribute name and the second being its new value. More typically, though, we supply
an object of key-value pairs, as we have in *Listing 5.1*. The following syntax allows us to
easily expand our example to modify multiple attributes at once:

```
$(() => {
  $('div.chapter a')
    .attr({
      rel: 'external',
```

```
        title: 'Learn more at Wikipedia'
    });
});
```

Listing 5.2

Value callbacks

The straightforward technique for passing `.attr()` a simple object is sufficient when we want the attribute or attributes to have the same value for each matched element. Often, though, the attributes we add or change must have different values each time. One common example is that for any given document, each `id` value must be unique if we want our JavaScript code to behave predictably. To set a unique `id` value for each link, we can harness another feature of jQuery methods such as `.css()` and `.each()`--**value callbacks**.

A value callback is simply a function that is supplied instead of the value for an argument. This function is then invoked once per element in the matched set. Whatever data is returned from the function is used as the new value for the attribute. For example, we can use the following technique to generate a different `id` value for each element:

```
$(() => {
  $('div.chapter a')
    .attr({
      rel: 'external',
      title: 'Learn more at Wikipedia',
      id: index => `wikilink-${index}`
    });
});
```

Listing 5.3

Each time our value callback is fired, it is passed an integer indicating the iteration count; we're using it here to give the first link an `id` value of `wikilink-0`, the second `wikilink-1`, and so on.

We are using the `title` attribute to invite people to learn more about the linked term at Wikipedia. In the HTML tags we have used so far, all of the links point to Wikipedia. However, to account for other types of links, we should make the selector expression a little more specific:

```
$(() => {
  $('div.chapter a[href*="wikipedia"]')
    .attr({
      rel: 'external',
```

```
      title: 'Learn more at Wikipedia',
      id: index => `wikilink-${index}`
   });
});
```

Listing 5.4

To complete our tour of the `.attr()` method, we'll enhance the `title` attribute of these links to be more specific about the link destination. Once again, a value callback is the right tool for the job:

```
$(() => {
   $('div.chapter a[href*="wikipedia"]')
     .attr({
        rel: 'external',
        title: function() {
           return `Learn more about ${$(this).text()} at Wikipedia.`;
        },
        id: index => `wikilink-${index}`
     });
});
```

Listing 5.5

This time we've taken advantage of the context of value callbacks. Just as with event handlers, the keyword `this` points to the DOM element we're manipulating each time the callback is invoked. Here, we're wrapping the element in a jQuery object so that we can use the `.text()` method (introduced in `Chapter 4`, *Styling and Animating*) to retrieve the textual content of the link. This makes each link title different from the rest, as we can see in the following screenshot:

Data attributes

HTML5 data attributes allow us to attach arbitrary data values to page elements. Our jQuery code can then use these values, as well as modify them. The reason for using data attributes is so that we can separate DOM attributes that control how they're displayed and how they behave, from data that's specific to our application.

You'll use the `data()` jQuery method to read data values and to change data values. Let's add some new functionality that allows the user to mark a paragraph as read by clicking on it. We'll also need a checkbox that hides paragraphs that have been marked as read. We'll use data attributes to help us remember which paragraphs have been marked as read:

```
$(() => {
  $('#hide-read')
    .change((e) => {
      if ($(e.target).is(':checked')) {
        $('.chapter p')
          .filter((i, p) => $(p).data('read'))
          .hide();
      } else {
        $('.chapter p').show();
      }
    });

  $('.chapter p')
    .click((e) => {
      const $elm = $(e.target);

      $elm
        .css(
          'textDecoration',
          $elm.data('read') ? 'none' : 'line-through'
        )
        .data('read', !$(e.target).data('read'));
    });
});
```

Listing 5.6

When you click on a paragraph, the text is marked with a like through it to indicate that it has been read:

Flatland: A Romance of Many Dimensions
by Edwin A. Abbott

Part 1, Section 3

Concerning the Inhabitants of Flatland
an excerpt
Hide read paragraphs ☐

~~Our Professional Men and Gentlemen are Squares (to which class I myself belong) and Five-Sided Figures or Pentagons.~~

Next above these come the Nobility, of whom there are several degrees, beginning at Six-Sided Figures, or <u>Hexagons</u>, and from thence rising in the number of the sides till they receive the honourable title of <u>Polygonal</u>, or many-Sided. Finally when the number of the sides becomes so numerous, and the sides themselves so small, that the figure cannot be distinguished from a <u>circle</u>, he is included in the Circular or Priestly order; and this is the highest class of all.

~~It is a Law of Nature with us that a male child shall have **one more side** than his father, so that each generation shall rise (as a rule) one step in the scale of development and nobility. Thus the son of a Square is a Pentagon; the son of a Pentagon, a Hexagon; and so on.~~

But this rule applies not always to the Tradesman, and still less often to the Soldiers, and to the Workmen; who indeed can hardly be said to deserve the name of human Figures, since they have not all their sides equal. With them therefore the Law of Nature does not hold; and the son of an Isosceles (i.e. a Triangle with two sides equal) remains Isosceles still. Nevertheless, all hope is not such out, even from the Isosceles, that his posterity may ultimately rise above his degraded condition....

As you can see, the click event handler changes the visual appearance of paragraphs when they're clicked on. But the handler does something else too--it toggles the `read` data for the element: `data('read', !$(e.target).data('read'))`. This lets us tie application-specific data to the element, in a way that doesn't interfere with other HTML attributes that we might set.

The change handler for the **Hide read paragraphs** checkbox looks for paragraphs that have this data. The `filter((i, p) => $(p).data('read'))` call will only return paragraphs that have a `read` data attribute with a value of `true`. We're now able to filter elements based on specific application data. Here's what the page looks like with read paragraphs hidden:

Flatland: A Romance of Many Dimensions
by Edwin A. Abbott

Part 1, Section 3

Concerning the Inhabitants of Flatland
an excerpt
Hide read paragraphs ☑

Next above these come the Nobility, of whom there are several degrees, beginning at Six-Sided Figures, or <u>Hexagons</u>, and from thence rising in the number of their sides till they receive the honourable title of <u>Polygonal</u>, or many-Sided. Finally when the number of the sides becomes so numerous, and the sides themselves so small, that the figure cannot be distinguished from a <u>circle</u>, he is included in the Circular or Priestly order; and this is the highest class of all.

But this rule applies not always to the Tradesman, and still less often to the Soldiers, and to the Workmen; who indeed can hardly be said to deserve the name of human Figures, since they have not all their sides equal. With them therefore the Law of Nature does not hold; and the son of an Isosceles (i.e. a Triangle with two sides equal) remains Isosceles still. Nevertheless, all hope is not such out, even from the Isosceles, that his posterity may ultimately rise above his degraded condition....

We'll revisit some advanced usage scenarios of data handling with jQuery later in the book.

DOM element properties

As mentioned previously, there is a subtle distinction between HTML **attributes** and DOM **properties**. Attributes are the values given in quotation marks in the HTML source for the page, while properties are the values as accessed by JavaScript. We can observe attributes and properties easily in a developer tool like Chrome's:

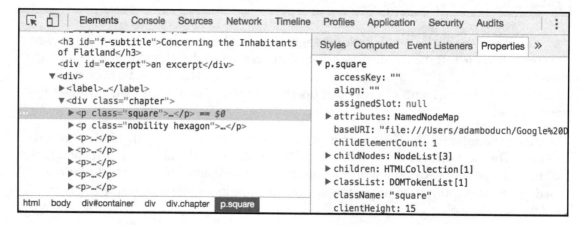

The Chrome Developer Tool's elements inspector shows us that the highlighted `<p>` element has an attribute called `class` with the value `square`. In the right panel, we can see that this element has a corresponding property called `className` with the value `square`. This illustrates one of the rare situations in which an attribute and its equivalent property have different names.

In most cases, attributes and properties are functionally interchangeable, and jQuery takes care of the naming inconsistencies for us. However, at times we do need to be mindful of the differences between the two. Some DOM properties, such as `nodeName`, `nodeType`, `selectedIndex`, and `childNodes`, have no equivalent attribute and therefore are not accessible via `.attr()`. Moreover, data types may differ: the `checked` attribute, for example, has a string value, while the `checked` property has a Boolean value. For these Boolean attributes, it is best to test and set the *property* rather than the *attribute* to ensure consistent cross-browser behavior.

We can get and set properties from jQuery using the `.prop()` method:

```
// Get the current value of the "checked" property
const currentlyChecked = $('.my-checkbox').prop('checked');

// Set a new value for the "checked" property
$('.my-checkbox').prop('checked', false);
```

The `.prop()` method has all the same features as `.attr()`, such as accepting an object of multiple values to set at the same time and taking value callback functions.

The value of form controls

Perhaps the most troublesome difference between attributes and properties arises when trying to get or set the value of a form control. For text inputs, the `value` attribute is equivalent to the `defaultValue` property, not the `value` property. For `select` elements, the value is usually obtained via the element's `selectedIndex` property or the `selected` property of its `option` elements.

Because of these discrepancies, we should avoid using `.attr()`--and, in the case of `select` elements, even `.prop()`--to get or set form element values. Instead, we can use the `.val()` method, which jQuery provides for these occasions:

```
// Get the current value of a text input
const inputValue = $('#my-input').val();
// Get the current value of a select list
const selectValue = $('#my-select').val();
//Set the value of a single select list
$('#my-single-select').val('value3');
// Set the value of a multiple select list
$('#my-multi-select').val(['value1', 'value2']);
```

As with `.attr()` and `.prop()`, `.val()` can take a function for its setter argument. With its multipurpose `.val()` method, jQuery yet again makes developing for the web much easier.

DOM tree manipulation

The `.attr()` and `.prop()` methods are very powerful tools, and with them we can make targeted changes to the document. We still haven't seen ways to change the overall structure of the document though. To actually manipulate the DOM tree, you'll need to learn a bit more about the function that lies at the very heart of the jQuery library.

The $() function revisited

From the start of this book, we've been using the $ () function to access elements in a document. As we've seen, this function acts as a factory, producing new jQuery objects that point to the elements described by CSS selectors.

This isn't all that the $ () function can do. It can also change the contents of a page. Simply by passing a snippet of HTML code to the function, we can create an entirely new DOM structure.

Accessibility reminder

We should keep in mind, once again, the inherent danger in making certain functionality, visual appeal, or textual information available only to those with web browsers capable of (and enabled for) using JavaScript. Important information should be accessible to all, not just people who happen to be using the right software.

Creating new elements

A feature commonly seen on FAQ pages is the **back to top** link that appears after each question-and-answer pair. It could be argued that these links serve no semantic purpose, and therefore they can be legitimately included via JavaScript as an enhancement for a subset of the visitors to a page. For our example, we'll add a **back to top** link after each paragraph, as well as the anchor to which the **back to top** links will take us. To begin, we simply create the new elements:

```
$(() => {
  $('<a href="#top">back to top</a>');
  $('<a id="top"></a>');
});
```

Listing 5.7

We've created a **back to top** link in the first line of code and a target anchor for the link in the second line. However, no **back to top** links appear on the page yet.

> Our Professional Men and Gentlemen are Squares (to which class I myself belong) and Five-Sided Figures or <u>Pentagons</u>.
>
> Next above these come the Nobility, of whom there are several degrees, beginning at Six-Sided Figures, or <u>Hexagons</u>, and from thence rising in the number of their sides till they receive the honourable title of <u>Polygonal</u>, or many-Sided. Finally when the number of the sides becomes so numerous, and the sides themselves so small, that the figure cannot be distinguished from a <u>circle</u>, he is included in the Circular or Priestly order; and this is the highest class of all.
>
> It is a Law of Nature with us that a male child shall have **one more**

While the two lines of code that we've written do indeed create the elements, they don't yet add the elements to the page. We need to tell the browser where these new elements should go. To do that, we can use one of the many jQuery **insertion methods**.

Inserting new elements

The `jQuery` library has a number of methods available for inserting elements into the document. Each one dictates the relationship the new content will have to the existing content. For example, we will want our **back to top** links to appear after each paragraph, so we'll use the appropriately named `.insertAfter()` method to accomplish this:

```
$(() => {
  $('<a href="#top">back to top</a>')
    .insertAfter('div.chapter p');
  $('<a id="top"></a>');
});
```

Listing 5.8

So, now that we've actually inserted the links into the page (and into the DOM) after each paragraph that appears within `<div class="chapter">`, the **back to top** links will appear:

> Our Professional Men and Gentlemen are Squares (to which class I myself belong) and Five-Sided Figures or Pentagons.
>
> back to top
>
> Next above these come the Nobility, of whom there are several degrees, beginning at Six-Sided Figures, or Hexagons, and from thence rising in the number of their sides till they receive the honourable title of Polygonal, or many-Sided. Finally when the number of the sides becomes so numerous, and the sides themselves so small, that the figure cannot be distinguished from a circle, he is included in the Circular or Priestly order; and this is the highest class of all.
>
> back to top
>
> It is a Law of Nature with us that a male child shall have **one more**

Note that the new links appear on their own line, not within the paragraph. This is because the `.insertAfter()` method, and its counterpart `.insertBefore()`, add content *outside* the specified element.

Unfortunately, the links won't work yet. We still need to insert the anchor with `id="top"`. This time, we'll use one of the methods that insert elements *inside* of other elements:

```
$(() => {
  $('<a href="#top">back to top</a>')
    .insertAfter('div.chapter p');
  $('<a id="top"></a>')
    .prependTo('body');
});
```

Listing 5.9

This additional code inserts the anchor right at the beginning of the `<body>` tag; in other words, at the top of the page. Now, with the `.insertAfter()` method for the links and the `.prependTo()` method for the anchor, we have a fully functioning set of **back to top** links for the page.

Once we add the corresponding .appendTo() method, we now have a complete set of options for inserting new elements before and after other elements:

- .insertBefore(): Adds content *outside of* and *before* existing elements
- .prependTo(): Adds content *inside of* and *before* existing elements
- .appendTo(): Adds content *inside of* and *after* existing elements
- .insertAfter(): Adds content *outside of* and *after* existing elements

Moving elements

When adding the **back to top** links, we created new elements and inserted them on the page. It's also possible to take elements from one place on the page and insert them into another place. A practical application of this type of insertion is the dynamic placement and formatting of footnotes. One footnote already appears in the original *Flatland* text that we are using for this example, but we'll also designate a couple of other portions of the text as footnotes for the purpose of this demonstration:

```
<p>How admirable is the Law of Compensation! <span
   class="footnote">And how perfect a proof of the natural
   fitness and, I may almost say, the divine origin of the
   aristocratic constitution of the States of Flatland!</span>
   By a judicious use of this Law of Nature, the Polygons and
   Circles are almost always able to stifle sedition in its
   very cradle, taking advantage of the irrepressible and
   boundless hopefulness of the human mind.&hellip;
</p>
```

Our HTML document contains three footnotes; the previous paragraph contains one example. The footnote text is inside the paragraph text, set apart using <span class="footnote"></span>. By marking up the HTML document in this way, we can preserve the context of the footnote. A CSS rule applied in the stylesheet italicizes the footnotes, so an affected paragraph initially looks like the following:

How admirable is the Law of Compensation! *And how perfect a proof of the natural fitness and, I may almost say, the divine origin of the aristocratic constitution of the States of Flatland!* By a judicious use of this Law of Nature, the Polygons and Circles are almost always able to stifle sedition in its very cradle, taking advantage of the irrepressible and boundless hopefulness of the human mind....

Now, we need to grab the footnotes and move them to the bottom of the document. Specifically, we'll insert them in between `<div class="chapter">` and `<div id="footer">`.

Keep in mind that even in cases of implicit iteration, the order in which elements are processed is precisely defined, starting at the top of the DOM tree and working down. Since it's important to maintain the correct order of the footnotes in their new place on the page, we should use `.insertBefore('#footer')`. This will place each footnote directly before the `<div id="footer">` element so that the first footnote is placed between `<div class="chapter">` and `<div id="footer">`, the second footnote is placed between the first footnote and `<div id="footer">`, and so on. Using `.insertAfter('div.chapter')`, on the other hand, would cause the footnotes to appear in reverse order.

So far, our code looks like the following:

```
$(() => {
  $('span.footnote').insertBefore('#footer');
});
```

Listing 5.10

The footnotes are in `<span>` tags, which means they display inline by default, one right after the other with no separation. However, we've anticipated this in the CSS, giving `span.footnote` elements a `display` value of `block` when they are outside of `<div class="chapter">`. So, the footnotes are now beginning to take shape:

---

to mutual warfare, and perish by one another's angles. No less than one hundred and twenty rebellions are recorded in our annals, besides minor outbreaks numbered at two hundred and thirty-five; and they have all ended thus.

back to top

"What need of a certificate?" a Spaceland critic may ask: "Is not the procreation of a Square Son a certificate from Nature herself, proving the Equal-sidedness of the Father?" I reply that no Lady of any position will marry an uncertified Triangle. Square offspring has sometimes resulted from a slightly Irregular Triangle; but in almost every such case the Irregularity of the first generation is visited on the third; which either fails to attain the Pentagonal rank, or relapses to the Triangular.

The Equilateral is bound by oath never to permit the child henceforth to enter his former home or so much as to look upon his relations again, for fear lest the freshly developed organism may, by force of unconscious imitation, fall back again into his hereditary level.

And how perfect a proof of the natural fitness and, I may almost say, the divine origin of the aristocratic constitution of the States of Flatland!

The footnotes are in the proper position now, yet there is still a lot of work that can be done to them. A more robust footnote solution should do the following:

1. Number each footnote.
2. Mark the location in the text from which each footnote is pulled using the number of the footnote.
3. Create a link from the text location to its matching footnote, and from the footnote back to the location in the text from which each footnote is pulled using the number of the footnote.

Wrapping elements

To number the footnotes, we could explicitly add numbers in the markup, but here we can take advantage of the standard ordered list element that takes care of numbering for us. To do this, we need to create a containing `<ol>` element surrounding all of the footnotes and an `<li>` element surrounding each one individually. To achieve this, we'll use **wrapping methods**.

When wrapping elements in another element, we need to be clear about whether we want each element wrapped in its own container or all elements wrapped in a single container. For our footnote numbering, we need both types of wrapper:

```
$(() => {
  $('span.footnote')
    .insertBefore('#footer')
    .wrapAll('<ol id="notes"></ol>')
    .wrap('<li></li>');
});
```

Listing 5.11

Once we have inserted the footnotes before the footer, we wrap the entire set inside a single `<ol>` element using `.wrapAll()`. We then proceed to wrap each individual footnote inside its own `<li>` element using `.wrap()`. We can see that this has created properly numbered footnotes:

---

have all ended thus.

back to top

1.   *"What need of a certificate?" a Spaceland critic may ask: "Is not the procreation of a Square Son a certificate from Nature herself, proving the Equal-sidedness of the Father?" I reply that no Lady of any position will marry an uncertified Triangle. Square offspring has sometimes resulted from a slightly Irregular Triangle; but in almost every such case the Irregularity of the first generation is visited on the third; which either fails to attain the Pentagonal rank, or relapses to the Triangular.*

2.   *The Equilateral is bound by oath never to permit the child henceforth to enter his former home or so much as to look upon his relations again, for fear lest the freshly developed organism may, by force of unconscious imitation, fall back again into his hereditary level.*

3.   *And how perfect a proof of the natural fitness and, I may almost say, the divine origin of the aristocratic constitution of the States of Flatland!*

Now, we're ready to mark and number the place from which we're pulling the footnote. To do this in a straightforward manner, though, we need to rewrite our existing code so that it doesn't rely on implicit iteration.

Explicit iteration

The `.each()` method, which acts as an **explicit iterator**, is very similar to the `forEach` array iterator that was recently added to the JavaScript language. The `.each()` method can be employed when the code we want to use on each of the matched elements is too complex for the implicit iteration syntax. It is passed a callback function that will be called once for each element in the matched set.

```
$(() => {
  const $notes = $('<ol id="notes"></ol>')
    .insertBefore('#footer');

  $('span.footnote')
    .each((i, span) => {
      $(span)
        .appendTo($notes)
        .wrap('<li></li>');
    });
});
```

Listing 5.12

The motivation for our change here will become clear shortly. First, we need to understand the information that's provided to our `.each()` callback.

In *Listing 5.12*, we use the `span` parameter to create a jQuery object pointing to a single footnote, `<span>`, then we append the element to the notes `<ol>`, and finally wrap the footnote inside an `<li>` element.

To mark the locations in the text from which the footnotes were pulled, we can take advantage of the `.each()` callback's parameter. This parameter provides the iteration count, starting at `0` and incrementing each time the callback is invoked. Therefore, this counter will always be 1 less than number of the footnote. We'll account for this fact when producing the appropriate labels in the text:

```
$(() => {
   const $notes = $('<ol id="notes"></ol>')
      .insertBefore('#footer');

   $('span.footnote')
      .each((i, span) => {
         $(`<sup>${i + 1}</sup>`)
            .insertBefore(span);
         $(span)
            .appendTo($notes)
            .wrap('<li></li>');
      });
});
```

Listing 5.13

Now, before each footnote is pulled out of the text to be placed at the bottom of the page, we create a new `<sup>` element containing the footnote's number and insert it into the text. The order of actions is important here; we need to make sure that the marker is inserted before the footnote is moved, or else we lose track of its initial position.

Looking at our page again, now we can see footnote markers where the inline footnotes used to be:

> subject of rejoicing in our country for many furlongs round. After a strict examination conducted by the Sanitary and Social Board, the infant, if certified as Regular, is with solemn ceremonial admitted into the class of Equilaterals. He is then immediately taken from his proud yet sorrowing parents and adopted by some childless Equilateral.②
>
> back to top
>
> How admirable is the Law of Compensation!③By a judicious use of this Law of Nature, the Polygons and Circles are almost always able to stifle sedition in its very cradle, taking advantage of the irrepressible and boundless hopefulness of the human mind....

Using inverted insertion methods

In *Listing 5.13*, we inserted content before an element, then appended that same element to another place in the document. Typically, when working with elements in jQuery, we can use chaining to perform multiple actions succinctly and efficiently. We weren't able to do that here, though, because `this` is the *target* of `.insertBefore()` and the *subject* of `.appendTo()`. The **inverted insertion methods** will help us get around this limitation.

Each of the insertion methods, such as `.insertBefore()` or `.appendTo()`, has a corresponding inverted method. The inverted methods perform exactly the same task as the standard ones, but the subject and target are reversed. For example:

```
$('<p>Hello</p>').appendTo('#container');
```

is the same as:

```
$('#container').append('<p>Hello</p>');
```

Using `.before()`, the inverted form of `.insertBefore()`, we can now re-factor our code to exploit chaining:

```
$(() => {
  const $notes = $('<ol id="notes"></ol>')
    .insertBefore('#footer');

  $('span.footnote')
    .each((i, span) => {
```

```
    $(span)
        .before(`<sup>${i + 1}</sup>`)
        .appendTo($notes)
        .wrap('<li></li>');
    });
});
```

Listing 5.14

Insertion method callbacks

The inverted insertion methods can accept a function as an argument, much like `.attr()` and `.css()` can. This function is invoked once per target element, and should return the HTML string to be inserted. We could use this technique here, but since we will encounter several such situations for each footnote, the single `.each()` call will end up being the cleaner solution.

We're now ready to take care of the final step in our checklist: create a link from the text location to its matching footnote, and from the footnote back to the text location. We'll need four pieces of markup per footnote to achieve this: two links, one in the text and one after the footnote, and two `id` attributes in those same locations. Because the argument to the `.before()` method is about to get complex, this is a good time to introduce a new notation for string creation.

In *Listing 5.14*, we prepare our footnote marker using a **template string**. This is a very useful technique, but for joining a large number of strings it can start to look cluttered. Instead, we can use the array method `.join()` to construct the larger string. The following statements have the same effect:

```
var str = 'a' + 'b' + 'c';
var str = `${'a'}${'b'}${'c'}`;
var str = ['a', 'b', 'c'].join('');
```

While it requires a few more characters to type in this example, the `.join()` method can add clarity when otherwise difficult to read string concatenation or string templates. Let's look at our code again, this time using `.join()` to create the string:

```
$(() => {
    const $notes = $('<ol id="notes"></ol>')
        .insertBefore('#footer');

    $('span.footnote')
        .each((i, span) => {
            $(span)
                .before([
                    '<sup>',
```

```
            i + 1,
            '</sup>'
        ].join(''))
        .appendTo($notes)
        .wrap('<li></li>');
    });
});
```

Listing 5.15

Using this technique, we can augment the footnote marker with a link to the bottom of the page as well as a unique `id` value. While we're at it, we'll also add an `id` for the `<li>` element, so the link has a destination to point at, as shown in the following code snippet:

```
$(() => {
    const $notes = $('<ol id="notes"></ol>')
        .insertBefore('#footer');

    $('span.footnote')
        .each((i, span) => {
            $(span)
                .before([
                    '<a href="#footnote-',
                    i + 1,
                    '" id="context-',
                    i + 1,
                    '" class="context">',
                    '<sup>',
                    i + 1,
                    '</sup></a>'
                ].join(''))
                .appendTo($notes)
                .wrap('<li></li>');
        });
});
```

Listing 5.16

With the additional markup in place, each footnote marker now links down to the corresponding footnote at the bottom of the document. All that remains is to create a link back from the footnote to its context. For this, we can employ the inverse of the `.appendTo()` method, `.append()`:

```
$(() => {
    const $notes = $('<ol id="notes"></ol>')
        .insertBefore('#footer');

    $('span.footnote')
```

```
    .each((i, span) => {
      $(span)
        .before([
          '<a href="#footnote-',
          i + 1,
          '" id="context-',
          i + 1,
          '" class="context">',
          '<sup>',
          i + 1,
          '</sup></a>'
        ].join(''))
        .appendTo($notes)
        .append([
          ' (<a href="#context-',
          i + 1,
          '">context</a>)'
        ].join(''))
        .wrap('<li></li>');
    });
});
```

Listing 5.17

Note that the `href` tag points back to the `id` value of the corresponding marker. In the following screenshot, you can see the footnotes again, except this time with the new link appended to each:

---

have all ended thus.

back to top

---

1. *"What need of a certificate?" a Spaceland critic may ask: "Is not the procreation of a Square Son a certificate from Nature herself, proving the Equal-sidedness of the Father?" I reply that no Lady of any position will marry an uncertified Triangle. Square offspring has sometimes resulted from a slightly Irregular Triangle; but in almost every such case the Irregularity of the first generation is visited on the third; which either fails to attain the Pentagonal rank, or relapses to the Triangular. (context)*

2. *The Equilateral is bound by oath never to permit the child henceforth to enter his former home or so much as to look upon his relations again, for fear lest the freshly developed organism may, by force of unconscious imitation, fall back again into his hereditary level. (context)*

3. *And how perfect a proof of the natural fitness and, I may almost say, the divine origin of the aristocratic constitution of the States of Flatland! (context)*

Copying elements

So far in this chapter, we have inserted newly created elements, moved elements from one location in the document to another, and wrapped new elements around existing ones. Sometimes, though, we may want to copy elements. For example, a navigation menu that appears in the page's header could be copied and placed in the footer as well. Whenever elements can be copied to enhance a page visually, we can let jQuery do the heavy lifting.

For copying elements, jQuery's `.clone()` method is just what we need; it takes any set of matched elements and creates a copy of them for later use. As in the case of the `$()` function's element creation process we explored earlier in this chapter, the copied elements will not appear in the document until we apply one of the insertion methods.

For example, the following line creates a copy of the first paragraph inside `<div class="chapter">`:

```
$('div.chapter p:eq(0)').clone();
```

This alone is not enough to change the content of the page. We can make the cloned paragraph appear before `<div class="chapter">` with an insertion method:

```
$('div.chapter p:eq(0)')
  .clone()
  .insertBefore('div.chapter');
```

This will cause the first paragraph to appear twice. So, to use a familiar analogy, `.clone()` is related to the insertion methods just as *copy* is to *paste*.

Clone with events

The `.clone()` method, by default, does not copy any events that are bound to the matching element or any of its descendants. However, it can take a single Boolean parameter that, when set to true (`.clone(true)`), clones events as well. This convenient event cloning allows us to avoid having to deal with manually rebinding events, as was discussed in Chapter 3, *Handling Events*.

Cloning for pull quotes

Many websites, like their print counterparts, use **pull quotes** to emphasize small portions of text and attract the reader's eye. A pull quote is simply an excerpt from the main document that is presented with a special graphical treatment alongside the text. We can easily accomplish this embellishment with the .clone() method. First, let's take another look at the third paragraph of our example text:

```
<p>
   <span class="pull-quote">It is a Law of Nature
   <span class="drop">with us</span> that a male child shall
   have <strong>one more side</strong> than his father</span>,
   so that each generation shall rise (as a rule) one step in
   the scale of development and nobility. Thus the son of a
   Square is a Pentagon; the son of a Pentagon, a Hexagon; and
   so on.
</p>
```

Note that the paragraph begins with <span class="pull-quote">. This is the class we will be targeting for cloning. Once the copied text inside that <span> tag is pasted into another place, we need to modify its style properties to set it apart from the rest of the text.

To accomplish this type of styling, we'll add a pulled class to the copied <span>. In our stylesheet, that class receives the following style rule:

```
.pulled {
   position: absolute;
   width: 120px;
   top: -20px;
   right: -180px;
   padding: 20px;
   font: italic 1.2em "Times New Roman", Times, serif;
   background: #e5e5e5;
   border: 1px solid #999;
   border-radius: 8px;
   box-shadow: 1px 1px 8px rgba(0, 0, 0, 0.6);
}
```

An element with this class is visually differentiated from the main content by applying style rules for background, border, font, and so on. Most importantly, it's absolutely positioned, 20 pixels above and 20 pixels to the right of the nearest (absolute or relative) positioned ancestor in the DOM. If no ancestor has positioning (other than static) applied, the pull quote will be positioned relative to the document <body>. Because of this, we need to make sure in the jQuery code that the cloned pull quote's parent element has position: relative set.

CSS position calculation

While the top positioning is fairly intuitive, it may not be clear at first how the pull quote box will be located 20 pixels to the right of its positioned parent. We derive the number first from the total width of the pull-quote box, which is the value of the `width` property plus the left and right padding, or `145px + 5px + 10px = 160px`. We then set the `right` property of the pull quote. A value of `0` would align the pull quote's right side with that of its parent. Therefore, to place its left side 20 pixels to the right of the parent, we need to move it in a negative direction 20 pixels more than its total width, or `-180px`.

Now, we can consider the jQuery code needed to apply this style. We'll start with a selector expression to find all of the `<span class="pull-quote">` elements and apply the `position: relative` style to each parent element as we just discussed:

```
$(() => {
  $('span.pull-quote')
    .each((i, span) => {
      $(span)
        .parent()
        .css('position', 'relative');
    });
});
```

Listing 5.18

Next, we need to create the pull quote itself, taking advantage of the CSS we've prepared. We need to clone each `<span>` tag, add the `pulled` class to the copy, and insert it into the beginning of its parent paragraph:

```
$(() => {
  $('span.pull-quote')
    .each((i, span) => {
      $(span)
        .clone()
        .addClass('pulled')
        .prependTo(
          $(span)
            .parent()
            .css('position', 'relative')
        );
    });
});
```

Listing 5.19

Because we're using absolute positioning for the pull quote, the placement of it within the paragraph is irrelevant. As long as it remains inside the paragraph, it will be positioned in relation to the top and the right of the paragraph, based on our CSS rules.

The pull quote now appears alongside its originating paragraph, as intended:

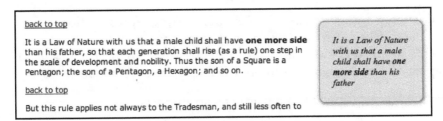

This is a good start. For our next enhancement, we'll clean up the content of the pull quotes a bit.

Content getter and setter methods

It would be nice to be able to modify the pull quote a bit by dropping some words and replacing them with ellipses to keep the content brief. To demonstrate this, we have wrapped a few words of the example text in a `<span class="drop">` tag.

The easiest way to accomplish this replacement is to directly specify the new HTML entity that is to replace the old one. The `.html()` method is perfect for this:

```
$(() => {
  $('span.pull-quote')
    .each((i, span) => {
      $(span)
        .clone()
        .addClass('pulled')
        .find('span.drop')
          .html('&hellip;')
          .end()
        .prependTo(
          $(span)
            .parent()
            .css('position', 'relative')
        );
    });
});
```

Listing 5.20

The new lines in *Listing 5.20* rely on the DOM traversal techniques we learned in Chapter 2, *Selecting Elements*. We use `.find()` to search inside the pull quote for any `<span class="drop">` elements, operate on them, and then return to the pull quote itself by calling `.end()`. In between these methods, we invoke `.html()` to change the content into an ellipsis (using the appropriate HTML entity).

When called without arguments, `.html()` returns a string representation of the HTML entity inside the matched element. With an argument, the contents of the element are replaced by the supplied HTML entity. We must take care to only specify a valid HTML entity, escaping special characters properly when using this technique.

The specified words have now been replaced by an ellipsis:

---

back to top

It is a Law of Nature with us that a male child shall have **one more side** than his father, so that each generation shall rise (as a rule) one step in the scale of development and nobility. Thus the son of a Square is a Pentagon; the son of a Pentagon, a Hexagon; and so on.

back to top

> *It is a Law of Nature ... that a male child shall have **one more side** than his father*

Pull quotes typically do not retain their original font formatting, such as the boldfaced **one more side** text in this example. What we really want to display is the text of `<span class="pull-quote">` stripped of any `<strong>`, `<em>`, `<a href>`, or other inline tags. To replace all of the pull-quote HTML entities with a stripped, text-only version, we can employ the `.html()` method's companion method, `.text()`.

Like `.html()`, the `.text()` method can either retrieve the content of the matched element or replace its content with a new string. Unlike `.html()`, however, `.text()` always gets or sets a plain text string. When `.text()` retrieves content, all of the included tags are ignored, and HTML entities are translated into plain characters. When it sets content, special characters such as < are translated into their HTML entity equivalents:

```
$(() => {
  $('span.pull-quote')
    .each((i, span) => {
      $(span)
        .clone()
        .addClass('pulled')
        .find('span.drop')
          .html('&hellip;')
          .end()
```

```
        .text((i, text) => text)
        .prependTo(
          $(span)
            .parent()
            .css('position', 'relative')
        );
    });
  });
```

Listing 5.21

When you retrieve values using `text()`, the markup is removed. This is exactly what we're trying to accomplish with this example. As with some of the other jQuery functions that you've learned about so far, `text()` accepts a function. The return value is used to set the text of the element, while the current text is passed in as the second argument. So to strip tags from element text, just call `text((i, text) => text)`. Awesome!

Here's the results of this approach:

back to top

It is a Law of Nature with us that a male child shall have **one more side** than his father, so that each generation shall rise (as a rule) one step in the scale of development and nobility. Thus the son of a Square is a Pentagon; the son of a Pentagon, a Hexagon; and so on.

back to top

But this rule applies not always to the Tradesman, and still less often to

It is a Law of Nature ... that a male child shall have one more side than his father

DOM manipulation methods in a nutshell

The extensive DOM manipulation methods that jQuery provides vary according to their task and their target location. We haven't covered them all here, but most are analogous to the ones we've seen, and more will be discussed in `Chapter 12`, *Advanced DOM Manipulation*. The following outline can serve as a reminder of which method we can use to accomplish which task:

- To *create* new elements from HTML, use the `$()` function
- To *insert* new elements *inside* every matched element, use the following functions:
  - `.append()`

- `.appendTo()`
- `.prepend()`
- `.prependTo()`

- To *insert* new elements *adjacent to* every matched element, use the following functions:
    - `.after()`
    - `.insertAfter()`
    - `.before()`
    - `.insertBefore()`

- To *insert* new elements *around* every matched element, use the following functions:
    - `.wrap()`
    - `.wrapAll()`
    - `.wrapInner()`

- To *replace* every matched element with new elements or text, use the following functions:
    - `.html()`
    - `.text()`
    - `.replaceAll()`
    - `.replaceWith()`

- To *remove* elements inside every matched element, use the following function:
    - `.empty()`

- To *remove* every matched element and descendants from the document without actually deleting them, use the following functions:
    - `.remove()`
    - `.detach()`

Summary

In this chapter, we have created, copied, reassembled, and embellished content using jQuery's DOM modification methods. We've applied these methods to a single web page, transforming a handful of generic paragraphs to a footnoted, pull-quoted, linked, and stylized literary excerpt. This chapter has shown us just how easy it is to add, remove, and rearrange the contents of a page with jQuery. In addition, you have learned how to make any changes we want to the CSS and DOM properties of page elements.

Next up, we'll take a round-trip journey to the server via jQuery's Ajax methods.

Further reading

The topic of DOM manipulation will be explored in more detail in Chapter 12, *Advanced DOM Manipulation*. A complete list of DOM manipulation methods is available in Appendix B, *Quick Reference*, of this book, or in the official jQuery documentation at http://api.jquery.com/.

Exercises

The challenge exercises may require the use of the official jQuery documentation at http://api.jquery.com/.

1. Alter the code that introduces the **back to top** links, so that the links only appear after the fourth paragraph.
2. When a **back to top** link is clicked on, add a new paragraph after the link containing the message **You were here**. Ensure that the link still works.
3. When the author's name is clicked, turn it bold (by adding an element, rather than manipulating classes or CSS attributes).
4. **Challenge**: On a subsequent click of the bolded author's name, remove the <b> element that was added (thereby toggling between bold and normal text).
5. **Challenge**: Add a class of inhabitants to each of the chapter's paragraphs without calling .addClass(). Make sure to preserve any existing classes.

6
Sending Data with Ajax

The term **Asynchronous JavaScript and XML (Ajax)** was coined by *Jesse James Garrett* in 2005. Since then, it has come to represent many different things, as the term encompasses a group of related capabilities and techniques. At its most basic level, an Ajax solution includes the following technologies:

- **JavaScript**: This is used to capture interactions with the user or other browser-related events and to interpret the data from the server and present it on the page
- **XMLHttpRequest**: This allows requests to be made to the server without interrupting other browser tasks
- **Textual data:** The server provides data in a format such as XML, HTML, or JSON

Ajax transforms static **web pages** into interactive **web applications**. Unsurprisingly, browsers are not entirely consistent with their implementations of the XMLHttpRequest object, but jQuery will assist us.

In this chapter, we will cover:

- Loading data from the server without a page refresh
- Sending data from JavaScript in the browser back to the server
- Interpreting data in a variety of formats, including HTML, XML, and JSON
- Providing feedback to the user about the status of an Ajax request

Loading data on demand

Ajax is just a means of loading data from the server into the web browser without a page refresh. This data can take many forms, and we have many options for what to do with it when it arrives. We'll see this by performing the same basic task, using different approaches.

We are going to build a page that displays entries from a dictionary, grouped by the starting letter of the dictionary entry. The HTML defining the content area of the page will look like this:

```
<div id="dictionary">
</div>
```

Our page will have no content to begin with. We are going to use jQuery's various Ajax methods to populate this `<div>` tag with dictionary entries.

Getting the example code

You can access the example code from the following GitHub repository: ht tps://github.com/PacktPublishing/Learning-jQuery-3.

We're going to need a way to trigger the loading process, so we'll add some links for our event handlers to latch onto:

```
<div class="letters">
  <div class="letter" id="letter-a">
    <h3><a href="entries-a.html">A</a></h3>
  </div>
  <div class="letter" id="letter-b">
    <h3><a href="entries-a.html">B</a></h3>
  </div>
  <div class="letter" id="letter-c">
    <h3><a href="entries-a.html">C</a></h3>
  </div>
  <div class="letter" id="letter-d">
    <h3><a href="entries-a.html">D</a></h3>
  </div>
  <!-- and so on -->
</div>
```

These simple links will lead us to pages that list the dictionary entries for that letter. We will use progressive enhancement to allow these links to manipulate the page without a full page load. With basic styling applied, this HTML will produce a page that looks like this:

The Devil's Dictionary

by Ambrose Bierce

<u>**A**</u>

<u>**B**</u>

<u>**C**</u>

<u>**D**</u>

Now, we can focus on getting content onto the page.

Appending HTML

Ajax applications are often no more than a request for a chunk of HTML. This technique, sometimes referred to as **Asynchronous HTTP and HTML (AHAH)**, is almost simple to implement with jQuery. First, we need some HTML to insert, which we'll place in a file called a.html alongside our main document. This secondary HTML file begins as follows:

```
<div class="entry">
  <h3 class="term">ABDICATION</h3>
  <div class="part">n.</div>
  <div class="definition">
    An act whereby a sovereign attests his sense of the high
    temperature of the throne.
    <div class="quote">
      <div class="quote-line">Poor Isabella's Dead, whose
      abdication</div>
      <div class="quote-line">Set all tongues wagging in the
      Spanish nation.</div>
      <div class="quote-line">For that performance 'twere
      unfair to scold her:</div>
      <div class="quote-line">She wisely left a throne too
      hot to hold her.</div>
      <div class="quote-line">To History she'll be no royal
      riddle &mdash;</div>
      <div class="quote-line">Merely a plain parched pea that
      jumped the griddle.</div>
```

```
        <div class="quote-author">G.J.</div>
      </div>
    </div>
</div>

<div class="entry">
  <h3 class="term">ABSOLUTE</h3>
  <div class="part">adj.</div>
  <div class="definition">
    Independent, irresponsible.  An absolute monarchy is one
    in which the sovereign does as he pleases so long as he
    pleases the assassins.  Not many absolute monarchies are
    left, most of them having been replaced by limited
    monarchies, where the sovereign's power for evil (and for
    good) is greatly curtailed, and by republics, which are
    governed by chance.
  </div>
</div>
```

The page continues with more entries in this HTML structure. Rendered on its own, a.html is quite plain:

ABDICATION

n.
An act whereby a sovereign attests his sense of the high temperature of the throne.
Poor Isabella's Dead, whose abdication
Set all tongues wagging in the Spanish nation.
For that performance 'twere unfair to scold her:
She wisely left a throne too hot to hold her.
To History she'll be no royal riddle —
Merely a plain parched pea that jumped the griddle.
G.J.

ABSOLUTE

adj.
Independent, irresponsible. An absolute monarchy is one in which the sovereign does as he pleases so long as he pleases the assassins. Not many absolute monarchies are left, most of them having been replaced by limited monarchies, where the sovereign's power for evil (and for good) is greatly curtailed, and by republics, which are governed by chance.

ACKNOWLEDGE

Note that a.html is not a true HTML document; it contains no <html>, <head>, or <body>, all of which are normally required. We usually call such a file a *partial* or *fragment*; its only purpose is to be inserted into another HTML document, which we'll do now:

```
$(() => {
  $('#letter-a a')
    .click((e) => {
      e.preventDefault()

      $('#dictionary').load('a.html');
    });
});
```

<div align="center">Listing 6.1</div>

The .load() method does all the heavy lifting for us. We specify the target location for the HTML snippet using a normal jQuery selector, and then pass the URL of the file to be loaded as a parameter. Now, when the first link is clicked on, the file is loaded and placed inside <div id="dictionary">. The browser will render the new HTML as soon as it is inserted:

The Devil's Dictionary

by Ambrose Bierce

A

B

C

D

ABDICATION   *n.*

An act whereby a sovereign attests his sense of the high temperature of the throne.

Poor Isabella's Dead, whose abdication
Set all tongues wagging in the Spanish nation.
For that performance 'twere unfair to scold her:
She wisely left a throne too hot to hold her.
To History she'll be no royal riddle —

Note that the HTML is now styled, whereas before it was plain. This is due to the CSS rules in the main document; as soon as the new HTML snippet is inserted, the rules apply to its elements as well.

When testing this example, the dictionary definitions will probably appear instantaneously when the button is clicked on. This is a hazard of working on our applications locally; it is hard to account for delays or interruptions in transferring documents across the network. Suppose we added an alert box to display after the definitions are loaded:

```
$(() => {
  $('#letter-a a')
```

```
    .click((e) => {
      e.preventDefault()

      $('#dictionary').load('a.html');
      alert('Loaded!');
    });
  });
```

We might assume from the structure of this code that the alert can only be displayed after the load has been performed. JavaScript execution is **synchronous**, working on one task after another in strict sequence.

However, when this particular code is tested on a production web server, the alert will have come and gone before the load has completed, due to network lag. This happens because all Ajax calls are by default **asynchronous**. Asynchronous loading means that once the HTTP request to retrieve the HTML snippet is issued, script execution immediately resumes without waiting. Some time later, the browser receives the response from the server and handles it. This is the desired behavior; it is unfriendly to lock up the whole web browser while waiting for data to be retrieved.

If actions must be delayed until the load has been completed, jQuery provides a callback for this. We've already seen callbacks in `Chapter 4`, *Styling and Animating*, using them to execute actions after an effect has completed. Ajax callbacks perform a similar function, executing after data arrives from the server. We will use this capability in our next example, as you learn how to read JSON data from the server.

Working with JavaScript objects

Pulling in fully formed HTML on demand is very convenient, but it means having to transfer a lot of information about the HTML structure along with the actual content. There are times when we would rather transfer as little data as possible and process it after it arrives. In this case, we need to retrieve the data in a structure that we can traverse with JavaScript.

With jQuery's selectors, we could traverse the HTML we get back and manipulate it, but a native JavaScript data format involves less data to transfer and less code to process it.

Retrieving JSON

As we have often seen, JavaScript objects are just sets of key-value pairs, and can be defined succinctly using curly braces ({ }). JavaScript arrays, on the other hand, are defined on the fly with square brackets ([]) and have implicit keys, which are incrementing integers. Combining these two concepts, we can easily express some very complex and rich data structures.

The term **JavaScript Object Notation (JSON)** was coined by *Douglas Crockford* to capitalize on this simple syntax. This notation can offer a concise alternative to the bulky XML format:

```
{
  "key": "value",
  "key 2": [
    "array",
    "of",
    "items"
  ]
}
```

While based on JavaScript object literals and array literals, JSON is more prescriptive about its syntax requirements and more restrictive about the values it allows. For example, JSON specifies that all object keys, as well as all string values must be enclosed in double quotes. Also, functions are not valid JSON values. Because of its strictness, developers should avoid hand-editing JSON and instead rely on software such as a server-side script to format it properly.

 For information on JSON's syntax requirements, some of its potential advantages and its implementations in many programming languages, visit http://json.org/.

We can encode our data using this format in many ways. To illustrate one approach, we'll place some dictionary entries in a JSON file that we'll call b.json:

```
[
  {
    "term": "BACCHUS",
    "part": "n.",
    "definition": "A convenient deity invented by the...",
    "quote": [
```

```
      "Is public worship, then, a sin,",
      "That for devotions paid to Bacchus",
      "The lictors dare to run us in,",
      "And resolutely thump and whack us?"
    ],
    "author": "Jorace"
  },
  {
    "term": "BACKBITE",
    "part": "v.t.",
    "definition": "To speak of a man as you find him when..."
  },
  {
    "term": "BEARD",
    "part": "n.",
    "definition": "The hair that is commonly cut off by..."
  },
  ... file continues ...
```

To retrieve this data, we'll use the $.getJSON() method, which fetches the file and processes it. When the data arrives from the server, it is simply a text string in JSON format. The $.getJSON() method parses this string and provides the calling code with the resulting JavaScript object.

Using global jQuery functions

Up until this point, all jQuery methods that we've used have been attached to a jQuery object that we've built with the $() function. The selectors have allowed us to specify a set of DOM nodes to work with, and the methods have operated on them in some way. This $.getJSON() function, however, is different. There is no logical DOM element to which it could apply; the resulting object has to be provided to the script, not injected into the page. For this reason, getJSON() is defined as a method of the global jQuery object (a single object called jQuery or $ defined once by the jQuery library), rather than of an individual jQuery object instance (the object returned by the $() function).

If $ were a class $.getJSON() would be a class method. For our purposes, we'll refer to this type of method as a **global function**; in effect, they are functions that use the jQuery namespace so as not to conflict with other function names.

To use this function, we pass it the filename as before:

```
$(() => {
  $('#letter-b a')
    .click((e) => {
```

```
    e.preventDefault();
    $.getJSON('b.json');
  });
});
```

Listing 6.3

This code has no apparent effect when we click on the link. The function call loads the file, but we have not told JavaScript what to do with the resulting data. For this, we need to use a callback function.

The `$.getJSON()` function takes a second argument, which is a function to be called when the load is complete. As mentioned earlier, Ajax calls are asynchronous, and the callback provides a way to wait for the data to be transmitted rather than executing code right away. The callback function also takes an argument, which is filled with the resulting data. So, we can write:

```
$(() => {
  $('#letter-b a')
    .click((e) => {
      e.preventDefault();
      $.getJSON('b.json', (data) => {});
    });
});
```

Listing 6.4

Inside this function, we can use the `data` parameter to traverse the JSON structure as necessary. We'll need to iterate over the top-level array, building the HTML for each item. We'll use the `reduce()` method of the data array to turn it into an HTML string that we can then insert into the document. The `reduce()` method takes a function as an argument and returns a section of the result for each item of the array:

```
$(() => {
  $('#letter-b a')
    .click((e) => {
      e.preventDefault();

      $.getJSON('b.json', (data) => {
        const html = data.reduce((result, entry) => `
          ${result}
          <div class="entry">
            <h3 class="term">${entry.term}</h3>
            <div class="part">${entry.part}</div>
            <div class="definition">
              ${entry.definition}
```

```
                </div>
              </div>
            `, '');

        $('#dictionary')
          .html(html);
      });
    });
  });
```

Listing 6.5

We use a template string to build the HTML content for each array item. The `result` argument is the value from the previous array item. Using this approach, it's a lot easier to see the HTML structure than would otherwise be using string concatenation. Once all of the HTML has been built for each entry, we insert it into `<div id="dictionary">` with `.html()`, replacing anything that may have already been there.

Safe HTML

This approach presumes that the data is safe for HTML consumption; it should not contain any stray < characters, for example.

All that's left is to handle the entries with quotations, which we can accomplish by implementing a couple of helper functions that use the `reduce()` technique to build a string:

```
$(() => {
  const formatAuthor = entry =>
    entry.author ?
      `<div class="quote-author">${entry.author}</div>` :
      '';

  const formatQuote = entry =>
    entry.quote ?
      `
      <div class="quote">
        ${entry.quote.reduce((result, q) => `
          ${result}
          <div class="quote-line">${q}</div>
        `, '')}
        ${formatAuthor(entry)}
      </div>
      ` : '';

  $('#letter-b a')
```

```
.click((e) => {
  e.preventDefault();

  $.getJSON('b.json', (data) => {
    const html = data.reduce((result, entry) => `
      ${result}
      <div class="entry">
        <h3 class="term">${entry.term}</h3>
        <div class="part">${entry.part}</div>
        <div class="definition">
          ${entry.definition}
          ${formatQuote(entry)}
        </div>
      </div>
    `, '');

    $('#dictionary')
      .html(html);
  });
});
});
```

Listing 6.6

With this code in place, we can click on the **B** link and confirm our results. The dictionary entries are displayed on the right-hand side of the page, as expected:

The Devil's Dictionary

by Ambrose Bierce

A

B

C

D

BACCHUS *n.*

A convenient deity invented by the ancients as an excuse for getting drunk.

Is public worship, then, a sin,
That for devotions paid to Bacchus
The lictors dare to run us in,
And resolutely thump and whack us?

Jorace

The JSON format is concise, but not forgiving. Every bracket, brace, quote, and comma must be present and accounted for, or the file will not load. In some cases, we won't even get an error message; the script will just silently fail.

Executing a script

Occasionally, we don't want to retrieve all the JavaScript we will need when the page is first loaded. We might not know what scripts will be necessary until some user interaction occurs. We could introduce the `<script>` tags on the fly when they are needed, but a more elegant way to inject additional code is to have jQuery load the `.js` file directly.

Pulling in a script is about as simple as loading an HTML fragment. In this case, we use the `$.getScript()` function, which--like its siblings--accepts a URL locating the script file:

```
$(() => {
  $('#letter-c a')
    .click((e) => {
      e.preventDefault();
      $.getScript('c.js');
    });
});
```

Listing 6.7

In our last example, we needed to process the result data so that we could do something useful with the loaded file. With a script file, though, the processing is automatic; the script is simply run.

Scripts that are fetched this way are run in the global context of the current page. This means they have access to all globally defined functions and variables, notably including jQuery itself. We can, therefore, mimic the JSON example to prepare and insert HTML on the page when the script is executed, and place this code in `c.js`:

```
const entries = [
  {
    "term": "CALAMITY",
    "part": "n.",
    "definition": "A more than commonly plain and..."
  },
  {
    "term": "CANNIBAL",
    "part": "n.",
    "definition": "A gastronome of the old school who..."
  },
  {
    "term": "CHILDHOOD",
    "part": "n.",
    "definition": "The period of human life intermediate..."
  }
  // and so on
```

```
];

const html = entries.reduce((result, entry) => `
  ${result}
  <div class="entry">
    <h3 class="term">${entry.term}</h3>
    <div class="part">${entry.part}</div>
    <div class="definition">
      ${entry.definition}
    </div>
  </div>
`, '');

$('#dictionary')
  .html(html);
```

Now, clicking on the **C** link has the expected result, showing the appropriate dictionary entries.

Loading an XML document

XML is part of the acronym Ajax, but we haven't actually loaded any XML yet. Doing so is straightforward, and mirrors the JSON technique closely. First, we'll need an XML file, d.xml, containing some data we wish to display:

```
<?xml version="1.0" encoding="UTF-8"?>
<entries>
  <entry term="DEFAME" part="v.t.">
    <definition>
      To lie about another.  To tell the truth about another.
    </definition>
  </entry>
  <entry term="DEFENCELESS" part="adj.">
    <definition>
      Unable to attack.
    </definition>
  </entry>
  <entry term="DELUSION" part="n.">
    <definition>
      The father of a most respectable family, comprising
      Enthusiasm, Affection, Self-denial, Faith, Hope,
      Charity and many other goodly sons and daughters.
    </definition>
    <quote author="Mumfrey Mappel">
      <line>All hail, Delusion!  Were it not for thee</line>
      <line>The world turned topsy-turvy we should see;
```

```
        </line>
      <line>For Vice, respectable with cleanly fancies,
        </line>
      <line>Would fly abandoned Virtue's gross advances.
        </line>
    </quote>
  </entry>
</entries>
```

This data could be expressed in many ways, of course, and some would more closely mimic the structure we established for the HTML or JSON used earlier. Here, however, we're illustrating some of the features of XML designed to make it more readable to humans, such as the use of attributes for `term` and `part` rather than tags.

We'll start off our function in a familiar manner:

```
$(() => {
  $('#letter-d a')
    .click((e) => {
      e.preventDefault();
      $.get('d.xml', (data) => {

      });
    });
});
```

Listing 6.8

This time, it's the `$.get()` function that does our work. In general, this function simply fetches the file at the supplied URL and provides the plain text to the callback. However, if the response is known to be XML because of its server-supplied MIME type, the callback will be handed to the XML DOM tree.

Fortunately, as we have already seen, jQuery has substantial DOM-traversing capabilities. We can use the normal `.find()`, `.filter()`, and other traversal methods on the XML document just as we would on HTML:

```
$(() => {
  $('#letter-d a')
    .click((e) => {
      const formatAuthor = entry =>
        $(entry).attr('author') ?
        `
          <div class="quote-author">
            ${$(entry).attr('author')}
          </div>
        ` : '';
```

```
const formatQuote = entry =>
  $(entry).find('quote').length ?
    `
    <div class="quote">
      ${$(entry)
        .find('quote')
        .get()
        .reduce((result, q) => `
          ${result}
          <div class="quote-line">
            ${$(q).text()}
          </div>
        `, '')}
      ${formatAuthor(entry)}
    </div>
    ` : '';

e.preventDefault();

$.get('d.xml', (data) => {
  const html = $(data)
    .find('entry')
    .get()
    .reduce((result, entry) => `
      ${result}
      <div class="entry">
        <h3 class="term">${$(entry).attr('term')}</h3>
        <div class="part">${$(entry).attr('part')}</div>
        <div class="definition">
          ${$(entry).find('definition').text()}
          ${formatQuote(entry)}
        </div>
      </div>
    `, '');

  $('#dictionary')
    .html(html);
});
});
});
```

Listing 6.9

This has the expected effect when the **D** link is clicked on:

The Devil's Dictionary

by Ambrose Bierce

A

B

C

D

DANCE *v.i.*

To leap about to the sound of tittering music, preferably with arms about your neighbor's wife or daughter. There are many kinds of dances, but all those requiring the participation of the two sexes have two characteristics in common: they are conspicuously innocent, and warmly loved by the vicious.

This is a new use for the DOM traversal methods we already know, shedding some light on the flexibility of jQuery's CSS selector support. CSS syntax is typically used to help beautify HTML pages, and thus selectors in standard `.css` files use HTML tag names such as `div` and `body` to locate content. However, jQuery can use arbitrary XML tag names, such as `entry` and `definition`, just as readily as the standard HTML ones.

The advanced selector engine inside jQuery facilitates finding parts of the XML document in much more complicated situations as well. For example, suppose we wanted to limit the displayed entries to those that have quotes that, in turn, have attributed authors. To do this, we can limit the entries to those with the nested `<quote>` elements by changing `entry` to `entry:has(quote)`. Then, we can further restrict the entries to those with `author` attributes on the `<quote>` elements by writing `entry:has(quote[author])`. The line in *Listing 6.9* with the initial selector now reads:

```
$(data).find('entry:has(quote[author])').each(function() {
```

This new selector expression restricts the returned entries correspondingly:

The Devil's Dictionary

by Ambrose Bierce

<u>**A**</u>

<u>**B**</u>

<u>**C**</u>

<u>**D**</u>

    DEBT *n.*

An ingenious substitute for the chain and whip of the slave-driver.

    As, pent in an aquarium, the troutlet
    Swims round and round his tank to find an outlet,
    Pressing his nose against the glass that holds him,
    Nor ever sees the prison that enfolds him;
    So the poor debtor, seeing naught around him,
    Yet feels the narrow limits that impound him,
    Grieves at his debt and studies to evade it,
    And finds at last he might as well have paid it.
                                    Barlow
                                   S. Vode

While we can use jQuery on XML data that's returned from the server, the downside is the size of our code has grown considerably.

Choosing a data format

We have looked at four formats for our external data, each of which is handled by jQuery's Ajax functions. We have also verified that all four can handle the task at hand, loading information onto an existing page when the user requests it and not before. How, then, do we decide which one to use in our applications?

HTML snippets require very little work to implement. The external data can be loaded and inserted into the page with one simple method that doesn't even require a callback function. No traversal of the data is necessary for the straightforward task of adding the new HTML into the existing page. On the other hand, the data is not necessarily structured in a way that makes it reusable for other applications. The external file is tightly coupled with its intended container.

JSON files are structured for simple reuse. They are compact and easy to read. The data structure must be traversed to pull out the information and present it on the page, but this can be done with standard JavaScript techniques. Since modern browsers parse the files natively with a single call to `JSON.parse()`, reading in a JSON file is extremely fast. Errors in the JSON file can cause silent failure or even side effects on the page, so the data must be crafted carefully by a trusted party.

JavaScript files offer the ultimate in flexibility, but are not really a data storage mechanism. Since the files are language-specific, they cannot be used to provide the same information to disparate systems. Instead, the ability to load a JavaScript file means that behaviors that are rarely needed can be factored out into external files, reducing code size unless and until it is needed.

While *XML* has fallen out of favor in the JavaScript community, with most developers preferring JSON, it is still so common that providing data in this format makes it very likely that the data can be reused elsewhere. The XML format is somewhat bulky, and can be a bit slower to parse and manipulate than other options.

With these characteristics in mind, it is typically easiest to provide external data as HTML snippets, as long as the data is not needed in other applications as well. In cases where the data will be reused but the other applications can also be influenced, JSON is often a good choice due to its performance and size. When the remote application is not known, XML may provide the greatest assurance that interoperability will be possible.

More than any other consideration, we should determine if the data is already available. If it is, chances are that it's in one of these formats to begin with, so the decision may be made for us.

Passing data to the server

Our examples to this point have focused on the task of retrieving static data files from the web server. However, the server can dynamically shape the data based on input from the browser. We're helped along by jQuery in this task as well; all of the methods we've covered so far can be modified so that data transfer becomes a two-way street.

Interacting with server-side code

Since demonstrating these techniques requires interaction with the web server, we'll need to use server-side code for the first time here. The examples given will use Node.js, which is very widely used as well as freely available. We will not cover any Node.js or Express specifics here, but there are plentiful resource on the web if you Google either of these technologies.

Performing a GET request

To illustrate the communication between client (using JavaScript) and server (also using JavaScript), we'll write a script that only sends one dictionary entry to the browser on each request. The entry chosen will depend on a parameter sent from the browser. Our script will pull its data from an internal data structure like this:

```
const E_entries = {
  EAVESDROP: {
    part: 'v.i.',
    definition: 'Secretly to overhear a catalogue of the ' +
                'crimes and vices of another or yourself.',
    quote: [
      'A lady with one of her ears applied',
      'To an open keyhole heard, inside,',
      'Two female gossips in converse free &mdash;',
      'The subject engaging them was she.',
      '"I think," said one, "and my husband thinks',
      'That she\'s a prying, inquisitive minx!"',
      'As soon as no more of it she could hear',
      'The lady, indignant, removed her ear.',
      '"I will not stay," she said, with a pout,',
      '"To hear my character lied about!"',
    ],
    author: 'Gopete Sherany',
  },
  EDIBLE: {
    part:'adj.',
    definition: 'Good to eat, and wholesome to digest, as ' +
                'a worm to a toad, a toad to a snake, a snake ' +
                'to a pig, a pig to a man, and a man to a worm.',
  },
  // Etc...
```

In a production version of this example, the data would probably be stored in a database and loaded on demand. Since the data is a part of the script here, the code to retrieve it is quite straightforward. We examine the query string part of the URL, then pass the term and entry to a function that returns the HTML snippet to display:

```
const formatAuthor = entry =>
  entry.author ?
    `<div class="quote-author">${entry.author}</div>` :
    '';

const formatQuote = entry =>
  entry.quote ?
    `
    <div class="quote">
      ${entry.quote.reduce((result, q) => `
        ${result}
        <div class="quote-line">${q}</div>
      `, '')}
      ${formatAuthor(entry)}
    </div>
    ` : '';

const formatEntry = (term, entry) => `
  <div class="entry">
    <h3 class="term">${term}</h3>
    <div class="part">${entry.part}</div>
    <div class="definition">
      ${entry.definition}
      ${formatQuote(entry)}
    </div>
  </div>
`;

app.use(express.static('./'));

app.get('/e', (req, res) => {
  const term = req.query.term.toUpperCase();
  const entry = E_entries[term];
  let content;

  if (entry) {
    content = formatEntry(term, entry);
  } else {
    content = '<div>Sorry, your term was not found.</div>';
  }

  res.send(content);
});
```

Now, requests to this /e handler, will return the HTML snippet corresponding to the term that was sent in the GET parameters. For example, when accessing the handler with /e?term=eavesdrop, we get back:

EAVESDROP

v.i.
Secretly to overhear a catalogue of the crimes and vices of another or yourself.
A lady with one of her ears applied
To an open keyhole heard, inside,
Two female gossips in converse free —
The subject engaging them was she.
"I think," said one, "and my husband thinks
That she's a prying, inquisitive minx!"
As soon as no more of it she could hear
The lady, indignant, removed her ear.
"I will not stay," she said, with a pout,
"To hear my character lied about!"
Gopete Sherany

Once again, we note the lack of formatting we saw with earlier HTML snippets, because CSS rules have not been applied.

Since we're showing how data is passed to the server, we will use a different method to request entries than the solitary buttons we've been relying on so far. Instead, we'll present a list of links for each term, and cause a click on any of them to load the corresponding definition. The HTML we'll add for this looks like the following:

```html
<div class="letter" id="letter-e">
  <h3>E</h3>
  <ul>
    <li><a href="e?term=Eavesdrop">Eavesdrop</a></li>
    <li><a href="e?term=Edible">Edible</a></li>
    <li><a href="e?term=Education">Education</a></li>
    <li><a href="e?term=Eloquence">Eloquence</a></li>
    <li><a href="e?term=Elysium">Elysium</a></li>
    <li><a href="e?term=Emancipation">Emancipation</a>
      </li>
    <li><a href="e?term=Emotion">Emotion</a></li>
```

```
      <li><a href="e?term=Envelope">Envelope</a></li>
      <li><a href="e?term=Envy">Envy</a></li>
      <li><a href="e?term=Epitaph">Epitaph</a></li>
      <li><a href="e?term=Evangelist">Evangelist</a></li>
    </ul>
  </div>
```

Now, we need to get our frontend JavaScript code to call the backend JavaScript with the right parameters. We could do this with the normal `.load()` mechanism, appending the query string right to the URL and fetching data with addresses such as `e?term=eavesdrop` directly. Instead, though, we can have jQuery construct the query string based on an object we provide to the `$.get()` function:

```
$(() => {
  $('#letter-e a')
    .click((e) => {
      e.preventDefault();

      const requestData = {
        term: $(e.target).text()
      };

      $.get('e', requestData, (data) => {
        $('#dictionary').html(data);
      });
    });
});
```

Listing 6.10

Now that we have seen other Ajax interfaces that jQuery provides, the operation of this function seems familiar. The only difference is the second parameter, which allows us to supply an object containing keys and values that become part of the query string. In this case, the key is always `term`, but the value is taken from the text of each link. Now, clicking on the first link in the list causes its definition to appear:

The Devil's Dictionary

by Ambrose Bierce

A

B

C

D

E

Eavesdrop
Edible
Education
Eloquence
Elysium
Emancipation

EAVESDROP *v.i.*

Secretly to overhear a catalogue of the crimes and vices of another or yourself.

A lady with one of her ears applied
To an open keyhole heard, inside,
Two female gossips in converse free —
The subject engaging them was she.
"I think," said one, "and my husband thinks
That she's a prying, inquisitive minx!"
As soon as no more of it she could hear
The lady, indignant, removed her ear.
"I will not stay," she said, with a pout,
"To hear my character lied about!"

**Gopete
Sherany**

All the links here have URLs, even though we are not using them in the code. To prevent the links from being followed normally when clicked on, we invoke the `.preventDefault()` method.

Return false or prevent default?
When writing the `click` handlers in this chapter, we have chosen to use `e.preventDefault()` rather than ending the handler with `return false`. This practice is recommended when the default action would otherwise reload the page or load another page. If our `click` handler, for example, contains a JavaScript error, calling `.preventDefault()` on the handler's first line (before the error is encountered) ensures that the form will not be submitted, and our browser's error console will properly report the error. Remember from Chapter 3, *Handling Events*, that return `false` calls both `event.preventDefault()` and `event.stopPropagation()`. If we wanted to stop the event from bubbling, we would need to call the latter as well.

Serializing a form

Sending data to the server often involves the user filling out forms. Rather than relying on the normal form submission mechanism, which will load the response in the entire browser window, we can use jQuery's Ajax toolkit to submit the form asynchronously and place the response inside the current page.

To try this out, we'll need to construct a simple form:

```
<div class="letter" id="letter-f">
  <h3>F</h3>
  <form action="f">
    <input type="text" name="term" value="" id="term" />
    <input type="submit" name="search" value="search"
      id="search" />
  </form>
</div>
```

This time, we'll return a set of entries from the server by having our /f handler search for the supplied search term as a substring of a dictionary term. We'll use our formatEntry() function from the /e handler to return the data in the same format as before. Here's the /f handler implementation:

```
app.post('/f', (req, res) => {
  const term = req.body.term.toUpperCase();
  const content = Object.keys(F_entries)
    .filter(k => k.includes(term))
    .reduce((result, k) => `
      ${result}
      ${formatEntry(k, F_entries[k])}
    `, '');

  res.send(content);
});
```

Now, we can react to a form submission and craft the proper query parameters by traversing the DOM tree:

```
$(() => {
  $('#letter-f form')
    .submit((e) => {
      e.preventDefault();

      $.post(
        $(e.target).attr('action'),
        { term: $('input[name="term"]').val() },
        (data) => { $('#dictionary').html(data); }
      );
    });
});
```

Listing 6.11

This code has the intended effect, but searching for input fields by name and appending them to a map one by one is cumbersome. In particular, this approach does not scale well as the form becomes more complex. Fortunately, jQuery offers a shortcut for this often-used idiom. The `.serialize()` method acts on a jQuery object and translates the matched DOM elements into a query string that can be passed along with an Ajax request. We can generalize our submission handler as follows:

```
$(() => {
  $('#letter-f form')
    .submit((e) => {
      e.preventDefault();

      $.post(
        $(e.target).attr('action'),
        $(e.target).serialize(),
        (data) => { $('#dictionary').html(data); }
      );
    });
});
```

Listing 6.12

The same script will work to submit the form, even as the number of fields increases. When we perform a search for `fid`, for example, the terms containing that substring are displayed as shown in the following screenshot:

The Devil's Dictionary

by Ambrose Bierce

A

B

C

D

E

FIDDLE *n.*

An instrument to tickle human ears by friction of a horse's tail on the entrails of a cat.
To Rome said Nero: "If to smoke you turn
I shall not cease to fiddle while you burn."
To Nero Rome replied: "Pray do your worst,
'Tis my excuse that you were fiddling first."
Orm Pludge

Eavesdrop
Edible
Education

FIDELITY *n.*

A virtue peculiar to those who are about to be betrayed.

Keeping an eye on the request

So far, it has been sufficient for us to make a call to an Ajax method and patiently await the response. At times, though, it is handy to know a bit more about the HTTP request as it progresses. If such a need arises, jQuery offers a suite of functions that can be used to register callbacks when various Ajax-related events occur.

The `.ajaxStart()` and `.ajaxStop()` methods are two examples of these observer functions. When an Ajax call begins with no other transfer in progress, the `.ajaxStart()` callback is fired. Conversely, when the last active request ends, the callback attached with `.ajaxStop()` will be executed. All of the observers are global, in that they are called when any Ajax communication occurs, regardless of what code initiates it. And all of them, can only be bound to `$(document)`.

We can use these methods to provide some feedback to the user in the case of a slow network connection. The HTML for the page can have a suitable loading message appended:

```
<div id="loading">
   Loading...
</div>
```

This message is just a piece of arbitrary HTML; it could include an animated GIF image as a loading indicator, for instance. In this case, we'll add a few simple styles to the CSS file so that when the message is displayed, the page will look like the following:

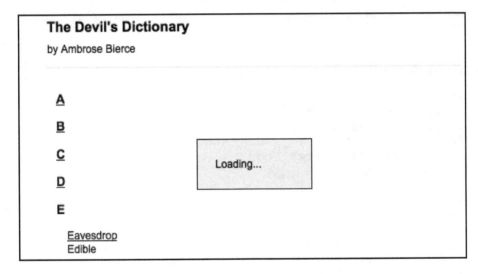

In keeping with the spirit of progressive enhancement, however, we won't put this HTML markup directly on the page. Instead, we'll insert it using jQuery:

```
$(() => {
  $('<div/>')
    .attr('id', 'loading')
    .text('Loading...')
    .insertBefore('#dictionary');
});
```

Our CSS file will give this `<div>` a `display: none;` style declaration so that the message is initially hidden. To display it at the right time, we just register it as an observer with `.ajaxStart()`:

```
$(() => {
  const $loading = $('<div/>')
    .attr('id', 'loading')
    .text('Loading...')
    .insertBefore('#dictionary');

  $(document)
    .ajaxStart(() => {
      $loading.show();
    });
});
```

We can chain the hiding behavior right onto this:

```
$(() => {
  const $loading = $('<div/>')
    .attr('id', 'loading')
    .text('Loading...')
    .insertBefore('#dictionary');

  $(document)
    .ajaxStart(() => {
      $loading.show();
    })
    .ajaxStop(() => {
      $loading.hide();
    });
});
```

Listing 6.13

We now have our loading feedback.

Once again, note that these methods have no association with the particular ways in which the Ajax communications begin. The `.load()` method attached to the **A** link and the `.getJSON()` method attached to the **B** link both cause these actions to occur.

In this case, this global behavior is desirable. If we need to get more specific, though, we have a few options at our disposal. Some of the observer methods, such as .ajaxError(), send their callback a reference to the XMLHttpRequest object. This can be used to differentiate one request from another and provide different behaviors. Other more specific handling can be achieved by using the low-level $.ajax() function, which we'll discuss a bit later.

The most common way of interacting with the request is the success callback, which we have already covered. We have used this in several of our examples to interpret the data coming back from the server and to populate the page with the results. It can be used for other feedback too, of course. Consider once again our .load() example from *Listing 6.1*:

```
$(() => {
  $('#letter-a a')
    .click((e) => {
      e.preventDefault();
      $('#dictionary')
        .load('a.html');
    });
});
```

We can create a small enhancement here by making the loaded content fade into view rather than appear suddenly. The .load() method can take a callback to be fired on completion:

```
$(() => {
  $('#letter-a a')
    .click((e) => {
      e.preventDefault();
      $('#dictionary')
        .hide()
        .load('a.html', function() {
          $(this).fadeIn();
        });
    });
});
```

Listing 6.14

First, we hide the target element and then initiate the load. When the load is complete, we use the callback to show the newly populated element by fading it in.

Error handling

So far, we have only dealt with successful responses to Ajax requests, loading the page with new content when everything goes as planned. Responsible developers, however, should account for the possibility of network or data errors and report them appropriately. Developing Ajax applications in a local environment can lull developers into a sense of complacency since, aside from a possible mistyped URL, Ajax errors don't just happen locally. The Ajax convenience methods such as $.get() and .load() do not provide an error callback argument themselves, so we need to look elsewhere for a solution to this problem.

Aside from using the global .ajaxError() method, we can react to errors by capitalizing on jQuery's deferred object system. We will discuss deferred objects more fully in Chapter 11, *Advanced Effects*, but, for now, we'll simply note that we can chain .done(), .always(), and .fail() methods to any Ajax function except .load(), and use these methods to attach the relevant callbacks. For example, if we take the code from *Listing 6.16* and change the URL to one that doesn't exist, we can test the .fail() method:

```
$(() => {
  $('#letter-e a')
    .click((e) => {
      e.preventDefault();

      const requestData = {
        term: $(e.target).text()
      };

      $.get('notfound', requestData, (data) => {
        $('#dictionary').html(data);
      }).fail((xhr) => {
        $('#dictionary')
          .html(`An error occurred:
            ${xhr.status}
            ${xhr.responseText}
          `);
      });
    });
});
```

Listing 6.15

Now, clicking on any of the links for terms beginning with E will produce an error message. The exact content of `jqXHR.responseText` will vary depending on the server configuration:

The Devil's Dictionary

by Ambrose Bierce

<u>**A**</u>

<u>**B**</u>

<u>**C**</u>

<u>**D**</u>

E

Sorry, but an error occurred: 404

Not Found

The requested URL /6549/06/z.php was not found on this server.

The `.status` property contains a numeric code provided by the server. These codes are defined in the HTTP specification, and when a `.fail()` handler is triggered, they will represent an error condition such as:

Response code	Description
400	Bad request
401	Unauthorized
403	Forbidden
404	Not found
500	Internal server error

A complete list of response codes can be found on the W3C's site: `http://www.w3.org/Protocols/rfc2616/rfc2616-sec10.html`.

We will examine error handling more closely in `Chapter 13`, *Advanced Ajax*.

Ajax and events

Suppose we wanted to allow each dictionary term name to control the display of the definition that follows; clicking on the term name would show or hide the associated definition. With the techniques we have seen so far, this should be pretty straightforward:

```
$(() => {
  $('h3.term')
    .click((e) => {
      $(e.target)
        .siblings('.definition')
        .slideToggle();
    });
});
```

Listing 6.16

When a term is clicked on, this code finds siblings of the element that have a class of `definition`, and slides them up or down as appropriate.

All seems in order, but a click does nothing with this code. Unfortunately, the terms have not yet been added to the document when we attach the `click` handlers. Even if we managed to attach `click` handlers to these items, once we clicked on a different letter the handlers would no longer be attached.

This is a common problem with areas of a page populated by Ajax. A popular solution is to rebind handlers each time the page area is refreshed. This can be cumbersome, however, as the event-binding code needs to be called each time anything causes the DOM structure of the page to change.

A superior alternative was introduced in Chapter 3, *Handling Events*. We can implement **event delegation**, actually binding the event to an ancestor element that never changes. In this case, we'll attach the `click` handler to the `<body>` element, using `.on()` to catch our clicks that way:

```
$(() => {
  $('body')
    .on('click', 'h3.term', (e) => {
      $(e.target)
        .siblings('.definition')
        .slideToggle();
    });
});
```

Listing 6.17

When used this way, the `.on()` method tells the browser to observe all clicks anywhere in the document. If (and only if) the clicked element matches the `h3.term` selector, then the handler is executed. Now, the toggling behavior will take place on any term, even if it is added by a later Ajax transaction.

Deferreds and promises

jQuery deferred objects were introduced at a time when there was no consistent way to handle asynchronous behavior in JavaScript code. Promises help us orchestrate asynchronous stuff, such as multiple HTTP requests, file reads, animations, and so on. Promises aren't exclusive to JavaScript, nor are they a new idea. The best way to think about a promise is as a contract that promises to resolve a value *eventually*.

Now that promises are officially part of JavaScript, jQuery now fully supports promises. That is, jQuery deferred objects behave just like any other promise. This is important, as we'll see in this section, because it means that we can use jQuery deferreds to compose complex asynchronous behavior with other code that return native promises.

Performing Ajax calls on page load

Right now, our dictionary doesn't show any definitions on the initial page load. Instead, it just shows some empty space. Let's change that by showing the "A" entries when the document is ready. How do we do this?

One approach is to simply add the `load('a.html')` call into our document ready handler (`$(() => {})`) along with everything else. The problem is that this is inefficient because we have to wait for the document to be ready before we can even make the Ajax request. Wouldn't it be better to make the Ajax request as soon as our JavaScript runs?

The challenge is then synchronizing the document ready event with the Ajax response ready event. There is a race condition here because we don't know which event will happen first. There's a good chance that the document will be ready first, but we can't make that assumption. This is where promises are super helpful:

```
Promise.all([
  $.get('a.html'),
  $.ready
]).then(([[content]]) => {
  $('#dictionary')
    .hide()
    .html(content)
```

```
        .fadeIn();
});
```

Listing 6.18

The `Promise.all()` method takes an array of other promises, and returns a new promise. This new promise is then resolved when everything in the array argument resolves. This is how promises handle asynchronous race conditions for us. It doesn't matter if the Ajax promise (`$.get('a.html')`) resolves first or the document ready promise (`$.ready`) resolves first.

The `then()` handler is where we want to execute any code that depends on asynchronous values. For example, the content value is the resolved Ajax call. The document being ready implicitly resolves the DOM. If the DOM isn't ready, we cannot run `$('#dictionary')....`

Using fetch()

Another recent addition to JavaScript is the `fetch()` function. This is a more flexible alternative to `XMLHttpRequest`. For example, it's much easier to use `fetch()` when making cross-domain requests, or when you need to tweak specific HTTP header values. Let's implement the *G* entries using `fetch()`:

```
$(() => {
  $('#letter-g a')
    .click((e) => {
      e.preventDefault();

      fetch('/g')
        .then(resp => resp.json())
        .then(data => {
          const html = data.reduce((result, entry) => `
            ${result}
            <div class="entry">
              <h3 class="term">${entry.term}</h3>
              <div class="part">${entry.part}</div>
              <div class="definition">
                ${entry.definition}
                ${formatQuote(entry)}
              </div>
            </div>
          `, '');

          $('#dictionary')
```

```
            .html(html);
        });
    });
});
```

Listing 6.19

The `fetch()` function returns a promise, just like the various jQuery Ajax functions. This means that if the `/g` URL that we're calling in this example were actually located in another domain, we could use `fetch()` to access it. If we want JSON data, which we do, we need to call `.json()` in the `.then()` handler. Then, in a second handler, we can populate the DOM, using the same functions we created earlier in the chapter.

The whole idea behind promises is consistency. If we need to synchronize asynchronous behavior, promises are the way to do it. Anything that jQuery does asynchronously, can be used with other promises.

Summary

You have learned that the Ajax methods provided by jQuery can help us to load data in several different formats from the server without a page refresh. We can execute scripts from the server on demand and send data back to the server.

You've also learned how to deal with common challenges of asynchronous loading techniques, such as keeping handlers bound after a load has occurred and loading data from a third-party server.

This concludes our tour of the basic components of the `jQuery` library. Next, we'll look at how these features can be expanded upon easily using jQuery plugins.

Further reading

The topic of Ajax will be explored in more detail in `Chapter 13`, *Advanced Ajax*. A complete list of Ajax methods is available in `Appendix B`, *Quick Reference*, of this book or in the official jQuery documentation at `http://api.jquery.com/`.

Exercises

The challenge exercise may require the use of the official jQuery documentation at `http://api.jquery.com/`:

1. When the page loads, pull the body content of `exercises-content.html` into the content area of the page.
2. Rather than displaying the whole document at once, create tooltips for the letters in the left-hand column by loading just the appropriate letter's content from `exercises-content.html` when the user's mouse is over the letter.
3. Add error handling for this page load, displaying the error message in the content area. Test this error handling code by changing the script to request `does-not-exist.html` rather than `exercises-content.html`.
4. Here's a challenge. When the page loads, send a JSONP request to GitHub and retrieve a list of repositories for a user. Insert the name and URL of each repository into the content area of the page. The URL to retrieve the jQuery project's repositories is `https://api.github.com/users/jquery/repos`.

7
Using Plugins

Throughout the first six chapters of this book, we examined jQuery's core components. Doing this has illustrated many of the ways in which the jQuery library can be used to accomplish a wide variety of tasks. Yet as powerful as the library is at its core, its elegant **plugin architecture** has allowed developers to extend jQuery, making it even more feature rich.

The jQuery community created hundreds of plugins--from small selector helpers to full-scale user-interface widgets. You will now learn how to tap into this vast resource.

In this chapter, we will cover:

- Downloading and setting up plugins
- Calling jQuery methods provided by plugins
- Finding elements using custom selectors defined by jQuery plugins
- Adding sophisticated user interface behaviors using jQuery UI
- Implementing mobile-friendly features using jQuery Mobile

Using a plugin

Using a jQuery plugin is very straightforward. We need to simply obtain the plugin code, reference the plugin from our HTML, and invoke the new capabilities from our own scripts.

We can easily demonstrate these tasks using the jQuery **Cycle** plugin. This plugin, by Mike Alsup, allows us to quickly transform a static set of page elements into an interactive slideshow. Like many popular plugins, it can handle complex, advanced needs well, but can also hide this complexity when our requirements are more straightforward.

Downloading and referencing the Cycle plugin

To install any jQuery plugins, we'll use the npm package manager. This is the de facto tool for declaring package dependencies for modern JavaScript projects. For example, we can use a package.json file to declare that we need jQuery, and a specific set of jQuery plugins.

 For help on installing npm, see https://docs.npmjs.com/getting-start ed/what-is-npm. For help on initializing a package.json file, see https ://docs.npmjs.com/getting-started/using-a-package.json.

Once you have a package.json file in the root of your project directory, you're ready to start adding dependencies. For example, you can add a jquery dependency from your command console as follows:

```
npm install jquery --save
```

And if we want to use the cycle plugin, we can install that as well:

```
npm install jquery-cycle --save
```

The reason we use the --save flag with this command is so to tell npm that we're always going to need these packages, and that it should save these dependencies to package.json. Now that we have jquery and jquery-cycle installed, let's include them on our page:

```
<head>
  <meta charset="utf-8">
  <title>jQuery Book Browser</title>
  <link rel="stylesheet" href="07.css" type="text/css" />
  <script src="node_modules/jquery/dist/jquery.js"></script>
  <script src="node_modules/jquery-cycle/index.js"></script>
  <script src="07.js"></script>
</head>
```

We have now loaded our first plugin. As we can see, this is no more complicated than setting up jQuery itself. The plugin's capabilities are now ours to use in our scripts.

Calling a plugin method

The Cycle plugin operates on any set of sibling elements on a page. To show it in action, we'll set up some simple HTML containing book cover images and related information in a list, adding it to the body of our HTML document as follows:

```
<ul id="books">
  <li>
    <img src="images/jq-game.jpg" alt="jQuery Game Development
      Essentials" />
    <div class="title">jQuery Game Development Essentials</div>
    <div class="author">Salim Arsever</div>
  </li>
  <li>
    <img src="images/jqmobile-cookbook.jpg" alt="jQuery Mobile
      Cookbook" />
    <div class="title">jQuery Mobile Cookbook</div>
    <div class="author">Chetan K Jain</div>
  </li>
  ...
</ul>
```

Some light styling in our CSS file presents the book covers one after the other as shown in the following screenshot:

The Cycle plugin will work its magic on this list, transforming it into an attractive animated slideshow. This transformation can be invoked by calling the `.cycle()` method on the appropriate container in the DOM as follows:

```
$(() => {
  $('#books').cycle();
});
```

Listing 7.1

This syntax could hardly be more simple. As we would with any built-in jQuery method, we apply `.cycle()` to a jQuery object instance, which in turn points to the DOM elements we want to manipulate. Even without providing any arguments to it, `.cycle()` does a lot of work for us. The styles on the page are altered to present only one list item at a time, and a new item is shown using a cross-fading transition every 4 seconds:

This simplicity is typical of well-written jQuery plugins. A straightforward method call is all it takes to achieve professional and useful results. However, like many other plugins, Cycle offers a large number of options for customizing and fine-tuning its behavior.

Specifying plugin method parameters

Passing parameters to plugin methods is no different than doing so with native jQuery methods. In many cases, parameters are passed as a single object of key-value pairs (as we saw with $.ajax() in Chapter 6, *Sending Data with Ajax*). The choices of options to provide can be quite daunting; .cycle() alone has over 50 potential configuration options. The documentation for each plugin details the effect of each option, often with detailed examples.

The Cycle plugin allows us to alter the speed and style of the animation between slides, affect how and when slide transitions are triggered, and react to completed animations using callbacks. To demonstrate some of these capabilities, we'll provide three simple options to the method call from *Listing 7.1* as follows:

```
$(() => {
  $('#books').cycle({
    timeout: 2000,
    speed: 200,
    pause: true
  });
});
```

Listing 7.2

The timeout option specifies the number of milliseconds to wait between each slide transition (2,000). In contrast, speed determines the number of milliseconds the transitions themselves will take (200). When set to true, the pause option causes the slideshow to suspend itself when the mouse is inside the cycling region, which is especially useful when the cycling items are clickable.

Modifying parameter defaults

The Cycle plugin is impressive even with no supplied arguments. To accomplish this, it needs a sensible set of defaults to use when options are not supplied.

A common pattern, and the one followed by Cycle, is to gather all of the defaults into a single object. In the case of Cycle, the `$.fn.cycle.defaults` object contains all of the default options. When a plugin collects its defaults in a publicly visible location like this, we can alter them in our own scripts. This can make our code more concise when calling the plugin multiple times since we don't have to specify the new value for the option each time. Redefining the defaults is simple, as can be seen in the following code:

```
$.fn.cycle.defaults.timeout = 10000;
$.fn.cycle.defaults.random = true;

$(() => {
  $('#books').cycle({
    timeout: 2000,
    speed: 200,
    pause: true
  });
});
```

Listing 7.3

Here we've set two defaults, `timeout` and `random`, prior to invoking `.cycle()`. Since we declare a value of 2000 for `timeout` in our `.cycle()` call, our new default of 10000 will be ignored. On the other hand, the new default of `true` for `random` does take effect, causing the slides to transition in a random order.

Other types of plugins

Plugins need not be limited to providing additional jQuery methods. They can extend the library in many ways and even alter the functionality of existing features.

Plugins can change the way other parts of the jQuery library operate. Some offer new animation easing styles, for instance, or trigger additional jQuery events in response to user actions. The Cycle plugin offers such an enhancement by adding a new custom selector.

Custom selectors

Plugins that add custom selector expressions increase the capabilities of jQuery's built-in selector engine so that we can find elements on the page in new ways. Cycle adds a custom selector of this kind, which gives us an opportunity to explore this capability.

Cycle's slideshows can be paused and resumed by calling `.cycle('pause')` and `.cycle('resume')`, respectively. We can easily add buttons that control the slideshow, as shown in the following code:

```
$(() => {
  const $books = $('#books').cycle({
    timeout: 2000,
    speed: 200,
    pause: true
  });
  const $controls = $('<div/>')
    .attr('id', 'books-controls')
    .insertAfter($books);

  $('<button/>')
    .text('Pause')
    .click(() => {
      $books.cycle('pause');
    })
    .appendTo($controls);
  $('<button/>')
    .text('Resume')
    .click(() => {
      $books.cycle('resume');
    })
    .appendTo($controls);
});
```

Listing 7.4

Now, suppose that we want our **Resume** button to resume any paused Cycle slideshow on the page, in case there were more than one. We want to find all the `<ul>` elements on the page that are paused slideshows and resume them all. Cycle's custom `:paused` selector allows us to do this easily:

```
$(() => {
  $('<button/>')
    .text('Resume')
    .click(() => {
      $('ul:paused').cycle('resume');
    })
    .appendTo($controls);
});
```

Listing 7.5

With Cycle loaded, `$('ul:paused')` will create a jQuery object referencing all of the paused slideshows on the page so that we can interact with them at will. Selector extensions such as this that are provided by plugins can be freely combined with any of the standard jQuery selectors. We can see that, with the choice of appropriate plugins, jQuery can be molded to suit our needs.

Global function plugins

Many popular plugins provide new global functions within the `jQuery` namespace. This pattern is common when plugins supply features that are not related to the DOM elements on the page and thus are not good candidates for standard jQuery methods. For example, the Cookie plugin (`https://github.com/carhartl/jquery-cookie`) offers an interface for reading and writing cookie values on a page. This functionality is provided through the `$.cookie()` function, which can get or set individual cookies.

Let's say, for example, that we want to remember when users press our slideshow's **Pause** button so that we can keep it paused if they leave the page and return to it later. After loading the Cookie plugin, reading a cookie is as simple as using the cookie's name as the sole argument as shown in the following code:

```
if ($.cookie('cyclePaused')) {
  $books.cycle('pause');
}
```

Listing 7.6

Here, we look for the existence of a `cyclePaused` cookie; it doesn't matter what the value is for our purpose. If the cookie exists, the cycle will pause. When we insert this conditional pause immediately after the call to `.cycle()`, the slideshow keeps the first image visible until the user at some point presses the **Resume** button.

Of course, because we haven't set the cookie yet, the slideshow is still cycling through the images. Setting a cookie is as simple as getting its value; we just supply a string for the second argument as follows:

```
$(() => {
  $('<button/>')
    .text('Pause')
    .click(() => {
      $books.cycle('pause');
      $.cookie('cyclePaused', 'y');
    })
    .appendTo($controls);
```

```
$('<button/>')
  .text('Resume')
  .click(() => {
    $('ul:paused').cycle('resume');
    $.cookie('cyclePaused', null);
  })
  .appendTo($controls);
});
```

Listing 7.7

The cookie is set to y when the **Pause** button is pressed, and it is deleted by passing `null` when the **Resume** button is pressed. By default, the cookie remains for the duration of the session (generally until the browser tab is closed). Also by default, the cookie is associated with the page on which it was set. To change these default settings, we can supply an options object for the function's third argument. This is a pattern typical to jQuery plugins as well as jQuery core functions.

For example, to make the cookie available throughout the site and have it expire after 7 days, we can call the function with `$.cookie('cyclePaused', 'y', { path: '/', expires: 7 })`. For information on these and other options available when calling `$.cookie()`, we can refer to the documentation for the plugin.

The jQuery UI plugin library

While most plugins, such as Cycle and Cookie, focus on a single task, jQuery UI tackles a wide variety of challenges. In fact, while the jQuery UI code may often be packaged as a single file, it is actually a comprehensive suite of related plugins.

The jQuery UI team has created a number of core interaction components and full-fledged widgets to help make the web experience more like that of a desktop application. Interaction components include methods for dragging, dropping, sorting, selecting, and resizing items. The current stable of widgets includes buttons, accordions, datepickers, dialogs, and so on. Additionally, jQuery UI provides an extensive set of advanced effects to supplement the core jQuery animations.

The full UI library is too extensive to be adequately covered within this chapter; indeed, there are entire books devoted to the subject. Fortunately, a major focus of the project is consistency among its features, so exploring a couple of pieces in detail will serve to get us started in using the rest of them as needed.

Downloads, documentation, and demos of all the jQuery UI modules are available at `http://jqueryui.com/`. The download page offers a combined download with all the features baked in, or a customizable download that can contain just the functionality we need. The downloadable ZIP file also contains a stylesheet and images, which we need to include when we use jQuery UI's interaction components and widgets.

Effects

The effects module of jQuery UI consists of a core and a set of independent effect components. The core file provides animations for colors and classes, as well as advanced easing.

Color animations

With jQuery UI's core effects component linked into the document, the `.animate()` method is extended to accept additional style properties, such as `borderTopColor`, `backgroundColor`, and `color`. For example, we can now gradually change an element from white text on a black background to black text on a light gray background as follows:

```
$(() => {
  $books.hover((e) => {
    $(e.target)
      .find('.title')
      .animate({
        backgroundColor: '#eee',
        color: '#000'
      }, 1000);
  }, (e) => {
    $(e.target)
      .find('.title')
      .animate({
        backgroundColor: '#000',
        color: '#fff'
      }, 1000);
  });
});
```

Listing 7.8

Now when the mouse cursor enters the book slideshow region of the page, the book title's text color and background color both smoothly animate over a period of one second (1000 ms):

Class animations

The three CSS class methods that we have worked with in previous chapters-- .addClass(), .removeClass(), and .toggleClass()--are extended by jQuery UI to take an optional second argument for the animation duration. When this duration is specified, the page behaves as if we had called .animate() and directly specified all of the style attributes that change as a result of applying the class to the element:

```
$(() => {
  $('h1')
    .click((e) => {
      $(e.target).toggleClass('highlighted', 'slow');
    });
});
```

Listing 7.9

By executing the code in *Listing 7.9*, we've caused a click on the page header to add or remove the highlighted class. Since we specified a slow speed, though, the resulting color, border, and margin changes animate into place rather than immediately taking effect:

Advanced easing

When we instruct jQuery to perform an animation over a specified duration, it does not do so at a constant rate. If, for example, we call `$('#my-div').slideUp(1000)`, we know it will take a full second for the height of the element to reach zero; however, at the beginning and end of that second the height will be changing slowly, and in the middle it will be changing quickly. This rate alteration, called **easing**, helps the animation to appear smooth and natural.

Advanced easing functions vary this acceleration and deceleration curve to provide distinctive results. For example, the `easeInExpo` function grows exponentially, ending an animation at many times the speed at which it started. We can specify a custom easing function in any of the core jQuery animation methods or jQuery UI effect methods. This can be done by either adding an argument or adding an option to a settings object, depending on the syntax being used.

To see this in action, we can provide `easeInExpo` as the easing style for the `.toggleClass()` method we just introduced in *Listing 7.9* as follows:

```
$(() => {
  $('h1')
    .click((e) => {
      $(e.target)
        .toggleClass(
          'highlighted',
          'slow',
          'easeInExpo'
        );
    });
});
```

Listing 7.10

Now whenever the header is clicked, the styles modified by toggling the class attribute begin appearing very gradually, then accelerate and complete the transition abruptly.

View easing functions in action
Demonstrations of the full set of easing functions are available at
`http://api.jqueryui.com/easings/`.

Additional effects

The individual effect files included in jQuery UI add various transitions, some of which can be substantially more complex than the simple sliding and fading animations offered by jQuery itself. These effects are invoked by calling the `.effect()` method, which is added by jQuery UI. Effects that cause an element to be hidden or shown can instead be invoked using `.show()` or `.hide()`, if desired.

The effects supplied by jQuery UI can serve a number of purposes. Some, like `transfer` and `size`, are useful when elements are to change shape and position. Others, such as `explode` and `puff`, offer attractive hiding animations. Still others, including `pulsate` and `shake`, call attention to an element.

View effects in action

All of the jQuery UI effects are showcased at `http://jqueryui.com/effect/#default`.

The `shake` behavior is particularly nice for reinforcing that an action is not currently applicable. We could make use of this effect on our page when the **Resume** button would have no effect:

```
$(() => {
  $('<button/>')
    .text('Resume')
    .click((e) => {
      const $paused = $('ul:paused');
      if ($paused.length) {
        $paused.cycle('resume');
        $.cookie('cyclePaused', null);
      } else {
        $(e.target)
          .effect('shake', {
            distance: 10
          });
      }
    })
    .appendTo($controls);
});
```

Listing 7.11

Our new code checks the length of $('ul:paused') to determine if there are any paused slideshows to resume. If so, it calls Cycle's resume action as before; otherwise, the shake effect is performed. We see here that shake, as with the other effects, has options available to fine-tune its appearance. Here we set the distance of the effect to a smaller number than the default, to make the button rapidly shake back and forth when clicked.

Interaction components

The next major feature of the jQuery UI is its interaction components, which are a set of behaviors that can be used to produce complex interactive applications. One such component, for example, is **Resizable**, which can allow the user to change the size of any element with natural dragging movements.

Applying an interaction to an element is as simple as calling the method that bears its name. For instance, we can make the book titles resizable with a call to .resizable() as follows:

```
(() => {
  $books
    .find('.title')
    .resizable();
});
```

Listing 7.12

With jQuery UI's CSS file referenced in the document, this code will add a resizing handle to the bottom-right corner of the title box. Dragging this box alters the region's width and height as shown in the following screenshot:

As we might expect by now, these methods can be customized with a host of options. If, say, we wish to constrain the resizing to only happen vertically, we can accomplish that by specifying which drag handle should be added as follows:

```
$(() => {
  $books
    .find('.title')
    .resizable({ handles: 's' });
});
```

Listing 7.13

With a drag handle only on the south (bottom) side of the region, only the height of the region can be altered:

Other interaction components
Other jQuery UI interactions include Draggable, Droppable, and Sortable. Like Resizable, they are highly configurable. We can view demos of all of them and their configuration options at `http://jqueryui.com/`.

Widgets

In addition to these building-block interaction components, jQuery UI includes a handful of robust user interface widgets that appear and function out-of-the-box like the full-fledged elements we are accustomed to seeing in desktop applications. Some of these are quite simple. The **Button** widget, for example, enhances buttons and links on the page with attractive styling and rollover states.

Granting this appearance and behavior to all button elements on the page is extremely simple:

```
$(() => {
  $('button').button();
});
```

Listing 7.14

When the stylesheet for the jQuery UI Smoothness theme is referenced, the buttons take on a glossy, beveled appearance:

As with other UI widgets and interactions, Button accepts several options. We may wish to provide appropriate icons for our two buttons, for example; the Button widget comes with a large number of predefined icons that we can use. To do so, we could separate our `.button()` call into two, and specify an icon for each as follows:

```
$(() => {
  $('<button/>')
    .text('Pause')
    .button({
      icons: { primary: 'ui-icon-pause' }
    })
    .click(() => {
      // ...
    })
    .appendTo($controls);
  $('<button/>')
    .text('Resume')
    .button({
      icons: { primary: 'ui-icon-play' }
    })
    .click((e) => {
      // ...
    })
    .appendTo($controls);
});
```

Listing 7.15

The `primary` icons that we specified correspond to standard class names in jQuery UI's theme framework. By default, `primary` icons are displayed to the left of the button text while `secondary` icons are displayed to the right:

On the other hand, other widgets are much more sophisticated. The **Slider** widget introduces a brand new form element, similar to an HTML5 range element but cross-compatible with all popular browsers. This supports a greater degree of customization, as shown in the following code:

```
$(() => {
  $('<div/>')
    .attr('id', 'slider')
    .slider({
      min: 0,
      max: $books.find('li').length - 1
    })
    .appendTo($controls);
});
```

Listing 7.16

A call to `.slider()` transforms a simple `<div>` element into a slider widget. The widget can be controlled by dragging or by pressing the arrow keys, to aid in accessibility:

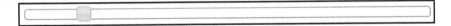

In *Listing 7.16* we've specified a minimum value of 0 for the slider, and a maximum of the index of the last book in our slideshow. We can use this as a manual control for the slideshow, by sending messages back and forth between the slideshow and slider when their respective states change.

To react to the slider's value changing, we can bind a handler to a custom event that is triggered by sliders. This event, `slide`, is not a native JavaScript event, but acts like one in our jQuery code. However, observing these events is so common that instead of calling `.on()` explicitly, we can just add our event handler to the `.slider()` call itself, as shown in the following code:

```
$(() => {
  $('<div/>')
    .attr('id', 'slider')
```

```
    .slider({
      min: 0,
      max: $books.find('li').length - 1,
      slide: (e, ui) => {
        $books.cycle(ui.value);
      }
    })
    .appendTo($controls);
});
```

Listing 7.17

Whenever the `slide` callback is invoked, its `ui` parameter is populated with information about the widget, including its current value. By passing this value along to the Cycle plugin, we can manipulate the current slide being shown.

We also need to update the slider widget whenever the slideshow advances to another slide. To communicate in this direction we can use Cycle's `before` callback, which is triggered before each slide transition:

```
$(() => {
  const $books = $('#books').cycle({
    timeout: 2000,
    speed: 200,
    pause: true,
    before: (li) => {
      $('#slider')
        .slider(
          'value',
          $('#books li').index(li)
        );
    }
  });
});
```

Listing 7.18

Inside the `before` callback, we call the `.slider()` method again. This time, we call it with `value` as its first parameter to set the new slider value. In jQuery UI parlance, we call `value` a *method* of slider, even though it is invoked by calling the `.slider()` method, not by its own dedicated method name.

Other widgets

Other jQuery UI widgets include Datepicker, Dialog, Tabs, and Accordion. Each widget has several associated options, events, and methods. For a full list, visit
`http://jqueryui.com/`.

jQuery UI ThemeRoller

One of the most exciting features of the jQuery UI library is ThemeRoller, a web-based interactive theme engine for the UI widgets. ThemeRoller makes creating highly customized, professional-looking elements quick and easy. The buttons and slider that we just created have the default theme applied to them; this theme will be output from *ThemeRoller* if no custom settings are supplied:

Generating a completely different set of styles is a simple matter of visiting `http://jqueryui.com/themeroller/`, modifying the various options as desired, and pressing the **Download Theme** button. A `.zip` file of stylesheets and images can then be unpacked into your site directory. For example, by choosing a few different colors and textures, we can within minutes create a new, coordinated look for our buttons, icons, and slider, as shown in the following screenshot:

The jQuery Mobile plugin library

We have seen how jQuery UI can assist us in assembling the user interface features needed for even a complex web application. The challenges it overcomes are varied and complex. A different set of hurdles exists, however, when preparing our pages for elegant presentation and interaction on mobile devices. To create a website or application for modern smart phones and tablets, we can turn to the jQuery Mobile project.

Like jQuery UI, jQuery Mobile consists of a suite of related components that can be used *ala carte* but which work together seamlessly. The framework provides an Ajax-driven navigation system, mobile-optimized interactive elements, and advanced touch event handlers. Again, as with jQuery UI, exploring all the features of jQuery Mobile is a daunting task, so instead we will provide some simple examples and refer to the official documentation for more details.

Downloads, documentation, and demos for jQuery Mobile are available at `http://jquerymobile.com/`.
Our jQuery Mobile example will use Ajax technology, so web server software will be required in order to try these examples. More information is available in `Chapter 6`, *Sending Data with Ajax*.

HTML5 custom data attributes

The code examples we've seen so far in this chapter have all used JavaScript APIs exposed by plugins in order to invoke the plugin functionality. We've seen jQuery object methods, global functions, and custom selectors as some ways that plugins offer their services to our scripts. The jQuery Mobile library has these entry points as well, but the most common way of interacting with it is instead via HTML5 data attributes.

The HTML5 specification allows us to insert any attribute we want into an element, so long as the attribute is prefixed by `data-`. Such attributes are completely ignored when rendering the page, but are available to us in our jQuery scripts. When we include jQuery Mobile on a page, the script scans the page for some `data-*` attributes, and adds mobile-friendly features to the corresponding elements.

The jQuery Mobile library looks for a few specific custom data attributes. We will examine more general ways of using this feature in our own scripts in `Chapter 12`, *Advanced DOM Manipulation*.

Because of this design choice, we will be able to demonstrate some powerful features of jQuery Mobile here without writing any JavaScript code ourselves.

Mobile navigation

One of the most prominent features of jQuery Mobile is its ability to simply transform the behavior of links on a page into Ajax-powered navigation. This transformation adds simple animation to the process, while preserving standard browser history navigation. To see this in action, we'll start with a document that presents links to information about several books (the same content we used for building a slideshow earlier) as follows:

```html
<!DOCTYPE html>
<html>
<head>
  <title>jQuery Book Browser</title>
  <link rel="stylesheet" href="booklist.css" type="text/css" />
  <script src="jquery.js"></script>
</head>
<body>

<div>
  <div>
    <h1>Selected jQuery Books</h1>
  </div>

  <div>
    <ul>
      <li><a href="jq-game.html">jQuery Game Development
        Essentials</a></li>
      <li><a href="jqmobile-cookbook.html">jQuery Mobile
        Cookbook</a></li>
      <li><a href="jquery-designers.html">jQuery for
        Designers</a></li>
      <li><a href="jquery-hotshot.html">jQuery Hotshot</a></li>
      <li><a href="jqui-cookbook.html">jQuery UI Cookbook</a></li>
      <li><a href="mobile-apps.html">Creating Mobile Apps with
        jQuery Mobile</a></li>
      <li><a href="drupal-7.html">Drupal 7 Development by
        Example</a></li>
      <li><a href="wp-mobile-apps.html">WordPress Mobile
        Applications with PhoneGap</a></li>
    </ul>
  </div>
</div>

</body>
</html>
```

In the downloadable code package for this chapter, the finished HTML example page can be found in the file called `mobile.html`.

So far we have not introduced jQuery Mobile at all, and the page is rendered in the default browser style, as we would expect. This is shown in the following screenshot:

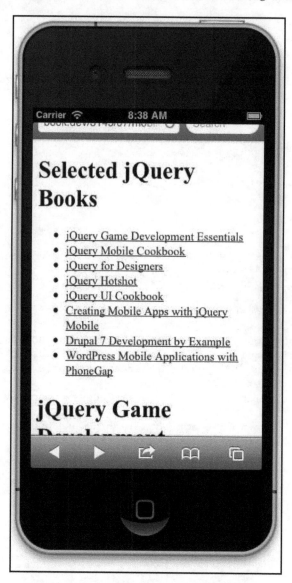

Our next step is to change the `<head>` section of the document so that it references jQuery Mobile and its stylesheet as follows:

```
<head>
  <title>jQuery Book Browser</title>
  <meta name="viewport"
    content="width=device-width, initial-scale=1">
  <link rel="stylesheet" href="booklist.css"
    type="text/css" />
  <link rel="stylesheet"
    href="jquery.mobile/jquery.mobile.css" type="text/css" />
  <script src="jquery.js"></script>
  <script src="jquery-migrate.js"></script>
  <script src="jquery.mobile/jquery.mobile.js"></script>
</head>
```

Note that we have also introduced a `<meta>` element defining the viewport of the page. This declaration tells mobile browsers to scale the content of the document in such a way that it completely fills the width of the device.

 We have to include the jquery-migrate plugin on the page, because without it, the latest stable version of jQuery doesn't work with the latest stable version of jQuery Mobile. Figure that one out. In any case, once the two officially work together, you can simply remove the jquery-migrate plugin from the page.

The jQuery Mobile styles are now applied to our document, displaying a larger sans-serif font and updating colors and spacing, as shown in the following screenshot:

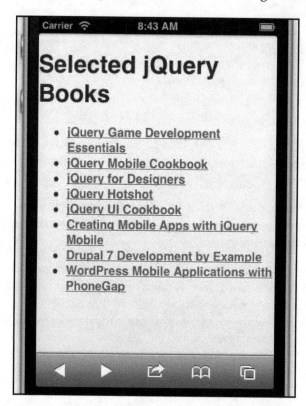

To properly handle navigation, jQuery Mobile needs to understand the structure of our page. We provide this information by using the `data-role` attribute:

```
<div data-role="page">
  <div data-role="header">
    <h1>Selected jQuery Books</h1>
  </div>

  <div data-role="content">
    <ul>
      <li><a href="jq-game.html">jQuery Game Development
        Essentials</a></li>
      <li><a href="jqmobile-cookbook.html">jQuery Mobile
        Cookbook</a></li>
      <li><a href="jquery-designers.html">jQuery for
        Designers</a></li>
      <li><a href="jquery-hotshot.html">jQuery Hotshot</a></li>
```

```
        <li><a href="jqui-cookbook.html">jQuery UI Cookbook</a></li>
        <li><a href="mobile-apps.html">Creating Mobile Apps with
          jQuery Mobile</a></li>
        <li><a href="drupal-7.html">Drupal 7 Development by
          Example</a></li>
        <li><a href="wp-mobile-apps.html">WordPress Mobile
          Applications with PhoneGap</a></li>
      </ul>
    </div>
  </div>
```

Now when the page loads, jQuery Mobile notices that we have a page header, and renders a standard-looking mobile header bar across the top of the page:

When the text is too long for the header bar, jQuery Mobile truncates it and adds an ellipsis at the end. In this case, we can rotate the mobile device to its landscape orientation to see the full title:

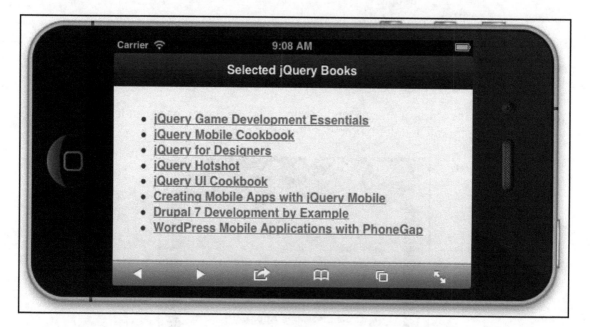

More importantly, this is all that is required in order to produce Ajax navigation. On the pages linked to from this list, we use similar markup:

```html
<div data-role="page">
  <div data-role="header">
    <h1>WordPress Mobile Applications with PhoneGap</h1>
  </div>
  <div data-role="content">
    <img src="images/wp-mobile-apps.jpg" alt="WordPress Mobile
      Applications with PhoneGap" />
    <div class="title">WordPress Mobile Applications with
      PhoneGap</div>
    <div class="author">Yuxian Eugene Liang</div>
  </div>
</div>
```

When the link to this page is clicked on, jQuery Mobile loads the page with an Ajax call, grabs the portion of the document marked with `data-role="page"`, and displays this content using a fading transition:

Delivering multiple pages in one document

In addition to offering Ajax functionality for loading other documents, jQuery Mobile provides the tools to deliver the same user experience even if all the content is contained within a single document. To implement this, we simply link the anchors within the page using standard # notation, and mark those sections of the page with data-role="page" just as if they were in separate documents, as follows:

```
<div data-role="page">
  <div data-role="header">
    <h1>Selected jQuery Books</h1>
  </div>

  <div data-role="content">
    <ul>
      <li><a href="#jq-game">jQuery Game Development
        Essentials</a></li>
      <li><a href="#jqmobile-cookbook">jQuery Mobile
        Cookbook</a></li>
```

```
    <li><a href="#jquery-designers">jQuery for
      Designers</a></li>
    <li><a href="#jquery-hotshot">jQuery Hotshot</a></li>
    <li><a href="#jqui-cookbook">jQuery UI Cookbook</a></li>
    <li><a href="#mobile-apps">Creating Mobile Apps with jQuery
      Mobile</a></li>
    <li><a href="#drupal-7">Drupal 7 Development by
      Example</a></li>
    <li><a href="wp-mobile-apps.html">WordPress Mobile
      Applications with PhoneGap</a></li>
    </ul>
  </div>
</div>

<div id="jq-game" data-role="page">
  <div data-role="header">
    <h1>jQuery Game Development Essentials</h1>
  </div>
  <div data-role="content">
    <img src="images/jq-game.jpg" alt="jQuery Game Development
      Essentials" />
    <div class="title">jQuery Game Development Essentials</div>
    <div class="author">Salim Arsever</div>
  </div>
</div>
```

We can freely choose between these two techniques at our convenience. Placing content in separate documents allows us to defer the loading of information until it is needed, at the cost of some higher overhead due to multiple page requests.

Interactive elements

The bulk of the features offered by jQuery Mobile are specific interactive elements for use on a page. These elements enhance basic web page functionality, making page components more user-friendly for a touch interface. Among these elements are accordion--style collapsible sections, toggle switches, sliding panels, and responsive tables.

 There is considerable overlap between the user interface elements offered by jQuery UI and jQuery Mobile. It is not recommended to use the two libraries together on the same page, but because the most important widgets are offered by both, there is rarely a need to do so.

List views

Due to their small, vertical screen layouts, smart phone applications are often heavily list-driven. We can use jQuery Mobile to easily enhance the lists on our pages to behave much more like these common native app elements. Once again, we simply introduce HTML5 custom data attributes:

```
<ul data-role="listview" data-inset="true">
  <li><a href="#jq-game">jQuery Game Development
    Essentials</a></li>
  <li><a href="#jqmobile-cookbook">jQuery Mobile Cookbook</a></li>
  <li><a href="#jquery-designers">jQuery for Designers</a></li>
  <li><a href="#jquery-hotshot">jQuery Hotshot</a></li>
  <li><a href="#jqui-cookbook">jQuery UI Cookbook</a></li>
  <li><a href="#mobile-apps">Creating Mobile Apps with jQuery
    Mobile</a></li>
  <li><a href="#drupal-7">Drupal 7 Development by Example</a></li>
  <li><a href="wp-mobile-apps.html">WordPress Mobile Applications
    with PhoneGap</a></li>
</ul>
```

Adding `data-role="listview"` tells jQuery Mobile to make the links within this list large and easy to activate with a finger in a touch interface, while `data-inset="true"` gives the list a nice border to separate it from surrounding content. The result is a familiar, native-looking control, as follows:

Now, we have large touch targets, but we can go a step further. List views like this in mobile apps are often paired with search fields to narrow down the items in the list. We can add such a field by introducing the `data-filter` attribute as follows:

```
<ul data-role="listview" data-inset="true" data-filter="true">
```

The result is a rounded input box with an appropriate icon, placed above the list:

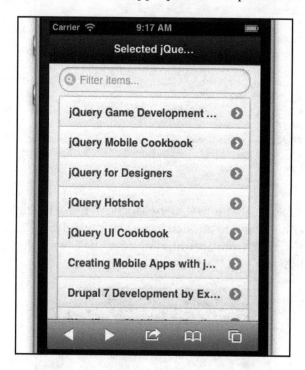

Not only does this search field look native, but it behaves correctly too, even though we have added no code of our own:

Toolbar buttons

Another user interface element enhanced by jQuery Mobile is the simple button. Just as jQuery UI allows us to standardize button appearances, jQuery Mobile increases the size and modifies the appearance of buttons to optimize them for touch input.

In some cases, jQuery Mobile even creates appropriate buttons for us where before there were none. For instance, there are often buttons in the toolbar of a mobile app. One standard button is the **Back** button in the upper-left corner of the screen, allowing the user to navigate up one level. If we add a `data-add-back-btn` attribute to our page `<div>` elements, we can have this feature without any scripting work:

```
<div data-role="page" data-add-back-btn="true">
```

Once this attribute has been added, a standard **Back** button is added to the toolbar of each page we navigate to:

 A complete listing of HTML5 data attributes for initializing and configuring jQuery Mobile widgets can be found at `http://jquerymobile.com/`.

Advanced features

As our mobile pages require more customized design elements and more complex interactions, jQuery Mobile provides robust tools to help us create them. All of the features are documented on the jQuery Mobile site (`http://jquerymobile.com/`). While these features are both too advanced and too numerous to discuss here in detail, a few deserve a brief mention:

- **Mobile-friendly events**: When jQuery Mobile is referenced on a page, our jQuery code has access to a number of special events including `tap`, `taphold`, and `swipe`. Handlers for these events can be bound with the same `.on()` method as for any other event. With `taphold` and `swipe` in particular, their default configurations, which include touch duration, can be modified by accessing properties of the `$.event.special.taphold` and `$.event.special.swipe` objects. In addition to touch-based events, jQuery Mobile provides special events that react to scrolling, orientation change, and various stages of its page navigation, as well as a set of virtualized mouse events that react to both mouse and touch.

- **Theming**: As with jQuery UI, jQuery Mobile offers a ThemeRoller (`http://jquerymobile.com/themeroller/`) for customizing the look and feel of widgets.

- **PhoneGap integration**: Sites built with jQuery Mobile are easy to convert to native mobile applications using PhoneGap (Cordova), with access to mobile device APIs (such as camera, accelerometer, and geolocation) and app stores. The `$.support.cors` and `$.mobile.allowCrossDomainPages` properties can even allow access to pages not contained within the application, such as those on a remote server.

Summary

In this chapter we have examined ways in which we can incorporate third-party plugins into our web pages. We've looked closely at the Cycle plugin, jQuery UI, and jQuery Mobile, and in the process have learned the patterns that we will encounter time and again in other plugins. In the next chapter, we'll take advantage of jQuery's plugin architecture to develop a few different types of plugins of our own.

Exercises

1. Increase the cycle transition duration to half a second, and change the animation such that each slide fades out before the next one fades in. Refer to the Cycle documentation to find the appropriate option to enable this.
2. Set the `cyclePaused` cookie to persist for 30 days.
3. Constrain the title box to resize only in ten pixel increments.
4. Make the slider animate smoothly from one position to the next as the slideshow advances.
5. Instead of letting the slideshow loop forever, cause it to stop after the last slide is shown. Disable the buttons and slider when this happens.
6. Create a new jQuery UI theme that has a light blue widget background and dark blue text and apply the theme to our sample document.
7. Modify the HTML in `mobile.html` so that the list view is divided up by the first letters of the book titles. See the jQuery Mobile documentation for `data-role="list-divider"` for details.

8
Developing Plugins

The available third-party plugins provide a bevy of options for enhancing our coding experience, but sometimes we need to reach a bit farther. When we write code that could be reused by others or even just ourselves, we may want to package it up as a new plugin. Fortunately, the process of developing a plugin is not much more involved than writing the code that uses it.

In this chapter, we will cover:

- Adding new global functions within the `jQuery` namespace
- Adding jQuery object methods that allow us to act on DOM elements
- Creating widget plugins using the jQuery UI widget factory
- Distributing plugins

Using the dollar ($) alias in plugins

When we write jQuery plugins, we must assume that the jQuery library is loaded. We cannot assume, however, that the dollar ($) alias is available. Recall from Chapter 3, *Handling Events*, that the `$.noConflict()` method can relinquish control of this shortcut. To account for this, our plugins should always call jQuery methods using the full jQuery name or internally define $ themselves.

Especially in larger plugins, many developers find that the lack of the dollar ($) shortcut makes code more difficult to read. To combat this, the shortcut can be locally defined for the scope of the plugin by defining a function and immediately invoking it. This syntax for defining and invoking a function at once, often referred to as an **Immediately Invoked Function Expression (IIFE)**, looks like this:

```
(($) => {
  // Code goes here
})(jQuery);
```

The wrapping function takes a single parameter to which we pass the global `jQuery` object. The parameter is named `$`, so within the function we can use the dollar ($) alias with no conflicts.

Adding new global functions

Some of the built-in capabilities of jQuery are provided via what we have been calling global functions. As we've seen, these are actually methods of the jQuery object, but practically speaking, they are functions within a `jQuery` namespace.

A prime example of this technique is the `$.ajax()` function. Everything that `$.ajax()` does could be accomplished with a regular global function called `ajax()`, but this approach would leave us open for function name conflicts. By placing the function within the `jQuery` namespace, we only have to worry about conflicts with other jQuery methods. This `jQuery` namespace also signals to those who might use the plugin that the jQuery library is required.

Many of the global functions provided by the core jQuery library are utility methods; that is, they provide shortcuts for tasks that are frequently needed, but not difficult to do by hand. The array-handling functions `$.each()`, `$.map()`, and `$.grep()` are good examples of these. To illustrate the creation of such utility methods, we'll add two simple functions to their number.

To add a function to the `jQuery` namespace, we can just assign the new function as a property of the `jQuery` object:

```
(($) => {
  $.sum = (array) => {
    // Code goes here
  };
})(jQuery);
```

Listing 8.1

Now, in any code that uses this plugin, we can write:

```
$.sum();
```

This will work just like a basic function call, and the code inside the function will be executed.

This `sum` method will accept an array, add the values in the array together, and return the result. The code for our plugin is quite brief:

```
(($) => {
  $.sum = array =>
    array.reduce(
      (result, item) =>
        parseFloat($.trim(item)) + result,
      0
    );
}) (jQuery);
```

Listing 8.2

To compute the sum, we're calling `reduce()` on the array, which simply iterates over each item in the array, and adding it to the `result`. In the preceding code, there's two callback functions that return values. Neither of them have a `return` statement because they're arrow functions. When we don't include the curly braces ({ }), the return value is implicit.

To test our plugins, we'll build a simple table with an inventory of groceries:

```
<table id="inventory">
  <thead>
    <tr class="one">
      <th>Product</th> <th>Quantity</th> <th>Price</th>
    </tr>
  </thead>
  <tfoot>
    <tr class="two" id="sum">
      <td>Total</td> <td></td> <td></td>
    </tr>
    <tr id="average">
      <td>Average</td> <td></td> <td></td>
    </tr>
  </tfoot>
  <tbody>
    <tr>
      <td><a href="spam.html" data-tooltip-text="Nutritious and
      delicious!">Spam</a></td> <td>4</td> <td>2.50</td>
    </tr>
```

```
    <tr>
      <td><a href="egg.html" data-tooltip-text="Farm fresh or
      scrambled!">Egg</a></td> <td>12</td> <td>4.32</td>
    </tr>
    <tr>
      <td><a href="gourmet-spam.html" data-tooltip-text="Chef
      Hermann's recipe.">Gourmet Spam</a></td> <td>14</td> <td>7.89
      </td>
    </tr>
  </tbody>
</table>
```

Getting the example code
You can access the example code from the following GitHub repository: ht
tps://github.com/PacktPublishing/Learning-jQuery-3.

Now, we'll write a short script that populates the appropriate table footer cell with the sum of all quantities:

```
$(() => {
  const quantities = $('#inventory tbody')
    .find('td:nth-child(2)')
    .map((index, qty) => $(qty).text())
    .get();
  const sum = $.sum(quantities);

  $('#sum')
    .find('td:nth-child(2)')
    .text(sum);
});
```

Listing 8.3

A look at the rendered HTML page verifies that our plugin is working correctly:

Inventory

Product	Quantity	Price
Spam	4	2.50
Egg	12	4.32
Gourmet Spam	14	7.89
Total	**30**	
Average		

Adding multiple functions

If our plugin needs to provide more than one global function, we could declare them independently. Here, we'll revise our plugin, adding a function to compute the average of an array of numbers:

```
(($) => {
  $.sum = array =>
    array.reduce(
      (result, item) =>
        parseFloat($.trim(item)) + result,
      0
    );

  $.average = array =>
    Array.isArray(array) ?
      $.sum(array) / array.length :
      '';
})(jQuery);
```

Listing 8.4

For convenience and brevity, we're using the `$.sum()` plugin to assist us in returning the value for `$.average()`. To decrease the chance of errors, we also check the argument to make sure it is an array before computing the average.

Now that a second method is defined, we can call it in the same fashion:

```
$(() => {
  const $inventory = $('#inventory tbody');
  const prices = $inventory
    .find('td:nth-child(3)')
    .map((index, qty) => $(qty).text())
    .get();
  const average = $.average(prices);

  $('#average')
    .find('td:nth-child(3)')
    .text(average.toFixed(2));
});
```

Listing 8.5

The average now appears in the third column:

Inventory

Product	Quantity	Price
Spam	4	2.50
Egg	12	4.32
Gourmet Spam	14	7.89
Total	**30**	
Average		*4.90*

Extending the global jQuery object

We can also employ an alternate syntax in defining our functions using the $.extend() function:

```
(($) => {
  $.extend({
    sum: array =>
      array.reduce(
        (result, item) =>
          parseFloat($.trim(item)) + result,
        0
      ),
    average: array =>
      Array.isArray(array) ?
        $.sum(array) / array.length :
        ''
  });
})(jQuery);
```

Listing 8.6

When called this way, $.extend() adds or replaces properties of the global jQuery object. This, therefore, produces the same results as the previous technique.

Isolating functions within namespaces

Our plugin now creates two separate global functions within the `jQuery` namespace. We risk a different kind of namespace pollution here, though; we could still have a conflict with function names defined in other jQuery plugins. To avoid this, it is best to encapsulate all the global functions for a given plugin into a single object:

```
(($) => {
  $.mathUtils = {
    sum: array =>
      array.reduce(
        (result, item) =>
          parseFloat($.trim(item)) + result,
        0
      ),
    average: array =>
      Array.isArray(array) ?
        $.mathUtils.sum(array) / array.length :
        ''
  };
})(jQuery);
```

Listing 8.7

This pattern essentially creates another namespace for our global functions, called `jQuery.mathUtils`. Though we will still informally call these functions global, they are now methods of the `mathUtils` object, which is itself a property of the global jQuery object. We, therefore, have to include the plugin name in our function calls:

```
$.mathUtils.sum(array);
$.mathUtils.average(array);
```

With this technique (and a sufficiently unique plugin name), we are protected from namespace collisions in our global functions. We now have the basics of plugin development in our repertoire. After saving our functions in a file called `jquery.mathutils.js`, we can include this script and use the functions from other scripts on the page.

Choosing a namespace

For functions that are solely for personal use, it often makes more sense to place them within our own project's global namespace. So, instead of using jQuery, we may instead choose to expose one global object of our own. We could, for example, have a global object called ljQ and define the ljQ.mathUtils.sum() and ljQ.mathUtils.average() methods instead of $.mathUtils.sum() and $.mathUtils.average(). This way, we completely remove the chance of namespace collisions with third-party plugins that we choose to include.

So, we've now seen the namespace protection and guaranteed library availability that jQuery plugins grant. These are just organizational benefits, though. To really tap into the power of jQuery plugins, we need to learn how to create new methods on individual jQuery object instances.

Adding jQuery object methods

Most of jQuery's built-in functionality is provided through its object instance methods, and this is where plugins shine as well. Whenever we would write a function that acts on part of the DOM, it is probably appropriate instead to create an **instance method**.

We have seen that adding global functions requires extending the jQuery object with new methods. Adding instance methods is similar, but we instead extend the jQuery.fn object:

```
jQuery.fn.myMethod = function() {
  alert('Nothing happens.');
};
```

The jQuery.fn object is an alias to jQuery.prototype, provided for conciseness.

We can then call this new method from our code after using any selector expression:

```
$('div').myMethod();
```

Our alert is displayed (once for each <div> in the document) when we invoke the method. We might as well have written a global function, though, as we haven't used the matched DOM nodes in any way. A reasonable method implementation acts on its context.

Object method context

Within any plugin method, the keyword `this` is set to the current jQuery object. Therefore, we can call any built-in jQuery method on `this` or extract its DOM nodes and work on them. To examine what we can do with object context, we'll write a small plugin to manipulate the classes on the matched elements.

Our new method will take two class names and swap which class is applied to each element with every invocation. While jQuery UI has a robust `.switchClass()` method that even permits animating the class change, we'll provide a simple implementation for demonstration purposes:

```
(function($) {
  $.fn.swapClass = function(class1, class2) {
    if (this.hasClass(class1)) {
      this
        .removeClass(class1)
        .addClass(class2);
    } else if (this.hasClass(class2)) {
      this
        .removeClass(class2)
        .addClass(class1);
    }
  };
})(jQuery);

$(() => {
  $('table')
    .click(() => {
      $('tr').swapClass('one', 'two');
    });
});
```

Listing 8.8

In our plugin, we first test for the presence of `class1` on the matched element and substitute `class2` if it is found. Otherwise, we test for `class2` and switch in `class1` if necessary. If neither class is currently present, we do nothing.

In the code that uses the plugin, we bind a `click` handler to the table, calling `.swapClass()` on every row when the table is clicked on. We'd expect this to change the class of the header row from `one` to `two` and to change the class of the sum row from `two` to `one`.

However, we observe a different result:

Inventory

Product	Quantity	Price
Spam	4	2.50
Egg	12	4.32
Gourmet Spam	14	7.89
Total	**30**	
Average		*4.90*

Every row has received the `two` class. To fix this, we need to correctly handle jQuery objects with multiple selected elements.

Implicit iteration

We need to remember that a jQuery selector expression can always match zero, one, or multiple elements. We must allow for any of these scenarios when designing a plugin method. In this case, we are calling `.hasClass()`, which only examines the first matched element. Instead, we need to check each element independently and act on it.

The easiest way to guarantee proper behavior, regardless of the number of matched elements, is to always call `.each()` on the method context; this enforces implicit iteration, which is important for maintaining consistency between plugin and built-in methods. Within the `.each()` callback function, the second argument refers to each DOM element in turn, so we can adjust our code to separately test for and apply classes to each matched element:

```
(function($) {
  $.fn.swapClass = function(class1, class2) {
    this
      .each((i, element) => {
        const $element = $(element);

        if ($element.hasClass(class1)) {
          $element
            .removeClass(class1)
            .addClass(class2);
        } else if ($element.hasClass(class2)) {
          $element
```

```
            .removeClass(class2)
            .addClass(class1);
      }
   });
};
})(jQuery);
```

Listing 8.9

Now, when we click on the table, the classes are switched without affecting the rows that have neither class applied:

Inventory

Product	Quantity	Price
Spam	4	2.50
Egg	12	4.32
Gourmet Spam	14	7.89
Total	30	
Average		4.90

Enabling method chaining

In addition to implicit iteration, jQuery users should be able to rely on chaining behavior. This means that we need to return a jQuery object from all plugin methods, unless the method is clearly intended to retrieve a different piece of information. The returned jQuery object is usually just the one provided as this. If we use .each() to iterate over this, we can just return its result:

```
(function($) {
  $.fn.swapClass = function(class1, class2) {
    return this
      .each((i, element) => {
        const $element = $(element);

        if ($element.hasClass(class1)) {
          $element
            .removeClass(class1)
            .addClass(class2);
        } else if ($element.hasClass(class2)) {
          $element
```

```
        .removeClass(class2)
        .addClass(class1);
    }
  });
};
}) (jQuery);
```

Listing 8.10

Previously, when we called .swapClass(), we had to start a new statement to do anything else with the elements. With the return statement in place, though, we can freely chain our plugin method with built-in methods.

Providing flexible method parameters

In Chapter 7, *Using Plugins,* we saw some plugins that can be fine-tuned to do exactly what we want through the use of parameters. We saw that a cleverly constructed plugin helps us by providing sensible defaults that can be independently overridden. When we make our own plugins, we should follow this example by keeping the user in mind.

To explore the various ways in which we can let a plugin's user customize its behavior, we need an example that has several settings that can be tweaked and modified. As our example, we'll replicate a feature of CSS by using a more brute-force JavaScript approach-- an approach that is more suitable for demonstration than for production code. Our plugin will simulate a shadow on an element by creating a number of copies that are partially transparent overlaid in different positions on the page:

```
(function($) {
  $.fn.shadow = function() {
    return this.each((i, element) => {
      const $originalElement = $(element);

      for (let i = 0; i < 5; i++) {
        $originalElement
          .clone()
          .css({
            position: 'absolute',
            left: $originalElement.offset().left + i,
            top: $originalElement.offset().top + i,
            margin: 0,
            zIndex: -1,
            opacity: 0.1
          })
          .appendTo('body');
```

```
      }
    });
  };
}) (jQuery);
```

For each element this method is called on, we make a number of clones of the element, adjusting their opacity. These clones are positioned absolutely at varying offsets from the original element. For the moment, our plugin takes no parameters, so calling the method is simple:

```
$(() => {
  $('h1').shadow();
});
```

This method call produces a very simple shadow effect on the header text:

Inventory

Product	Quantity	Price
Spam	4	2.50
Egg	12	4.32
Gourmet Spam	14	7.89
Total	**30**	
Average		*4.90*

Next, we can introduce some flexibility to the plugin method. The operation of the method relies on several numeric values that the user might want to modify. We can turn these into parameters so they can be changed on demand.

Options objects

We have seen many examples in the jQuery API of `options` objects being provided as parameters of methods such as `.animate()` and `$.ajax()`. This can be a much friendlier way to expose options to a plugin user than the simple parameter list we just used with the `.swapClass()` plugin. An object literal provides a visual label for each parameter and also makes the order of the parameters irrelevant. In addition, any time we can mimic the jQuery API in our plugins, we should do so. This will increase the consistency and therefore ease of use:

```javascript
(($) => {
  $.fn.shadow = function(options) {
    return this.each((i, element) => {
      const $originalElement = $(element);

      for (let i = 0; i < options.copies; i++) {
        $originalElement
          .clone()
          .css({
            position: 'absolute',
            left: $originalElement.offset().left + i,
            top: $originalElement.offset().top + i,
            margin: 0,
            zIndex: -1,
            opacity: options.opacity
          })
          .appendTo('body');
      }
    });
  };
}) (jQuery);
```

Listing 8.12

The number of copies made and their opacity are now customizable. Within our plugin, each value is accessed as a property of the `options` argument to the function.

Calling this method now requires us to provide an object containing the option values:

```javascript
$(() => {
  $('h1')
    .shadow({
      copies: 3,
      opacity: 0.25
    });
});
```

The configurability is an improvement, but we now have to provide both options every time. Next, we'll take a look at how we can allow our plugin users to omit either option.

Default parameter values

As the number of parameters for a method grows, it becomes less likely that we will always want to specify each one. A sensible set of default values can make a plugin interface much more usable. Fortunately, using an object to pass in our parameters helps with this task; it is simple to omit any item from the object and replace it with a default:

```
(($) => {
  $.fn.shadow = function(opts) {
    const defaults = {
      copies: 5,
      opacity: 0.1
    };
    const options = $.extend({}, defaults, opts);

    // ...
  };
})(jQuery);
```

Listing 8.13

Here, we have defined a new object called `defaults`. The utility function `$.extend()` lets us take the `opts` object provided as an argument and use it to create a new `options` object using `defaults` where necessary. The `extend()` function merges any objects passed to it into the first argument. This is why we've passed an empty object as the first argument, so that we create a new object for options, rather than accidentally destroying existing data. For example, what if defaults were defined somewhere else in the code and we accidentally replaced it's values?

We still call our method using an object literal, but now we can specify only the parameters that need to take different values than their defaults:

```
$(() => {
  $('h1')
    .shadow({
      copies: 3
    });
});
```

Unspecified parameters use their default values. The `$.extend()` method even accepts null values, so if the default parameters are all acceptable, our method can be called without producing JavaScript errors:

```
$(() => {
  $('h1').shadow();
});
```

Callback functions

Of course, some method parameters can be more complicated than a simple numeric value. One common parameter type we have seen frequently throughout the jQuery API is the callback function. The callback function can lend flexibility to a plugin without requiring a great deal of preparation when creating the plugin.

To use a callback function in our method, we need to simply accept the function object as a parameter and call that function wherever appropriate in our method implementation. As an example, we can extend our text shadow method to allow the user to customize the position of the shadow relative to the text:

```
(($) => {
  $.fn.shadow = function(opts) {
    const defaults = {
      copies: 5,
      opacity: 0.1,
      copyOffset: index => ({
        x: index,
        y: index
      })
    };
    const options = $.extend({}, defaults, opts);

    return this.each((i, element) => {
      const $originalElement = $(element);

      for (let i = 0; i < options.copies; i++) {
        const offset = options.copyOffset(i);

        $originalElement
          .clone()
          .css({
            position: 'absolute',
            left: $originalElement.offset().left + offset.x,
            top: $originalElement.offset().top + offset.y,
            margin: 0,
```

```
        zIndex: -1,
        opacity: options.opacity
      })
      .appendTo('body');
    }
  });
};
}) (jQuery);
```

Listing 8.14

Each slice of the shadow has a different offset from the original text. Previously, this offset has simply been equal to the index of the copy. Now, though, we're calculating the offset using the `copyOffset()` function, which is an option that the user can override. So, for example, we could provide negative values for the offset in both dimensions:

```
$(() => {
  $('h1').shadow({
    copyOffset: index => ({
      x: -index,
      y: -2 * index
    })
  });
});
```

This will cause the shadow to be cast up and to the left-hand side rather than down and to the right-hand side:

The callback allows simple modifications to the shadow's direction, or much more sophisticated positioning if the plugin user supplies the appropriate callback. If the callback is not specified, then the default behavior is once again used.

Customizable defaults

We can improve the experience of using our plugins by providing reasonable default values for our method parameters, as we have seen. However, sometimes it can be difficult to predict what a reasonable default value will be. If a script author needs to call our plugin multiple times with a different set of parameters than we set as the defaults, the ability to customize these defaults could significantly reduce the amount of code that needs to be written.

To make the defaults customizable, we need to move them out of our method definition and into a location that is accessible by outside code:

```
(() => {
  $.fn.shadow = function(opts) {
    const options = $.extend({}, $.fn.shadow.defaults, opts);
    // ...
  };

  $.fn.shadow.defaults = {
    copies: 5,
    opacity: 0.1,
    copyOffset: index => ({
      x: index,
      y: index
    })
  };
})(jQuery);
```

Listing 8.15

The defaults are now in the namespace of the shadow plugin, and can be directly referred to with `$.fn.shadow.defaults`. Now, code that uses our plugin can change the defaults that all subsequent calls to `.shadow()` will use. Options can also still be supplied at the time the method is invoked:

```
$(() => {
  $.fn.shadow.defaults.copies = 10;
  $('h1')
    .shadow({
      copyOffset: index => ({
        x: -index,
        y: index
      })
    });
});
```

This script will create a shadow using `10` copies of the element, because that is the new default value, but will also cast the shadow to the left-hand side and down due to the `copyOffset` callback that is provided along with the method call:

Inventory

Product	Quantity	Price
Spam	4	2.50
Egg	12	4.32
Gourmet Spam	14	7.89
Total	**30**	
Average		*4.90*

Creating plugins with the jQuery UI widget factory

As we saw in `Chapter 7`, *Using Plugins*, jQuery UI has an assortment of widgets--plugins that present a particular kind of UI element, such as a button or slider. These widgets present a consistent API to JavaScript programmers. This consistency makes learning to use one easy. When a plugin that we're writing will create a new user interface element, extending the jQuery UI library with a widget plugin is often the right choice.

A widget is an intricate piece of functionality, but fortunately we are not left to our own devices in creating one. The jQuery UI core contains a `factory` method called `$.widget()`, which does a lot of the work for us. Using this factory will help ensure that our code meets the API standards shared by all jQuery UI widgets.

Plugins we create using the widget factory have many nice features. We get all of these perks (and more) with very little effort on our part:

- The plugin becomes **stateful**, meaning that we can examine, alter, or even completely reverse the effects of the plugin after it has been applied
- User-supplied options are merged with customizable default options automatically

- Multiple plugin methods are seamlessly combined into a single jQuery method, accepting a string to identify which submethod is being called
- Custom event handlers triggered by the plugin get access to the widget instance's data

In fact, these advantages are so nice that we may wish to use the widget factory to construct any suitably complex plugin, UI-related or otherwise.

Creating a widget

For our example, we'll craft a plugin that adds custom tooltips to elements. A simple tooltip implementation creates a `<div>` container for each element on the page that gets a tooltip and positions that container next to the element when the mouse cursor hovers over the target.

The jQuery UI library contains its own built-in tooltip widget that is more advanced than the one we'll develop here. Our new widget will override the built-in `.tooltip()` method, which is not something we would likely do in a real project, but it will allow us to demonstrate several important concepts without needless complexity.

A jQuery UI plugin is created by the widget factory each time `$.widget()` is called. This function accepts the name of the widget and an object containing widget properties. The name of the widget must be namespaced; we'll use the namespace `ljq` and the plugin name `tooltip`. As a result, our plugin will be invoked by calling `.tooltip()` on a jQuery object.

The first widget property we'll define is `._create()`:

```
(($) => {
  $.widget('ljq.tooltip', {
    _create() {
      this._tooltipDiv = $('<div/>')
        .addClass([
          'ljq-tooltip-text',
          'ui-widget',
          'ui-state-highlight',
          'ui-corner-all'
        ].join(' '))
        .hide()
        .appendTo('body');
      this.element
        .addClass('ljq-tooltip-trigger')
        .on('mouseenter.ljq-tooltip', () => { this._open(); })
```

```
        .on('mouseleave.ljq-tooltip', () => { this._close(); });
    }
  });
}) (jQuery);
```

Listing 8.16

This property is a function that will be invoked by the widget factory whenever
`.tooltip()` is called, once per matched element in the jQuery object.

> Widget properties, such as _create, which begin with an underscore, are
> considered private. We will discuss public functions later.

Inside this creation function, we set up our tooltip for future displaying. To do this, we
make the new `<div>` element and add it to the document. We're storing the created element
in `this._tooltipDiv` for later use.

In the context of our function, `this` refers to the current widget instance and we can add
whatever properties we want to this object. The object has some built-in properties that can
be handy for us as well; in particular, `this.element` gives us a jQuery object pointing to
the element that was originally selected.

We use `this.element` to bind the `mouseenter` and `mouseleave` handlers to the tooltip
trigger element. We need these handlers to open the tooltip when the mouse begins
hovering over the trigger and to close it when the mouse leaves. Note that the events are
namespaced with the name of our plugin. As we discussed in Chapter 3, *Handling Events*,
namespacing makes it easier for us to add and remove event handlers without stepping on
the toes of other code that also wants to bind handlers to the elements.

Next, we need to define the `._open()` and `._close()` methods that we bound to the
`mouseenter` and `mouseleave` handlers:

```
(() => {
  $.widget('ljq.tooltip', {
    _create() {
      // ...
    },

    _open() {
      const elementOffset = this.element.offset();
      this._tooltipDiv
        .css({
          position: 'absolute',
```

```
        left: elementOffset.left,
        top: elementOffset.top + this.element.height()
      })
      .text(this.element.data('tooltip-text'))
      .show();
  },

  _close() {
    this._tooltipDiv.hide();
  }
});
})(jQuery);
```

Listing 8.17

The `._open()` and `._close()` methods themselves are self-explanatory. These are not special names, but rather illustrate that we can create whatever private functions we need within our widget, so long as their names begin with underscores. When the tooltip is opened, we position it with CSS and show it; when it is closed, we simply hide it.

During the opening process, we need to populate the tooltip with information. We're using the `.data()` method for this, which can get and set arbitrary data associated with any element. In this case, we are using the method to fetch the value of the `data-tooltip-text` attribute of each element.

With our plugin in place, the code `$('a').tooltip()` will cause a tooltip to be displayed when the mouse is over any anchor:

The plugin, thus far, is not very long, but densely packed with sophisticated concepts. To make this sophistication pay off, the first thing we can do is to make our widget stateful. The widget's state will allow users to enable and disable it as needed, or even destroy it entirely after creation.

Destroying widgets

We've seen that the widget factory creates a new jQuery method, in our case called
`.tooltip()`, that can be called with no arguments to apply the widget to a set of elements.
There's much more that this method can do, though. When we give this method a string
argument, it calls the method with the appropriate name.

One of the built-in methods is called `destroy`. Calling `.tooltip('destroy')` will remove
the tooltip widget from the page. The widget factory does most of the work, but if we have
modified parts of the document inside `._create()` (as we have here, by creating the
tooltip text `<div>`), we need to clean up after ourselves:

```
(($) => {
  $.widget('ljq.tooltip', {
    _create() {
      // ...
    },

    destroy() {
      this._tooltipDiv.remove();
      this.element
        .removeClass('ljq-tooltip-trigger')
        .off('.ljq-tooltip');
      this._superApply(arguments);
    },

    _open() {
      // ...
    },

    _close() {
      // ...
    }
  });
}) (jQuery);
```

Listing 8.18

This new code is added as a new property of the widget. The function undoes the
modifications we performed, then calls the prototype's version of destroy so that the
automatic cleanup occurs. The `_super()` and `_superApply()` methods call the base
widget methods of the same name. It's always a good idea to do this, so that the proper
initialization actions in the base widget are performed.

Note that destroy is not preceded with an underscore; this is a `public` method that we can call with `.tooltip('destroy')`.

Enabling and disabling widgets

In addition to being destroyed completely, any widget can be temporarily disabled and later re-enabled. The base widget methods, `enable` and `disable`, help us by setting the value of `this.options.disabled` to `true` or `false` as appropriate. All we have to do to support these methods is to check this value before our widget takes any action:

```
_open() {
  if (this.options.disabled) {
    return;
  }

  const elementOffset = this.element.offset();
  this._tooltipDiv
    .css({
      position: 'absolute',
      left: elementOffset.left,
      top: elementOffset.top + this.element.height()
    })
    .text(this.element.data('tooltip-text'))
    .show();
}
```

Listing 8.19

With this extra check in place, the tooltips stop displaying once `.tooltip('disable')` is called and display once again after `.tooltip('enable')` is invoked.

Accepting widget options

Now it's time to make our widget customizable. As we saw when constructing the `.shadow()` plugin, it's friendly to provide a customizable set of defaults for a widget, and then to override those defaults with options the user specifies. Nearly all of the work in this process is performed by the widget factory. All we need to do is to provide an `options` property:

```
options: {
```

```
    offsetX: 10,
    offsetY: 10,
    content: element => $(element).data('tooltip-text')
  },
```

Listing 8.20

The `options` property is a plain object. All the valid options for our widget should be represented, so that none of them are mandatory for the user to provide. Here we're supplying x and y coordinates for the tooltip relative to its trigger element, as well as a function that generates the tooltip text for each element.

The only piece of our code that needs to examine these options is `._open()`:

```
_open() {
  if (this.options.disabled) {
    return;
  }

  const elementOffset = this.element.offset();
  this._tooltipDiv
    .css({
      position: 'absolute',
      left: elementOffset.left + this.options.offsetX,
      top:
        elementOffset.top +
        this.element.height() +
        this.options.offsetY
    })
    .text(this.options.content(this.element))
    .show();
}
```

Listing 8.21

Inside the _open method, we can access these properties using `this.options`. We will always get the correct value for the option this way: the default value or the overridden value if the user has provided one.

We can still add our widget without arguments, such as `.tooltip()`, and get the default behavior. Now we can supply options that override the default behavior: `.tooltip({ offsetX: -10, offsetX: 25 })`. The widget factory even lets us change these options after the widget is instantiated: `.tooltip('option', 'offsetX', 20)`. The next time the option is accessed, we will see the new value.

Reacting to option changes
If we need to immediately react to an option change, we can add a
`_setOption` function to our widget that handles the change and then calls
the default implementation of `_setOption`.

Adding methods

The built-in methods are convenient, but often we will want to expose more hooks to the
users of our plugin, as we've done with the built-in `destroy` method. We've already seen
how to create new private functions inside our widget. Creating public methods is just the
same, except that the widget property names do not begin with an underscore. We can use
this to create methods that manually open and close the tooltip quite simply:

```
open() {
  this._open();
},
close() {
  this._close();
}
```

Listing 8.22

That's it! By adding public methods that call the private functions, we can now open a
tooltip with `.tooltip('open')` and close it with `.tooltip('close')`. The widget
factory even takes care of details for us like ensuring that chaining continues to work even if
we don't return anything from our method.

Triggering widget events

A great plugin not only extends jQuery, but also offers plenty of opportunities for other
code to extend the plugin itself. One simple way to offer this extensibility is to support a set
of custom events related to the plugin. The widget factory makes this process
straightforward:

```
_open() {
  if (this.options.disabled) {
    return;
  }

  const elementOffset = this.element.offset();
  this._tooltipDiv
    .css({
```

```
      position: 'absolute',
      left: elementOffset.left + this.options.offsetX,
      top:
        elementOffset.top +
        this.element.height() +
        this.options.offsetY
    })
    .text(this.options.content(this.element))
    .show();
  this._trigger('open');
},

_close: function() {
  this._tooltipDiv.hide();
  this._trigger('close');
}
```

Listing 8.23

Calling `this._trigger()` in one of our functions allows code to listen for the new custom event. The event's name will be prefixed with our widget name, so we don't have to worry much about conflicts with other events. If we call `this._trigger('open')` in our tooltip's opening function, for example, the event called `tooltipopen` will be issued each time the tooltip opens. We can listen for this event by calling `.on('tooltipopen')` on the element.

This only scratches the surface of what's possible with a full-fledged widget plugin, but gives us the tools we need to build a widget that has the features and conforms to the standards that jQuery UI users have come to expect.

Plugin design recommendations

Now that we have examined common ways to extend jQuery and jQuery UI by creating plugins, we can review and supplement what we've learned with a list of recommendations:

- Protect the dollar (`$`) alias from potential interference from other libraries by using `jQuery` instead or passing `$` into an IIFE, so that it can be used as a local variable.

- Whether extending the jQuery object with `$.myPlugin` or the jQuery prototype with `$.fn.myPlugin`, add no more than one property to the `$` namespace. Additional public methods and properties should be added to the plugin's namespace (for example, `$.myPlugin.publicMethod` or `$.fn.myPlugin.pluginProperty`).
- Provide an object containing default options for the plugin: `$.fn.myPlugin.defaults = {size: 'large'}`.
- Allow the plugin user to optionally override any of the default settings for all subsequent calls to the method (`$.fn.myPlugin.defaults.size = 'medium';`) or for a single call (`$('div').myPlugin({size: 'small'});`).
- In most cases when extending the jQuery prototype (`$.fn.myPlugin`), return `this` to allow the plugin user to chain additional jQuery methods to it (for example, `$('div').myPlugin().find('p').addClass('foo')`).
- When extending the jQuery prototype (`$.fn.myPlugin`), enforce implicit iteration by calling `this.each()`.
- Use callback functions when appropriate to allow for flexible modification of the plugin's behavior without having to change the plugin's code.
- If the plugin calls for user interface elements or needs to track elements' state, create it with the jQuery UI widget factory.
- Maintain a set of automated unit tests for the plugin with a testing framework such as QUnit to ensure that it works as expected. See Appendix A for more information about QUnit.
- Use a version control system such as Git to track revisions to the code. Consider hosting the plugin publicly on GitHub (`http://github.com/`) and allowing others to contribute.
- If making the plugin available for others to use, make the licensing terms clear. Consider using the MIT license, which jQuery also uses.

Distributing a plugin

By following the previous recommendations, we can produce a clean, maintainable plugin that follows time-tested conventions. If it performs a useful, reusable task, we may want to share it with the jQuery community.

In addition to properly preparing plugin code as defined earlier, we should be sure to adequately document the operation of the plugin prior to distribution. We can choose a documentation format that suits our style, but may want to consider a standard such as JSDoc (described at `http://usejsdoc.org/`). Several automatic documentation generators, including docco (`http://jashkenas.github.com/docco/`) and dox (`https://github.com/visionmedia/dox`) are available. Regardless of format, we must ensure that our documentation covers every parameter and option available for use with our plugin's methods.

Plugin code and documentation can be hosted anywhere; npm (`https://www.npmjs.com/`) is the standard option. For more information about publishing jQuery plugins as npm packages, take a look at this page: `http://blog.npmjs.org/post/112064849860/using-jq uery-plugins-with-npm`.

Summary

In this chapter, we have seen how the functionality that is provided by the jQuery core need not limit the library's capabilities. In addition to the readily available plugins we explored in `Chapter 7`, *Using Plugins*, we now know how to extend the menu of features ourselves.

The plugins we've created contain various features, including global functions that use the jQuery library, new methods of the jQuery object for acting on DOM elements, and sophisticated jQuery UI widgets. With these tools at our disposal, we can shape jQuery-- and our own JavaScript code--into whatever form we desire.

Exercises

The challenge exercises may require the use of the official jQuery documentation at `http://api.jquery.com/`.

1. Create new plugin methods called `.slideFadeIn()` and `.slideFadeOut()`, combining the opacity animations of `.fadeIn()` and `.fadeOut()` with the height animations of `.slideDown()` and `.slideUp()`.
2. Extend the customizability of the `.shadow()` method so that the z-index of the cloned copies can be specified by the plugin user.
3. Add a new submethod called `isOpen` to the tooltip widget. This submethod should return `true` if the tooltip is currently displayed and `false` otherwise.

4. Add code that listens for the `tooltipopen` event that our widget fires and logs a message to the console.

5. **Challenge**: Provide an alternative `content` option for the tooltip widget that fetches the content of the page that an anchor's `href` points to via Ajax, and displays that content as the tooltip text.

6. **Challenge**: Provide a new `effect` option for the tooltip widget that, if specified, applies the named jQuery UI effect (such as `explode`) to the showing and hiding of the tooltip.

9

Advanced Selectors and Traversing

In January 2009, jQuery's creator John Resig introduced a new open source JavaScript project called **Sizzle**. A standalone **CSS selector engine**, Sizzle was written to allow any JavaScript library to adopt it with little or no modification to its codebase. In fact, jQuery has been using Sizzle as its own selector engine ever since version 1.3.

Sizzle is the component within jQuery that is responsible for parsing the CSS selector expressions we put into the `$()` function. It determines which native DOM methods to use as it builds a collection of elements that we can then act on with other jQuery methods. The combination of Sizzle and jQuery's set of traversal methods makes jQuery an extremely powerful tool for finding elements on the page.

In `Chapter 2`, *Selecting Elements*, we looked at each of the basic types of selector and traversal method so that we have a roadmap of what's available to us in the jQuery library. In this more advanced chapter, we will cover:

- Using selectors to find and filter data in various ways
- Writing plugins that add new selectors and DOM traversal methods
- Optimizing our selector expressions for better performance
- Understanding some of the inner workings of the Sizzle engine

Selecting and traversing revisited

To kick off this more in-depth look into selectors and traversing, we'll build a script that will provide yet more selecting and traversing examples to inspect. For our sample, we'll build an HTML document containing a list of news items. We'll place those items in a table so that we can experiment with selecting rows and columns in several ways:

```
<div id="topics">
  Topics:
  <a href="topics/all.html" class="selected">All</a>
  <a href="topics/community.html">Community</a>
  <a href="topics/conferences.html">Conferences</a>
  <!-- continued... -->
</div>
<table id="news">
  <thead>
    <tr>
      <th>Date</th>
      <th>Headline</th>
      <th>Author</th>
      <th>Topic</th>
    </tr>
  </thead>
  <tbody>
    <tr>
      <th colspan="4">2011</th>
    </tr>
    <tr>
      <td>Apr 15</td>
      <td>jQuery 1.6 Beta 1 Released</td>
      <td>John Resig</td>
      <td>Releases</td>
    </tr>
    <tr>
      <td>Feb 24</td>
      <td>jQuery Conference 2011: San Francisco Bay Area</td>
      <td>Ralph Whitbeck</td>
      <td>Conferences</td>
    </tr>
    <!-- continued... -->
  </tbody>
</table>
```

Getting the example code
You can access the example code from the following GitHub repository: `ht tps://github.com/PacktPublishing/Learning-jQuery-3`.

From this code fragment, we can see the structure of the document. The table has four columns, representing date, headline, author, and topic, but some table rows contain a subheading of a calendar year instead of those four items:

jQuery News

Topics: `All` Community   Conferences   Documentation   Plugins   Releases   Miscellaneous

Date	Headline	Author	Topic
2011			
Apr 15	jQuery 1.6 Beta 1 Released	John Resig	Releases
Feb 24	jQuery Conference 2011: San Francisco Bay Area	Ralph Whitbeck	Conferences
Feb 7	New Releases, Videos & a Sneak Peek at the jQuery UI Grid	Addy Osmani	Plugins
Jan 31	jQuery 1.5 Released	John Resig	Releases
Jan 30	API Documentation Changes	Karl Swedberg	Documentation
2010			
Nov 23	Team Spotlight: The jQuery Bug Triage Team	Paul Irish	Community
Oct 4	New Official jQuery Plugins Provide Templating, Data Linking and Globalization	John Resig	Plugins
Sep 4	The Official jQuery Podcast Has a New Home	Ralph Whitbeck	Documentation

Between the title and table, there are sets of links representing each of the news topics in the table. For our first task, we'll change the behavior of these links to filter the table *in place* rather than requiring navigation to different pages.

Dynamic table filtering

In order to use the topic links to filter the table, we need to prevent their default linking behavior. We should also give the user some feedback about the currently selected topic:

```
$(() => {
  $('#topics a')
    .click((e) => {
      e.preventDefault();
      $(e.target)
```

```
        .addClass('selected')
        .siblings('.selected')
        .removeClass('selected');
    });
  });
```

Listing 9.1

We remove the `selected` class from all the topic links when one is clicked on, then add the `selected` class to the new topic. The call to `.preventDefault()` prevents the link from being followed.

Next, we need to actually perform the filtering operation. As a first pass at this problem, we can hide every row of the table that doesn't contain the text of the topic:

```
$(() => {
  $('#topics a')
    .click((e) => {
      e.preventDefault();
      const topic = $(e.target).text();

      $(e.target)
        .addClass('selected')
        .siblings('.selected')
        .removeClass('selected');

      $('#news tr').show();
      if (topic != 'All') {
        $(`#news tr:has(td):not(:contains("${topic}"))`)
          .hide();
      }
    });
});
```

Listing 9.2

We're now storing the text of the link in the constant `topic` so that we can compare it against the text in the table itself. First, we show all the table rows and then, if the topic is not **All**, we hide the irrelevant ones. The selector we're using for this process is a little complex, though:

```
#news tr:has(td):not(:contains("topic"))
```

The selector starts off straightforwardly, with `#news tr` locating all of the rows in the table. We then filter this element set using the `:has()` custom selector. This selector winnows the currently selected elements down to those that contain the specified descendant. In this case, we're eliminating the header rows (such as the calendar years) from consideration, since they do not contain `<td>` cells.

Once we have found the rows of the table where the actual content lies, we need to find out which ones relate to the selected topic. The `:contains()` custom selector matches just the elements that have the given text string somewhere inside them; wrapping this in a `:not()` selector then gives us all the rows that don't have the topic string so we can hide them.

This code works well enough, unless the topic happens to appear as part of a news headline, for instance. We also need to take care of the eventuality that one topic is a substring of another. To handle these cases, we will need to execute code for each of the rows:

```
$(() => {
  $('#topics a')
    .click((e) => {
      e.preventDefault();
      const topic = $(e.target).text();

      $(e.target)
        .addClass('selected')
        .siblings('.selected')
        .removeClass('selected');

      $('#news tr').show();
      if (topic != 'All') {
        $('#news')
          .find('tr:has(td)')
          .not((i, element) =>
            $(element)
              .children(':nth-child(4)')
              .text() == topic
          )
          .hide();
      }
    });
});
```

Listing 9.3

This new code eliminates some of the complex selector expression text by adding DOM traversal methods. The `.find()` method acts just like the space previously separating `#news` and `tr`, but the `.not()` method does something that `:not()` can't do. Just as we saw with the `.filter()` method back in `Chapter 2`, *Selecting Elements*, `.not()` can accept a callback function invoked once per element to be tested. If that function returns `true`, the element is excluded from the result set.

 Selectors versus traversal methods
The choice of using a selector or its equivalent traversal method has performance ramifications as well. We'll explore this choice in more detail later in this chapter.

Inside the `.not()` method's filtering function, we examine the child elements of the row to find the fourth one (which is the cell in the `Topic` column). A simple check of the text of this cell tells us whether the row should be hidden. Only the matching rows are displayed:

Topics:	All	Community	Conferences	Documentation	Plugins	Releases	Miscellaneous		
Date	**Headline**							**Author**	**Topic**
2011									
Feb 24	jQuery Conference 2011: San Francisco Bay Area							Ralph Whitbeck	Conferences
2010									
Aug 24	jQuery Conference 2010: Boston							Ralph Whitbeck	Conferences
Jun 14	Seattle jQuery Open Space and Hack Attack with John Resig							Rey Bango	Conferences
Mar 15	jQuery Conference 2010: San Francisco Bay Area							Mike Hostetler	Conferences
2009									
Oct 22	jQuery Summit							John Resig	Conferences

Striping table rows

In `Chapter 2`, *Selecting Elements*, one of our selector examples illustrated the ways in which we can apply alternating row colors to a table. We saw that the `:even` and `:odd` custom selectors can make short work of this task, and that the CSS-native `:nth-child()` pseudo-class can accomplish it as well:

```
$(() => {
  $('#news tr:nth-child(even)')
    .addClass('alt');
});
```

Listing 9.4

This straightforward selector finds every other table row, and since each year's news articles reside in their own `<tbody>` element, the alternation starts over again with each section.

Date	Headline	Author	Topic
2011			
Apr 15	jQuery 1.6 Beta 1 Released	John Resig	Releases
Feb 24	jQuery Conference 2011: San Francisco Bay Area	Ralph Whitbeck	Conferences
Feb 7	New Releases, Videos & a Sneak Peek at the jQuery UI Grid	Addy Osmani	Plugins
Jan 31	jQuery 1.5 Released	John Resig	Releases
Jan 30	API Documentation Changes	Karl Swedberg	Documentation
2010			
Nov 23	Team Spotlight: The jQuery Bug Triage Team	Paul Irish	Community
Oct 4	New Official jQuery Plugins Provide Templating, Data Linking and Globalization	John Resig	Plugins

For a more complicated row-striping challenge, we can attempt to give the `alt` class to sets of two rows at a time. The first two rows will receive the class, then the next two will not, and so on. To achieve this, we will need to revisit **filtering functions**:

```
$(() => {
  $('#news tr')
    .filter(i => (i % 4) < 2)
    .addClass('alt');
});
```

Listing 9.5

In our `.filter()` examples in `Chapter 2`, *Selecting Elements*, as well as the `.not()` example in *Listing 9.3*, our filtering functions examined each element to determine whether to include it in the result set. Here, though, we don't need information about the element to determine if it should be included. Instead, we need to know its position within the original set of elements. This information is passed as an argument to the function, and we're calling it `i`.

The `i` parameter now holds the zero-based index of the element. With this, we can use the modulo operator (`%`) to determine whether we are in a pair of elements that should receive the `alt` class or not. Now, we have stripes of two rows throughout the table.

There are a couple of loose ends to clean up, however. Because we're no longer using the :nth-child() pseudo-class, the alternation does not begin again within each <tbody>. Also, we should be skipping table header rows for a consistent appearance. These goals can be achieved by making a couple of small modifications:

```
$(() => {
  $('#news tbody')
    .each((i, element) => {
      $(element)
        .children()
        .has('td')
        .filter(i => (i % 4) < 2)
        .addClass('alt');
    });
});
```

Listing 9.6

To treat each group of rows independently, we can loop over the <tbody> elements with an .each() call. Within the loop, we then exclude subheading rows just as we did in *Listing 9.3*, using .has(). This results in a table striped in sets of two rows:

Date	Headline	Author	Topic
2011			
Apr 15	jQuery 1.6 Beta 1 Released	John Resig	Releases
Feb 24	jQuery Conference 2011: San Francisco Bay Area	Ralph Whitbeck	Conferences
Feb 7	New Releases, Videos & a Sneak Peek at the jQuery UI Grid	Addy Osmani	Plugins
Jan 31	jQuery 1.5 Released	John Resig	Releases
Jan 30	API Documentation Changes	Karl Swedberg	Documentation
2010			
Nov 23	Team Spotlight: The jQuery Bug Triage Team	Paul Irish	Community

Combining filtering and striping

Our advanced table striping now works nicely, but behaves strangely when the topic filter is used. For the two functions to play together well, we need to re-stripe the table each time a filter is used. We will also need to consider whether rows are currently hidden when calculating where to apply the alt class:

```
$(() => {
  function stripe() {
    $('#news')
```

```
        .find('tr.alt')
        .removeClass('alt')
        .end()
        .find('tbody')
        .each((i, element) => {
          $(element)
            .children(':visible')
            .has('td')
            .filter(i => (i % 4) < 2)
            .addClass('alt');
        });
    }
    stripe();

    $('#topics a')
      .click((e) => {
        e.preventDefault();
        const topic = $(e.target).text();

        $(e.target)
          .addClass('selected')
          .siblings('.selected')
          .removeClass('selected');

        $('#news tr').show();
        if (topic != 'All') {
          $('#news')
            .find('tr:has(td)')
            .not((i, element) =>
              $(element)
                .children(':nth-child(4)')
                .text() == topic
            )
            .hide();
        }

        stripe();
      });
  });
```

Listing 9.7

Combining the filtering code from *Listing 9.3* with our row striping routine, this script now defines a function called `stripe()`, which is called once when the document is loaded, and again each time a topic link is clicked. Within the function, we take care of removing the `alt` class from rows that no longer need it, as well as limiting the selected rows to those that are currently shown. We accomplish this with the `:visible` pseudo-class, which (along with its counterpart `:hidden`) respects whether elements are hidden for a variety of reasons, including having a `display` value of `none`, or `width` and `height` values of `0`.

We can now filter the rows of our table while preserving our row striping:

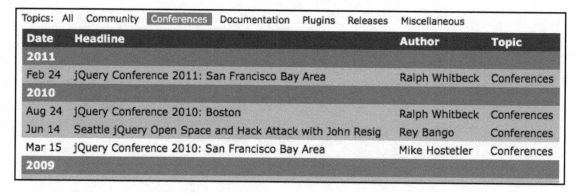

More selector and traversal methods

Even after all the examples we've seen, we have not come close to exploring every way to find elements on a page using jQuery. There are dozens of selectors and DOM traversal methods available to us, and each has a particular utility we may need to call upon.

To find the appropriate selector or method for our needs, many resources are available to us. The quick reference at the end of this book lists each selector and method with a very brief description of each. For lengthier descriptions and usage examples, though, we will need a more thorough guide, such as the online jQuery API reference. This site lists all the selectors at `http://api.jquery.com/category/selectors/`, and the traversal methods at `http://api.jquery.com/category/traversing/`.

Customizing and optimizing selectors

Many techniques that we've seen give us a tool chest that can be used to find any page element we want to work with. The story doesn't end here though; there is much to learn about performing our element-finding tasks efficiently. This efficiency can take the form of both code that is easier to write and read, and code that executes more quickly inside the web browser.

Writing a custom selector plugin

One way to improve legibility is to encapsulate code snippets in reusable components. We do this all the time by creating functions. In Chapter 8, *Developing Plugins*, we expanded this idea by crafting jQuery plugins that added methods to jQuery objects. This isn't the only way plugins can help us reuse code, though. Plugins can also provide additional **selector expressions**, such as the :paused selector that Cycle gave us in Chapter 7, *Using Plugins*.

The easiest type of selector expression to add is a **pseudo-class**. This is an expression that starts with a colon, such as :checked or :nth-child(). To illustrate the process of creating a selector expression, we'll build a pseudo-class called :group(). This new selector will encapsulate the code we used to find table rows to stripe back in *Listing 9.6*.

When using a selector expression to find elements, jQuery looks for instructions in an internal object called expr. The values in this object behave much like the filtering functions that we pass to .filter() or .not(), containing JavaScript code that causes each element to be contained in the result set if and only if the function returns true. We can add new expressions to this object using the $.extend() function:

```
(($) => {
  $.extend($.expr[':'], {
    group(element, index, matches) {
      const num = parseInt(matches[3], 10);

      return Number.isInteger(num) &&
        ($(element).index() - 1) % (num * 2) < num;
    }
  });
})(jQuery);
```

Listing 9.8

This code tells jQuery that `group` is a valid string that can follow a colon in a selector expression, and that, when it is encountered, the given function should be called to determine whether the element should be included in the result set.

The function that is evaluated here is passed four parameters:

- `element`: The DOM element under consideration. This is needed for most selectors, but not ours.
- `index`: The index of the DOM element within the result set. Unfortunately, this is always 0, and we cannot rely on it. The only reason it's included here is because we need positional access to the matches argument.
- `matches`: An array containing the result of the regular expression that was used to parse this selector. Typically, `matches[3]` is the only relevant item in the array; in a selector of the form `:group(2)`, the `matches[3]` item contains 2, the text within the parentheses.

Pseudo-class selectors can use some or all of the information contained in these three arguments to determine whether or not the element belongs in the result set. In this case, `element` and `matches` are all that we require. We actually do require the index position of every element that's passed to this function. Since the `index` argument cannot be relied upon, we simply use the `.index()` jQuery method to get the index for us.

With the new `:group` selector, we now have a flexible way to select alternating groups of elements. For example, we could combine the selector expression and `.filter()` function from *Listing 9.5* into a single selector expression: `$('#news tr:group(2)')`, or we could preserve the per-section behavior from *Listing 9.7*, and use `:group()` as an expression within a `.filter()` call. We can even change the number of rows to group by simply changing the number within the parentheses:

```
$(() => {
  function stripe() {
    $('#news')
      .find('tr.alt')
      .removeClass('alt')
      .end()
      .find('tbody')
      .each((i, element) => {
        $(element)
          .children(':visible')
          .has('td')
          .filter(':group(3)')
          .addClass('alt');
      });
```

```
    }

    stripe();
});
```

Listing 9.9

Now we can see that the row striping alternates by groups of three:

Date	Headline	Author	Topic
2011			
Apr 15	jQuery 1.6 Beta 1 Released	John Resig	Releases
Feb 24	jQuery Conference 2011: San Francisco Bay Area	Ralph Whitbeck	Conferences
Feb 7	New Releases, Videos & a Sneak Peek at the jQuery UI Grid	Addy Osmani	Plugins
Jan 31	jQuery 1.5 Released	John Resig	Releases
Jan 30	API Documentation Changes	Karl Swedberg	Documentation
2010			
Nov 23	Team Spotlight: The jQuery Bug Triage Team	Paul Irish	Community

Selector performance

In planning any web development project, we need to keep in mind the time it takes to create the site, the ease and speed with which we can maintain our code, and the performance of the site as users interact with it. Often the first two of these concerns are more important than the third. Especially with client-side scripting, developers can easily fall into the traps of **premature optimization** and **micro-optimization**. These pitfalls can cause us to spend countless hours tweaking our code to shave milliseconds from the JavaScript execution time, even when there was no noticeable performance lag in the first place.

 A good rule of thumb is to consider the developer's time more valuable than the computer's time, unless users notice slowness in our application.

Even when performance is an issue, pinpointing the bottlenecks in our jQuery code can be difficult. As we hinted at earlier in this chapter, some selectors are generally faster than others, and moving part of a selector to a traversal method can help speed up the time it takes to find elements on the page. Selector and traversal performance is therefore often a good place to start examining our code to reduce the amount of delay that users may experience when interacting with the page.

 Any decrees made about the relative speed of selectors and traversal methods are likely to become outdated with the release of newer, faster browsers and clever speed tweaks introduced in newer jQuery versions. In matters of performance, it is a good idea to routinely question our assumptions and to optimize code after performing measurements using a tool such as **jsPerf** (http://jsperf.com).

With this in mind, we'll examine a couple of simple guidelines for producing optimized jQuery selector code.

Sizzle selector implementation

As noted in the beginning of this chapter, when we pass a selector expression into the $() function, jQuery's Sizzle implementation parses the expression and determines how to gather the elements represented by it. In its basic form, Sizzle applies the most efficient native **DOM method** that the browser supports to obtain a nodeList, a native array-like object of DOM elements that jQuery ultimately converts to a true array and adds to the jQuery object. The following is a list of DOM methods that jQuery uses internally, along with the recent browser versions that support them:

Method	Selects	Supported by
.getElementById()	The unique element with an ID that matches the given string.	All browsers
.getElementsByTagName()	All elements with a tag name that matches the given string.	All browsers
.getElementsByClassName()	All elements that have one of their class names matching the given string.	IE9+, Firefox 3+, Safari 4+, Chrome 4+, and Opera 10+
.querySelectorAll()	All elements that match the given selector expression.	IE8+, Firefox 3.5+, Safari 3+, Chrome 4+, and Opera 10+

If a part of the selector expression cannot be handled by one of these methods, Sizzle falls back to looping through each element that has already been collected and testing each one against the expression part. If *no* part of the selector expression can be handled by a DOM method, Sizzle starts with a collection of *all* elements in the document, represented by `document.getElementsByTagName('*')`, and loops through each one in turn.

This looping and testing of each element is much more costly in terms of performance than any of the native DOM methods. Fortunately, the most recent versions of all modern desktop browsers include the native `.querySelectorAll()` method, and Sizzle uses it when it can't use other, even speedier, native methods--with one exception. When the selector expression contains a custom jQuery selector such as `:eq()` or `:odd` or `:even` that has no CSS counterpart, Sizzle has no choice but to loop and test.

Testing selector speed

To get an idea of the performance difference between `.querySelectorAll()` and the *loop-and-test* procedure, consider a document in which we wish to select all the `<input type="text">` elements. We could write the selector expression in one of two ways: `$('input[type="text"]')`, which uses a *CSS attribute selector*, or `$('input:text')`, which uses a *custom jQuery selector*. To test just the portions of the selectors we are interested in here, we will remove the `input` parts and compare the speeds of `$('[type="text"]')` and `$(':text')`. The JavaScript benchmarking site `http://jsperf.com/` lets us make this comparison, yielding dramatic results.

In jsPerf tests, each test case is cycled to see how many times it can be completed in a certain amount of time, so the higher the number, the better. When tested in modern browsers that support .querySelectorAll() (Chrome 26, Firefox 20, and Safari 6), the selector that can take advantage of it is remarkably faster than the custom jQuery selector:

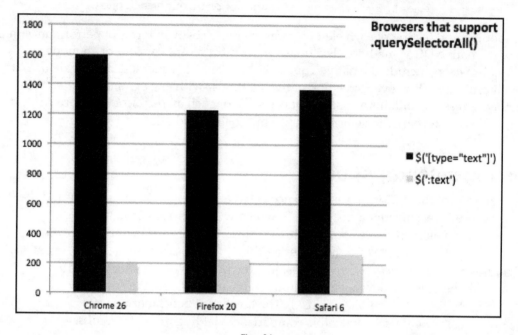

Figure 9.1

However, in a browser that does not support .querySelectorAll(), such as IE 7, the two selectors perform almost identically. In this case, both selectors force jQuery to loop through every element on the page and test each one individually:

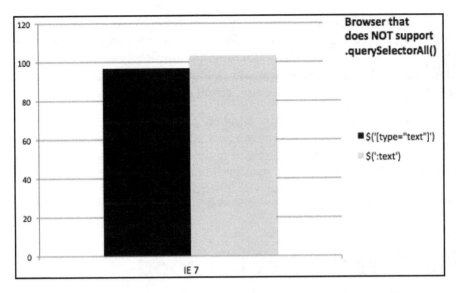

Figure 9.2

The performance difference between a selector that uses a native method and one that doesn't is also apparent when we look at $('input:eq(1)') and $('input') .eq(1):

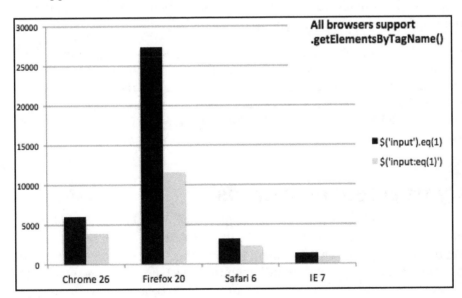

Figure 9.3

While the raw number of operations per second varies greatly from browser to browser, all of the tested browsers show a significant performance boost when we move the custom `:eq()` selector out into the `.eq()` method. Using the simple `input` tag name as the argument for the `$()` function allows for a quick lookup, and the `.eq()` method then simply calls an array function to retrieve the second element in the jQuery collection.

As a general rule of thumb, we should prefer selectors that are part of the CSS specification over jQuery's custom selectors whenever possible. Still, before changing our selectors, it makes sense to first confirm that there is a need to increase performance, and then test just how much the change would boost performance with a benchmarking tool such as `http://jsperf.com`.

DOM traversal under the hood

In `Chapter 2`, *Selecting Elements*, and again at the beginning of this chapter, we looked at ways of traveling from one set of DOM elements to another by calling DOM traversal methods. Our (far from exhaustive) survey of such methods included simple ways to reach neighboring cells, such as `.next()` and `.parent()`, and more complex ways of combining selector expressions, such as `.find()` and `.filter()`. By now, we should have a fairly strong grasp to these approaches of getting from one DOM element to another step by step.

Each time we take one of these steps, though, jQuery takes note of our travels, laying down a trail of breadcrumbs we can follow back home if needed. A couple of the methods we briefly touched on in that chapter, `.end()` and `.addBack()`, take advantage of this record keeping. To be able to get the most out of these methods, and in general to write efficient jQuery code, we need to understand a bit more about how the DOM traversal methods do their jobs.

jQuery traversal properties

As we know, we typically construct a jQuery object instance by passing a selector expression to the `$()` function. Within the resulting object, there lies an array structure containing references to each DOM element that matched that selector. What we haven't seen, though, are the other properties hidden in the object. For example, when a DOM traversal method is called, the `.prevObject` property holds a reference to the jQuery object the traversal method was called upon.

The jQuery object used to expose `selector` and `context` properties as well. Since they don't provide any value to us, they've been removed in jQuery 3.

To see the `prevObject` property in action, we can highlight an arbitrary cell of our table and examine its value:

```
$(() => {
  const $cell = $('#release');
    .addClass('highlight');
  console.log('prevObject', $cell.prevObject);
});
```

Listing 9.10

This snippet will highlight the single selected cell, as shown in the following screenshot:

Date	Headline	Author	Topic
2011			
Apr 15	jQuery 1.6 Beta 1 Released	John Resig	Releases
Feb 24	jQuery Conference 2011: San Francisco Bay Area	Ralph Whitbeck	Conferences
Feb 7	New Releases, Videos & a Sneak Peek at the jQuery UI Grid	Addy Osmani	Plugins
Jan 31	*jQuery 1.5 Released*	John Resig	Releases
Jan 30	API Documentation Changes	Karl Swedberg	Documentation

We can see that `.prevObject` is undefined since this is a newly created object. If we add a traversal method to the mix, though, things get more interesting:

```
$(() => {
  const $cell = $('#release')
    .nextAll()
    .addClass('highlight');
  console.log('prevObject', $cell.prevObject);
});
```

Listing 9.11

This change alters which cells are highlighted, as shown in the following screenshot:

Date	Headline	Author	Topic
2011			
Apr 15	jQuery 1.6 Beta 1 Released	John Resig	Releases
Feb 24	jQuery Conference 2011: San Francisco Bay Area	Ralph Whitbeck	Conferences
Feb 7	New Releases, Videos & a Sneak Peek at the jQuery UI Grid	Addy Osmani	Plugins
Jan 31	jQuery 1.5 Released	*John Resig*	*Releases*
Jan 30	API Documentation Changes	Karl Swedberg	Documentation

Now, the two cells following the one we initially selected are highlighted. Within the jQuery object, `.prevObject` now refers to the original jQuery object instance before the call to `.nextAll()`.

The DOM element stack

Since each jQuery object instance has a `.prevObject` property pointing to the previous one, we have a linked list structure that implements a **stack**. Each traversal method call finds a new set of elements and pushes this set onto the stack. This is only useful if we can do something with this stack, which is where the `.end()` and `.addBack()` methods come into play.

The `.end()` method simply pops one element off the end of the stack, which is the same as fetching the value of the `.prevObject` property. We saw an example of this in Chapter 2, *Selecting Elements*, and we will see more later in this chapter. For a more interesting example, though, we'll investigate how `.addBack()` manipulates the stack:

```
$(() => {
  $('#release')
    .nextAll()
    .addBack()
    .addClass('highlight');
});
```

Listing 9.12

Once again, the highlighted cells have changed:

Date	Headline	Author	Topic
2011			
Apr 15	jQuery 1.6 Beta 1 Released	John Resig	Releases
Feb 24	jQuery Conference 2011: San Francisco Bay Area	Ralph Whitbeck	Conferences
Feb 7	New Releases, Videos & a Sneak Peek at the jQuery UI Grid	Addy Osmani	Plugins
Jan 31	*jQuery 1.5 Released*	*John Resig*	*Releases*
Jan 30	API Documentation Changes	Karl Swedberg	Documentation

When `.addBack()` is called, jQuery looks back one step on the stack and combines the two element sets. In our example, this means that the highlighted cells include both the two cells found by the `.nextAll()` call and the original cell located using the selector. This new, merged element set is then pushed onto the stack.

This kind of stack manipulation is useful. To make sure these techniques work when they are needed, each traversal method implementation must properly update the stack; this means that we need to understand some of the system's inner workings if we want to provide traversal methods of our own.

Writing a DOM traversal method plugin

Like any other jQuery object method, traversal methods can be added to jQuery by adding properties to `$.fn`. We saw in Chapter 8, *Developing Plugins*, that new jQuery methods we define should operate on the matched set of elements and then return the jQuery object so that users can chain on additional methods. When we create DOM traversal methods, the process is similar, but the jQuery object we return needs to point to a new set of matched elements.

As an example, we'll build a plugin that finds all of the table cells in the same column as a given cell. First we'll look at the plugin code in its entirety, then examine it piece by piece to understand how it works:

```
(($) => {
  $.fn.column = function() {
    var $cells = $();

    this.each(function(i, element) {
      const $td = $(element).closest('td, th');
```

```
      if ($td.length) {
        const colNum = $td[0].cellIndex + 1;
        const $columnCells = $td
          .closest('table')
          .find('td, th')
          .filter(`:nth-child(${colNum})`);

        $cells = $cells.add($columnCells);
      }
    });

    return this.pushStack($cells);
  };
})(jQuery);
```

Listing 9.13

Our .column() method could be called on a jQuery object pointing to zero, one, or more DOM elements. To account for all of these possibilities, we use the .each() method to loop over the elements, adding the columns of cells one by one into the variable $cells. This $cells variable starts out as an empty jQuery object, but then is expanded with the .add() method to point to more and more DOM elements as needed.

This explains the outer loop of the function; inside the loop, we need to understand how $columnCells gets populated with the DOM elements in the table column. First, we get a reference to the table cell being examined. We want to allow the .column() method to be called on table cells or on elements inside table cells. The .closest() method takes care of this for us; it travels up the DOM tree until it finds an element matching the selector we provide. This method will prove very useful to us in event delegation, which we'll revisit in Chapter 10, *Advanced Events*.

With our table cell in hand, we find its column number using the DOM .cellIndex property. This gives us a zero-based index of the cell's column; we add 1 to this number since we'll be using it in a one-based context later. Then, from the cell, we travel up to the nearest <table> element, back down to the <td> and <th> elements, and filter these cells down to the appropriate column with an :nth-child() selector expression.

The plugin we're writing is limited to simple, non-nested tables due to the .find('td, th') call. To support nested tables, we would need to determine whether <tbody> tags are present and move up and down the DOM tree by the appropriate amount, which would add more complexity than is appropriate for this example.

Once we've found all the cells in the column or columns, we need to return the new jQuery object. We could just return `$cells` from our method, but this wouldn't properly respect the DOM element stack. Instead, we pass `$cells` to the `.pushStack()` method and return the result. This method accepts an array of DOM elements and adds them to the stack, so that later calls to methods such as `.addBack()` and `.end()` behave correctly.

To see our plugin in action, we can react to clicks on cells and highlight the corresponding column:

```
$(() => {
  $('#news td')
    .click((e) => {
      $(e.target)
        .siblings('.active')
        .removeClass('active')
        .end()
        .column()
        .addClass('active');
    });
});
```

Listing 9.14

The `active` class is added to the selected column, resulting in different shading when, for instance, one of the author's names is clicked:

Date	Headline	Author	Topic
2011			
Apr 15	jQuery 1.6 Beta 1 Released	John Resig	Releases
Feb 24	jQuery Conference 2011: San Francisco Bay Area	Ralph Whitbeck	Conferences
Feb 7	New Releases, Videos & a Sneak Peek at the jQuery UI Grid	Addy Osmani	Plugins
Jan 31	*jQuery 1.5 Released*	*John Resig*	*Releases*
Jan 30	API Documentation Changes	Karl Swedberg	Documentation

DOM traversal performance

The rule of thumb about selector performance applies equally to DOM traversal performance: we should prioritize ease of code writing and code maintenance when possible, only sacrificing legibility for optimization when performance is a measurable problem. Again, sites such as `http://jsperf.com/` are helpful in determining the best approach given several options.

While premature optimization should be avoided, it is good practice to minimize repetition of selectors and traversal methods. As these can be potentially expensive tasks, the fewer times we do them, the better. Two strategies for avoiding this repetition are **chaining** and **object caching**.

Improving performance using chaining

We have used chaining many times now, and it has allowed us to keep our code concise. There can be a performance benefit to chaining as well.

Our `stripe()` function from *Listing 9.9* located the element with the ID `news` once instead of twice. It needed to remove the `alt` class from rows that no longer needed it, and to apply that class to the new set of rows. Using chaining, we combined these two thoughts into one and prevented this repetition:

```
$(() => {
  function stripe() {
    $('#news')
      .find('tr.alt')
      .removeClass('alt')
      .end()
      .find('tbody')
      .each((i, element) => {
        $(element)
          .children(':visible')
          .has('td')
          .filter(':group(3)')
          .addClass('alt');
      });
  }

  stripe();
});
```

Listing 9.15

In order to merge the two uses of `$('#news')`, we once again exploit the DOM element stack within the jQuery object. The first call to `.find()` pushes the table rows onto the stack, but then `.end()` pops this off the stack so that the next `.find()` call is operating on the `news` table once again. This kind of clever manipulation of the stack is a handy way of avoiding selector duplication.

Improving performance with caching

Caching is simply storing the result of an operation so that it can be used multiple times without running the operation again. In the context of selector and traversal performance, we can cache a jQuery object in a constant for later use rather than creating a new one.

Returning to our example, we can rewrite the `stripe()` function to avoid selector duplication with caching rather than chaining:

```
$(() => {
  const $news = $('#news');

  function stripe() {
    $news
      .find('tr.alt')
      .removeClass('alt');
    $news
      .find('tbody')
      .each((i, element) => {
        $(element)
          .children(':visible')
          .has('td')
          .filter(':group(3)')
          .addClass('alt');
      });
  }

  stripe();
});
```

Listing 9.16

The two operations are separate JavaScript statements once again, rather than being chained together. We're still executing the `$('#news')` selector only once, though, by storing the result in `$news`. This caching approach is a little more verbose than chaining, since we need to separately create the variable storing the jQuery object. Obviously, creating more constants to manage in our code is less desirable than chaining together function calls. But sometimes, chaining is simply too complex, and caching objects like this is the better choice.

Because selecting elements on the page by ID is extremely fast, neither of these examples will have a big performance impact, and in practice we'd choose the approach that seemed the most legible and maintainable. These techniques are useful tools, though, when performance is found to be a concern.

Summary

In this chapter, we delved more deeply into jQuery's extensive capabilities for finding elements in a document. We've looked at some of the details of how the Sizzle selector engine works, and the implications this has on designing effective and efficient code. In addition, we have explored the ways in which we can extend and enhance jQuery's selectors and DOM traversal methods.

Further reading

A complete list of selectors and traversal methods is available in Appendix B, *Quick Reference* in this book, or in the official jQuery documentation at http://api.jquery.com/.

Exercises

The challenge exercises may require the use of the official jQuery documentation at http://api.jquery.com/.

1. Modify the table row striping routine so that it gives no class to the first row, a class of alt to the second row, and a class of alt-2 to the third row. Repeat this pattern for every set of three rows in a section.
2. Create a new selector plugin called :containsExactly() that selects elements with text content that exactly matches what is put inside the parentheses.
3. Use this new :containsExactly() selector to rewrite the filtering code from *Listing 9.3*.
4. Create a new DOM traversal plugin method called .grandparent() that moves from an element or elements to their grandparent elements in the DOM.
5. **Challenge**: Using http://jsperf.com/, paste in the content of index.html and compare the performance of finding the closest ancestor table element of <td id="release"> using the following:

   - The .closest() method
   - The .parents() method, limiting the result to the first table found

6. **Challenge**: Using `http://jsperf.com/`, paste in the content of `index.html` and compare the performance of finding the final `<td>` element in each row using the following:

- The `:last-child` pseudo-class
- The `:nth-child()` pseudo-class
- The `.last()` method within each row (using `.each()` to loop over the rows)
- The `:last` pseudo-class within each row (using `.each()` to loop over the rows)

10
Advanced Events

To build interactive web applications, we need to observe the user's activities and respond to them. We have seen that jQuery's event system can simplify this task, and we have already used this event system many times.

In Chapter 3, *Handling Events*, we touched upon a number of features that jQuery provides for reacting to events. In this more advanced chapter, we will cover:

- Event delegation and the challenges it presents
- Performance pitfalls associated with certain events and how to address them
- Custom events that we define ourselves
- The special event system that jQuery uses internally for sophisticated interactions

Revisiting events

For our sample document, we will create a simple photo gallery. The gallery will display a set of photos with an option to display additional photos upon the click of a link. We'll also use jQuery's event system to display textual information about each photo when the cursor is over it. The HTML that defines the gallery is as follows:

```
<div id="container">
  <h1>Photo Gallery</h1>

  <div id="gallery">
    <div class="photo">
      <img src="photos/skyemonroe.jpg">
      <div class="details">
        <div class="description">The Cuillin Mountains,
          Isle of Skye, Scotland.</div>
        <div class="date">12/24/2000</div>
```

```
        <div class="photographer">Alasdair Dougall</div>
      </div>
    </div>
    <div class="photo">
      <img src="photos/dscn1328.jpg">
      <div class="details">
        <div class="description">Mt. Ruapehu in summer</div>
        <div class="date">01/13/2005</div>
        <div class="photographer">Andrew McMillan</div>
      </div>
    </div>
    <div class="photo">
      <img src="photos/024.JPG">
      <div class="details">
        <div class="description">midday sun</div>
        <div class="date">04/26/2011</div>
        <div class="photographer">Jaycee Barratt</div>
      </div>
    </div>
    <!-- Code continues -->
  </div>
  <a id="more-photos" href="pages/1.html">More Photos</a>
</div>
```

Getting the example code

You can access the example code from the following GitHub repository: ht
tps://github.com/PacktPublishing/Learning-jQuery-3.

When we apply styles to the photos, arranging them into rows of three will make the gallery look like the following screenshot:

Loading additional pages of data

By now, we are experts at the common task of reacting to a click on a page element. When the **More Photos** link is clicked on, we need to perform an Ajax request for the next set of photos and append them to `<div id="gallery">` as follows:

```
$(() => {
  $('#more-photos')
    .click((e) => {
      e.preventDefault();
      const url = $(e.target).attr('href');

      $.get(url)
        .then((data) => {
          $('#gallery')
            .append(data);
```

```
    })
    .catch(({ statusText }) => {
      $('#gallery')
        .append(`<strong>${statusText}</strong>`)
    });
  });
});
```

Listing 10.1

We also need to update the destination of the **More Photos** link to point to the next page of photos:

```
$(() => {
  var pageNum = 1;

  $('#more-photos')
    .click((e) => {
      e.preventDefault();
      const $link = $(e.target);
      const url = $link.attr('href');

      if (pageNum > 19) {
        $link.remove();
        return;
      }

      $link.attr('href', `pages/${++pageNum}.html`);

      $.get(url)
        .then((data) => {
          $('#gallery')
            .append(data);
        })
        .catch(({ statusText }) => {
          $('#gallery')
            .append(`<strong>${statusText}</strong>`)
        });
    });
});
```

Listing 10.2

Our `.click()` handler now uses the pageNum variable to track the next page of photos to request, and uses this to build the new href value for the link. Since pageNum is defined outside the function, its value persists between the clicks of the link. We remove the link once we have reached the last page of photos.

We should also consider using the HTML5 history API to allow the user to bookmark our Ajax-loaded content. You can learn about this API at Dive into HTML5 (`http://diveintohtml5.info/history.html`) and implement it quite easily using the History plugin (`https://github.com/browserstate/history.js`).

Displaying data on hover

The next feature we want to provide on this page is to display the details relating to each photo when the user's mouse is in that area of the page. For our first pass at displaying this information, we can use the `.hover()` method:

```
$(() => {
  $('div.photo')
    .hover((e) => {
      $(e.currentTarget)
        .find('.details')
        .fadeTo('fast', 0.7);
    }, (e) => {
      $(e.currentTarget)
        .find('.details')
        .fadeOut('fast');
    });
});
```

Listing 10.3

When the cursor enters a photo's boundary, the associated information fades in to 70 percent opacity, and when it leaves, the information fades back out:

There are, of course, multiple ways to perform this task. Since a portion of each handler is the same, it's possible to combine the two handlers. We can bind a handler to both `mouseenter` and `mouseleave` at the same time by separating the event names with a space, as follows:

```
$('div.photo')
  .on('mouseenter mouseleave', (e) => {
    const $details = $(e.currentTarget).find('.details');

    if (e.type == 'mouseenter') {
      $details.fadeTo('fast', 0.7);
    } else {
      $details.fadeOut('fast');
    }
  });
```

Listing 10.4

With the same handler bound to both events, we check for the event's type to determine whether to fade the details in or out. The code locating `<div>`, however, is the same for both events, so we can write it just once.

This example is admittedly a little contrived, since the shared code in this instance is so brief. In other cases, though, this technique can significantly reduce code complexity. If we had chosen to add a class on `mouseenter` and remove it on `mouseleave`, for example, rather than animate opacity, we could have taken care of it with a single statement inside the handler, as follows:

```
$(e.currentTarget)
  .find('.details')
  .toggleClass('entered', e.type == 'mouseenter');
```

In any case, our script is now working as intended, except that we haven't accounted for the additional photos that we load when the user clicks the **More Photos** link. As we noted in Chapter 3, *Handling Events*, event handlers are only attached to the elements that are there when we make the `.on()` call. Elements added later, such as from an Ajax call, won't have the behavior. We saw that two approaches to addressing this issue are to *rebind* event handlers after the new content is introduced, or to initially bind the handlers to a containing element and rely on event bubbling. The second approach, *event delegation*, is the one we'll pursue here.

Event delegation

Recall that to implement event delegation by hand, we check the `target` property of the `event` object to see if it matches the element that we want to trigger the behavior. The event target represents the innermost, or most deeply nested, element that is receiving the event. With our sample HTML this time, however, we're presented with a new challenge. The `<div class="photo">` elements are unlikely to be the event target, since they contain other elements, such as the image itself and the image details.

What we need is the `.closest()` method, which works its way up the DOM from parent to parent until it finds an element that matches a given selector expression. If no elements are found, it acts like any other DOM traversal method, returning a new empty jQuery object. We can use `.closest()` to find `<div class="photo">` from any element it contains, as follows:

```
$(() => {
  $('#gallery')
    .on('mouseover mouseout', (e) => {
      const $target = $(e.target)
        .closest('div.photo');
      const $related = $(e.relatedTarget)
        .closest('div.photo');
      const $details = $target
        .find('.details');

      if (e.type == 'mouseover' && $target.length) {
        $details.fadeTo('fast', 0.7);
      } else if (e == 'mouseout' && !$related.length) {
        $details.fadeOut('fast');
      }
    });
});
```

Listing 10.5

Note that we also needed to change the event types from `mouseenter` and `mouseleave` to `mouseover` and `mouseout`, because the former types are only triggered when the mouse first enters the gallery `<div>` and finally leaves it, we need the handlers to be fired whenever the mouse enters any of the photos *within* that wrapping `<div>`. But the latter types introduce yet another scenario, in that the detail `<div>` will fade in and out repeatedly unless we include an additional check for the `event` object's `relatedTarget` property. Even with the additional code, repeated quick mouse movements over and out of photos are handled unsatisfactorily, leaving an occasional detail `<div>` visible when it should have faded out.

Using jQuery's delegation capabilities

Event delegation can be frustratingly difficult to manage by hand when tasks become more complex. Fortunately, jQuery's .on() method has delegation built into it, which can make life easier for us. Using this capability, our code can return to the simplicity of *Listing 10.4*:

```
$(() => {
  $('#gallery')
    .on('mouseenter mouseleave', 'div.photo', (e) => {
      const $details = $(e.currentTarget).find('.details');

      if (e.type == 'mouseenter') {
        $details.fadeTo('fast', 0.7);
      } else {
        $details.fadeOut('fast');
      }
    });
});
```

Listing 10.6

The selector, #gallery, remains the same as in *Listing 10.5*, but the event types return to the mouseenter and mouseleave of *Listing 10.4*. When we pass in 'div.photo' as the second argument to .on(), jQuery maps e.currentTarget to the element(s) matched by that selector within '#gallery'.

Choosing a delegation scope

Because all of the photo elements we are dealing with are contained inside <div id="gallery">, we have used #gallery as our delegation scope in the previous example. However, any element that is an ancestor of all of the photos could be used as this scope. For example, we could bind our handler to document, which is the common ancestor of everything on the page:

```
$(() => {
  $(document)
    .on('mouseenter mouseleave', 'div.photo', (e) => {
      const $details = $(e.currentTarget).find('.details');

      if (e.type == 'mouseenter') {
        $details.fadeTo('fast', 0.7);
      } else {
        $details.fadeOut('fast');
      }
```

```
    });
  });
```

It can be convenient to attach event handlers directly to document when setting up event delegation. Since all page elements descend from document, we don't need to worry about picking the right container. However, this convenience comes at a potential performance cost.

In a DOM of deeply nested elements, relying on events to bubble all the way up a multitude of ancestor elements could be costly. Regardless of which elements we are actually observing (by passing in their selector as the second argument of .on()), if we bind our handler to document then an event happening anywhere on the page needs to be examined. In *Listing 10.6*, for example, whenever the mouse enters any element on the page, jQuery needs to check to see whether it is entering a <div class="photo"> element or not. This can grow costly on large pages, especially if delegation is used a lot. By being more specific in our delegation context, this work can be reduced.

Delegating early

Despite these efficiency concerns, there are reasons we may yet choose to use document as our delegation context. In general, we can only bind event handlers once the DOM elements they are attached to are loaded, which is why we typically place our code inside $(() => {}). However, the document element is available immediately, so we don't need to wait for the whole DOM to be ready before we bind to it. Even if the script is referenced in the <head> of the document, as it is in our example, we can call .on() right away, as follows:

```
(function($) {
  $(document)
    .on('mouseenter mouseleave', 'div.photo', (e) => {
      const $details = $(e.currentTarget).find('.details');

      if (e.type == 'mouseenter') {
        $details.fadeTo('fast', 0.7);
      } else {
        $details.fadeOut('fast');
      }
    });
}) (jQuery);
```

Because we're not waiting for the entire DOM to be ready, we can be assured that the `mouseenter` and `mouseleave` behaviors will apply to all `<div class="photo">` elements as soon as they are rendered on the page.

To see the benefit of this technique, consider a `click` handler directly bound to a link. Suppose this handler performs some actions, and also prevents the default action of the link (navigating to another page). If we were to wait until the whole document was ready, we would run the risk of the user clicking on that link before the handler was registered, thereby leaving the current page rather than getting the enhanced treatment provided by the script. In contrast, binding a delegated event handler to `document` gives us the benefit of binding the event early without the cost of having to scan through a complex DOM structure.

Defining custom events

The events that get triggered naturally by the DOM implementations of browsers are crucial to any interactive web application. However, we aren't limited to this set of events in our jQuery code. We can also add our own custom events. We saw this briefly in `Chapter 8`, *Developing Plugins*, when we saw how jQuery UI widgets trigger events, but here we will investigate how we can create and use custom events outside of plugin development.

Custom events must be triggered manually by our code. In a sense, they are like regular functions that we define, in that we can cause a block of code to be executed when we invoke it from another place in the script. The `.on()` call for a custom event behaves like a function definition, while the `.trigger()` call acts like a function invocation.

However, event handlers are decoupled from the code that triggers them. This means that we can trigger events at any time, without knowing in advance what will happen when we do. A regular function call causes a single piece of code to be executed. A custom event, however, could have no handlers, one handler, or many handlers bound to it. In any case, all of the bound handlers will be executed when the event is triggered.

To illustrate this, we can revise our Ajax loading feature to use a custom event. We will trigger a `nextPage` event whenever the user requests more photos, and bind handlers that watch for this event and perform the work previously done by the `.click()` handler:

```
$(() => {
  $('#more-photos')
    .click((e) => {
      e.preventDefault();
      $(e.target).trigger('nextPage');
    });
});
```

Listing 10.9

The `.click()` handler now does very little work itself. It triggers the custom event and also prevents the default link behavior by calling `.preventDefault()`. The heavy lifting is transferred to the new event handlers for the `nextPage` event, as follows:

```
(($) => {
  $(document)
    .on('nextPage', (e) => {
      $.get($(e.target).attr('href'))
        .then((data) => {
          $('#gallery')
            .append(data);
        })
        .catch(({ statusText }) => {
          $('#gallery')
            .append(`<strong>${statusText}</strong>`)
        });
    });

  var pageNum = 1;

  $(document)
    .on('nextPage', () => {
      if (pageNum > 19) {
        $('#more-photos').remove();
        return;
      }

      $('#more-photos')
        .attr('href', `pages/${++pageNum}.html`);
    });
})(jQuery);
```

Listing 10.10

Our code really hasn't changed much since *Listing 10.2*. The largest difference is that we've split what was once a single function into two. This is simply to illustrate that a single event trigger can cause multiple bound handlers to fire. Clicking on the **More Photos** link results in the next group of pictures being appended and the link's `href` attribute being updated, as shown in the following screenshot:

With the code changed in *Listing 10.10,* we are also illustrating another application of event bubbling. The `nextPage` handlers could be bound to the link that triggers the event, but we would need to wait to do this until the DOM was ready. Instead, we are binding the handlers to the document itself, which is available immediately, so we can do the binding outside of `$(() => {})`. This is, in fact, the same principle we took advantage of in *Listing 10.8,* when we moved the `.on()` method outside of `$(() => {})`. The event bubbles up and, so long as another handler doesn't stop the event propagation, our handlers will be fired.

Infinite scrolling

Just as multiple event handlers can react to the same triggered event, the same event can be triggered in multiple ways. We can demonstrate this by adding an infinite scrolling feature to our page. This technique lets the user's scroll bar manage the loading of content, fetching additional content whenever the user reaches the end of what has been loaded thus far.

We'll begin with a simple implementation, then improve it in successive examples. The basic idea is to observe the `scroll` event, measure the current scroll bar position when scrolling occurs, and load new content if needed. The following code will trigger the `nextPage` event we defined in *Listing 10.10*:

```
(($) => {
  const checkScrollPosition = () => {
    const distance = $(window).scrollTop() +
      $(window).height();

    if ($('#container').height() <= distance) {
      $(document).trigger('nextPage');
    }
  }

  $(() => {
    $(window)
      .scroll(checkScrollPosition)
      .trigger('scroll');
  });
}) (jQuery);
```

Listing 10.11

The `checkScrollPosition()` function we've introduced here is set as a handler for the window's `scroll` event. This function computes the distance from the top of the document to the bottom of the window and then compares this distance to the total height of the main container in the document. As soon as these reach equality, we need to fill the page with additional photos, so we trigger the `nextPage` event.

As soon as we bind the `scroll` handler, we immediately trigger it with a call to `.trigger('scroll')`. This kick-starts the process, so that if the page is not initially filled with photos, an Ajax request is made right away to append more photos:

Custom event parameters

When we define functions, we can set up any number of parameters to be filled with argument values when we actually call the function. Similarly, when triggering a custom event, we may want to pass along additional information to any registered event handlers. We can accomplish this by using custom event parameters.

The first parameter defined for any event handler, as we've seen, is the DOM event object, as enhanced and extended by jQuery. Any additional parameters we define are available for our discretionary use.

To see this in action, we'll add a new option to the `nextPage` event from *Listing 10.10*, allowing us to scroll the page down to display the newly-added content:

```
(($) => {
```

```
$(document)
  .on('nextPage', (e, scrollToVisible) => {
    if (pageNum > 19) {
      $('#more-photos').remove();
      return;
    }

    $.get($('#more-photos').attr('href'))
      .then((data) => {
        const $data = $('#gallery')
          .append(data);

        if (scrollToVisible) {
          $(window)
            .scrollTop($data.offset().top);
        }

        checkScrollPosition();
      })
      .catch(({ statusText }) => {
        $('#gallery')
          .append(`<strong>${statusText}</strong>`)
      });
  });
}) (jQuery);
```

Listing 10.12

We have now added a `scrollToVisible` parameter to the event callback. The value of this parameter determines whether we perform the new functionality, which entails measuring the position of the new content and scrolling to it. Measurement is easy using the `.offset()` method, which returns the top and left coordinates of the new content. To move down the page, we call the `.scrollTop()` method.

Now, we need to pass an argument into the new parameter. All that is required is providing an extra value when invoking the event using `.trigger()`. When `newPage` is triggered via scrolling, we don't want the new behavior to occur, as the user is already manipulating the scroll position directly. When the **More Photos** link is clicked, on the other hand, we want the newly added photos to be displayed on screen, so we will pass a value of `true` to the handler:

```
$(() => {
  $('#more-photos')
    .click((e) => {
      e.preventDefault();
      $(e.target).trigger('nextPage', [true]);
```

```
        });
    });
```

Listing 10.13

In the call to `.trigger()`, we are now providing an array of values to pass to event handlers. In this case, the value of `true` will be given to the `scrollToVisible` parameter of the event handler in *Listing 10.12*.

Note that custom event parameters are optional on both sides of the transaction. We have two calls to `.trigger('nextPage')` in our code, only one of which provides argument values; when the other is called, this does not result in an error, but rather each parameter in the handler has the value `undefined`. Similarly, the lack of a `scrollToVisible` parameter in one of our `.on('nextPage')` calls is not an error; if a parameter does not exist when an argument is passed, that argument is simply ignored.

Throttling events

A major issue with the infinite scrolling feature as we've implemented it in *Listing 10.10* is its performance impact. While our code is brief, the `checkScrollPosition()` function does need to do some work to measure the dimensions of the page and window. This effort can accumulate rapidly, because in some browsers the `scroll` event is triggered repeatedly during the scrolling of the window. The result of this combination could be choppy or sluggish performance.

Several native events have the potential for frequent triggering. Common culprits include `scroll`, `resize`, and `mousemove`. To account for this, we will implement **event throttling**. This technique involves limiting our expensive calculations so that they only occur after some of the event occurrences, rather than each one. We can update our code from *Listing 10.13* to implement this technique as follows:

```
$(() => {
  var timer = 0;

  $(window)
    .scroll(() => {
      if (!timer) {
        timer = setTimeout(() => {
          checkScrollPosition();
          timer = 0;
        }, 250);
      }
    })
```

```
      .trigger('scroll');
});
```

Listing 10.14

Rather than setting checkScrollPosition() directly as the scroll event handler, we are using the JavaScript setTimeout function to defer the call by 250 milliseconds. More importantly, we are checking for a running timer first before doing any work. Since checking the value of a simple variable is extremely fast, most of the calls to our event handler will return almost immediately. The checkScrollPosition() call will only happen when a timer completes, which will at most be every 250 milliseconds.

We can easily adjust the setTimeout() value to a comfortable number that strikes a reasonable compromise between instant feedback and low performance impact. Our script is now a good web citizen.

Other ways to perform throttling

The throttling technique we've implemented is efficient and simple, but it is not the only solution. Depending on the performance characteristics of the action being throttled and typical interaction with the page, we may, for instance, want to institute a single timer for the page rather than create one when an event begins:

```
$(() => {
  var scrolled = false;

  $(window)
    .scroll(() => {
      scrolled = true;
    });

  setInterval(() => {
    if (scrolled) {
      checkScrollPosition();
      scrolled = false;
    }
  }, 250);

  checkScrollPosition();
});
```

Listing 10.15

Unlike our previous throttling code, this polling solution uses a single call to the JavaScript `setInterval()` function to begin checking the state of the `scrolled` variable every `250` milliseconds. Any time a scroll event occurs, `scrolled` is set to `true`, ensuring that the next time the interval passes, `checkScrollPosition()` will be called. The result is similar to that of *Listing 10.14*.

A third solution for limiting the amount of processing performed during frequently-repeated events is **debouncing**. This technique, named after the post-processing required to handle repeated signals sent by electrical switches, ensures that only a single, final event is acted upon even when many have occurred. We will see an example of this technique in `Chapter 13`, *Advanced Ajax*.

Extending events

Some events, such as `mouseenter` and `ready`, are designated as **special events** by the jQuery internals. These events use the elaborate event extension framework offered by jQuery. Such events get the opportunity to take action at various times in the life cycle of an event handler. They may react to handlers being bound or unbound, and they can even have preventable default behaviors like clicked links or submitted forms do. The event extension API lets us create sophisticated new events that act much like native DOM events.

The throttling behavior we implemented for scrolling in *Listing 10.13* is useful, and we may want to generalize it for use in other projects. We can accomplish this by creating a new event that encapsulates the throttling technique within the special event hooks.

To implement special behavior for an event, we add a property to the `$ .event.special` object. This added property, which is itself an object, has our event name as its key. It can contain callbacks called at many different specific times in an event's life cycle, including the following:

- `add`: This is called every time a handler for this event is bound
- `remove`: This is called every time a handler for the event is unbound
- `setup`: This is called when a handler is bound for the event, but only if no other handlers for that event are bound to the element
- `teardown`: This is the converse of `setup`, called when the last handler for the event is unbound from an element
- `_default`: This becomes the default behavior of the event, called unless the default action is prevented by an event handler

These callbacks can be used in some very creative ways. A fairly common scenario, which we'll explore in our example code, is to automatically trigger the event in response to a browser condition. It would be wasteful to monitor the state and trigger events if no handlers are listening for the event, so we can use the `setup` callback to initiate this work only when needed:

```
(($) => {
  $.event.special.throttledScroll = {
    setup(data) {
      var timer = 0;
      $(this).on('scroll.throttledScroll', () => {
        if (!timer) {
          timer = setTimeout(() => {
            $(this).triggerHandler('throttledScroll');
            timer = 0;
          }, 250);
        }
      });
    },
    teardown() {
      $(this).off('scroll.throttledScroll');
    }
  };
}) (jQuery);
```

Listing 10.16

For our scroll throttling event, we need to bind a regular `scroll` handler that uses the same `setTimeout` technique as the one we developed in *Listing 10.14*. Whenever a timer completes, the custom event will be triggered. Since we only need one timer per element, the `setup` callback will serve our needs. By supplying a custom namespace for the `scroll` handler, we can easily remove the handler when `teardown` is called.

To use this new behavior, all we have to do is bind handlers to the `throttledScroll` event. This greatly simplifies the event binding code, and gives us a nicely reusable throttling mechanism, as follows:

```
(($) => {
  $.event.special.throttledScroll = {
    setup(data) {
      var timer = 0;
      $(this)
        .on('scroll.throttledScroll', () => {
          if (!timer) {
            timer = setTimeout(() => {
              $(this).triggerHandler('throttledScroll');
```

```
              timer = 0;
          }, 250);
        }
      });
    },
    teardown() {
      $(this).off('scroll.throttledScroll');
    }
};

$(document)
    .on('mouseenter mouseleave', 'div.photo', (e) => {
      const $details = $(e.currentTarget).find('.details');

      if (e.type == 'mouseenter') {
        $details.fadeTo('fast', 0.7);
      } else {
        $details.fadeOut('fast');
      }
    });

var pageNum = 1;

$(document)
    .on('nextPage', (e, scrollToVisible) => {
      if (pageNum > 19) {
        $('#more-photos').remove();
        return;
      }

      $.get($('#more-photos').attr('href'))
        .then((data) => {
          const $data = $(data)
            .appendTo('#gallery');

          if (scrollToVisible) {
            $(window)
              .scrollTop($data.offset().top);
          }

          checkScrollPosition();
        })
      .catch(({ statusText }) => {
        $('#gallery')
          .append(`<strong>${statusText}</strong>`)
      });
    });
```

```
$(document)
  .on('nextPage', () => {
    if (pageNum < 20) {
      $('#more-photos')
        .attr('href', `pages/${++pageNum}.html`);
    }
  });

const checkScrollPosition = () => {
  const distance = $(window).scrollTop()
    + $(window).height();

  if ($('#container').height() <= distance) {
    $(document).trigger('nextPage');
  }
};

$(() => {
  $('#more-photos')
    .click((e) => {
      e.preventDefault();
      $(e.target).trigger('nextPage', [true]);
    });

  $(window)
    .on('throttledScroll', checkScrollPosition)
    .trigger('throttledScroll');
});
}) (jQuery);
```

Listing 10.17

More about special events

While this chapter covers advanced techniques for dealing with events, the event extension API is very advanced indeed, and a detailed investigation is beyond the scope of this book. The previous `throttledScroll` example covers the simplest and most common usage of the facility. Other possible applications include the following:

- Modifying the event object, so that event handlers have different information available to them
- Causing events that occur in one place in the DOM to trigger behaviors associated with different elements

- Reacting to new and browser-specific events that are not standard DOM events and allowing jQuery code to react to them as if they are standard
- Changing the way event bubbling and delegation are handled

Many of these tasks can be quite complicated. For an in-depth take on the possibilities offered by the event extension API, we can investigate the jQuery Learning Center's documentation at `http://learn.jquery.com/events/event-extensions/`.

Summary

The jQuery event system can be very powerful if we choose to leverage it fully. In this chapter, we have seen several aspects of the system, including event delegation methods, custom events, and the event extension API. We have also found ways of sidestepping pitfalls associated with delegation and with events that are triggered frequently.

Further reading

A complete list of event methods is available in `Appendix B`, *Quick Reference*, of this book, or in the official *jQuery documentation* at `http://api.jquery.com/`.

Exercises

The following challenge exercise may require the use of the official jQuery documentation at `http://api.jquery.com/`.

1. When the user clicks on a photo, add or remove the `selected` class on the photo `<div>`. Make sure this behavior works even for photos added later using the **Next Page** link.
2. Add a new custom event called `pageLoaded` that fires when a new set of images has been added to the page.
3. Using the `nextPage` and `pageLoaded` handlers, show a **Loading** message at the bottom of the page only while a new page is being loaded.
4. Bind a `mousemove` handler to photos that logs the current mouse position (using `console.log()`).

5. Revise this handler to perform the logging no more than five times a second.

6. **Challenge:** Create a new special event named `tripleclick` that fires when the mouse button is clicked on three times within 500 milliseconds. To test the event, bind a `tripleclick` handler to the `<h1>` element which hides and reveals the contents of `<div id="gallery">`.

11
Advanced Effects

Since learning about jQuery's animation capabilities, we have found many uses for them. We can hide and reveal objects on the page with ease, we can gracefully resize elements, and we can smoothly reposition elements. This effects library is versatile, and contains even more techniques and specialized abilities than we have seen so far.

In Chapter 4, *Styling and Animating*, you learned about jQuery's basic animation capabilities. In this more advanced chapter, we will cover:

- Ways to gather information about the state of animations
- Methods for interrupting active animations
- Global effect options that can affect all animations on the page at once
- Deferred objects, which allow us to act once animations have completed
- Easing, which alters the rate at which animations occur

Animation revisited

To refresh our memory about jQuery's effect methods, we'll set up a baseline from which to build in this chapter, starting with a simple hover animation. Using a document with photo thumbnails on it, we'll make each photo *grow* slightly when the user's mouse is over it, and shrink back to its original size when the mouse leaves. The HTML tags we'll use also contain some textual information that's hidden for now, which we'll use later in the chapter:

```
<div class="team">
  <div class="member">
    <img class="avatar" src="photos/rey.jpg" alt="" />
    <div class="name">Rey Bango</div>
    <div class="location">Florida</div>
    <p class="bio">Rey Bango is a consultant living in South Florida,
    specializing in web application development...</p>
  </div>
  <div class="member">
    <img class="avatar" src="photos/scott.jpg" alt="" />
    <div class="name">Scott González</div>
    <div class="location">North Carolina</div>
    <div class="position">jQuery UI Development Lead</div>
    <p class="bio">Scott is a web developer living in Raleigh, NC...
</p>
  </div>
  <!-- Code continues ... -->
</div>
```

Getting the example code

You can access the example code from the following GitHub repository: `ht tps://github.com/PacktPublishing/Learning-jQuery-3.`

The text associated with each image is initially hidden by the CSS by moving each `<div>` to the left of its `overflow: hidden` container:

```
.member {
  position: relative;
  overflow: hidden;
}

.member div {
  position: absolute;
  left: -300px;
  width: 250px;
}
```

The HTML and CSS together produce a vertically arranged list of images:

Executive Board

The Executive Board is responsible for the day-to-day operations of the jQuery project, and has powers delegated to it by our governance plan or a regular vote of the voting membership. The Executive Board is made up of seven members of the voting membership, elected twice annually by the voting membership, in October and April.

To alter the size of the image, we will increase its height and width from 75 pixels to 85 pixels. At the same time, to keep the image centered, we will decrease its padding from 5 pixels to 0 pixels:

```
$(() => {
  $('div.member')
    .on('mouseenter mouseleave', ({ type, target }) => {
      const width = height = type == 'mouseenter' ?
        85 : 75;
      const paddingTop = paddingLeft = type == 'mouseenter' ?
        0 : 5;

      $(target)
        .find('img')
        .animate({
          width,
          height,
          paddingTop,
          paddingLeft
```

```
            });
        });
    });
```

Listing 11.1

Here we repeat a pattern we saw in `Chapter 10`, *Advanced Events*, because much of the work we are performing when the mouse enters the region, is the same as when it leaves; we are combining the handlers for `mouseenter` and `mouseleave` into one function rather than calling `.hover()` with two separate callbacks. Inside this handler, we determine the values of `size` and `padding` based on which of the two events is being triggered, and pass these property values on to the `.animate()` method.

> **TIP** When you see the object literal notation surrounding function arguments (`{{ type, target }}`), it's called **object destructuring**. This is simply a convenient way to get the exact properties we need out of the event object, leading to more concise code in the function itself.

Now when the mouse cursor is over an image, it is slightly larger than the rest:

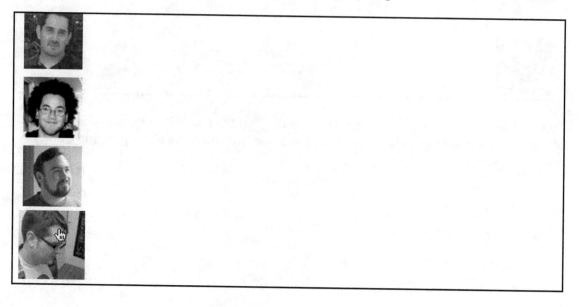

Observing and interrupting animations

Our basic animation already reveals a problem. As long as there is enough time for the animation to complete after each `mouseenter` or `mouseleave` event, the animations proceed as intended. When the mouse cursor moves rapidly and the events are triggered quickly, however, we see that the images also grow and shrink repeatedly, well after the last event is triggered. This occurs because, as discussed in `Chapter 4`, *Styling and Animating*, animations on a given element are added to a queue and called in order. The first animation is called immediately, completes in the allotted time, and then is removed from the queue, at which point the next animation becomes first in line, is called, completes, is shifted, and so on until the queue is empty.

There are many cases in which this animation queue, known within jQuery as `fx`, causes desirable behavior. In the case of hover actions such as ours, though, it needs to be circumvented.

Determining the animation state

One way to avoid the undesirable queuing of animations is to use jQuery's custom `:animated` selector. Inside the `mouseenter`/`mouseleave` event handler, we can use the selector to check the image and see if it is currently being animated:

```
$(() => {
  $('div.member')
    .on('mouseenter mouseleave', ({ type, target }) => {
      const width = height = type == 'mouseenter' ?
        85 : 75;
      const paddingTop = paddingLeft = type == 'mouseenter' ?
        0 : 5;

      $(target)
        .find('img')
        .not(':animated')
        .animate({
          width,
          height,
          paddingTop,
          paddingLeft
        });
    });
});
```

Listing 11.2

When the user's mouse enters the member `<div>`, the image will only animate if it isn't already being animated. When the mouse leaves, the animation will occur regardless of its state, because we always want it to ultimately restore the image to its original dimensions and padding.

We've successfully avoided the runaway animations that occur in *Listing 11.1*, but the animations still need improvement. When the mouse quickly enters and leaves the `<div>` tag, the image still has to complete the entire `mouseenter` animation (growing) before it starts the `mouseleave` animation (shrinking). This is not ideal, for sure, but the test of the `:animated` pseudo-class has introduced an even greater problem: if the mouse enters the `<div>` tag while the image is *shrinking*, the image will fail to grow again. Only a subsequent `mouseleave` and `mouseenter` animation after the animation has stopped will execute another animation. While using the `:animated` selector can be useful in some situations, here it doesn't help enough.

Halting a running animation

Fortunately, jQuery has a method to help us with both of the problems evident in *Listing 11.2*. The `.stop()` method can halt an animation in its tracks. To use it, we can return the code to the way it was in *Listing 11.1* and simply insert `.stop()` between `.find()` and `.animate()`:

```
$(() => {
  $('div.member')
    .on('mouseenter mouseleave', ({ type, currentTarget }) => {
      const width = height = type == 'mouseenter' ?
        85 : 75;
      const paddingTop = paddingLeft = type == 'mouseenter' ?
        0 : 5;

      $(currentTarget)
        .find('img')
        .stop()
        .animate({
          width,
          height,
          paddingTop,
          paddingLeft
        });
    });
});
```

Listing 11.3

It's worth noting that we stop the current animation *before* proceeding with the new one. Now when the mouse enters and leaves repeatedly, the undesirable effect of our previous attempts is gone. The current animation always completes immediately, so there is never more than one in the `fx` queue. When the mouse finally rests, the final animation completes, so the image is either fully grown (`mouseenter`) or restored to its original dimensions (`mouseleave`) depending on the last triggered event.

Caution when halting animations

Because the `.stop()` method, by default, halts animations at their current position, it can lead to surprising results when used with shorthand animation methods. Before animating, these shorthand methods determine the final value and then animate to that value. For example, if `.slideDown()` is halted with `.stop()` midway through its animation and then `.slideUp()` is called, the next time `.slideDown()` is called on the element, it will only slide down to the height at which it stopped the previous time. To mitigate this type of problem, the `.stop()` method can accept two Boolean (`true`/`false`) arguments, the second of which is known as `goToEnd`. If we set this argument to `true`, the current animation not only stops, but also jumps immediately to the final value. Still, the `goToEnd` feature can make the animation look *jerky*, so a better solution might be to store the final value in a variable and animate to it explicitly using `.animate()` rather than rely on jQuery to determine that value.

Another jQuery method, `.finish()`, is available for halting animations. It's similar to `.stop(true, true)` in that it clears all queued animations and jumps the current animation to the final value. However, unlike `.stop(true, true)`, it jumps all the *queued* animations to their final values as well.

Using global effect properties

The effects module in jQuery includes a handy `$.fx` object that we can access when we want to change the characteristics of our animations across the board. Although some of this object's properties are undocumented and intended to use solely within the library itself, others are provided as tools for globally altering the way our animations run. In the following examples, we'll take a look at a few of the documented properties.

Disabling all effects

We have already discussed a way to halt animations that are currently running, but what if we need to disable all animations entirely? We may, for example, wish to provide animations by default, but disable those animations for low-resource devices where animations could look choppy, or for users who find animations distracting. To do so, we can simply set the $.fx.off property to true. For our demonstration, we will display a previously hidden button to allow the user to toggle animations on and off:

```
$(() => {
  $('#fx-toggle')
    .show()
    .on('click', () => {
      $.fx.off = !$.fx.off;
    });
});
```

Listing 11.4

The hidden button is displayed between the introductory paragraph and the subsequent images:

Executive Board

The Executive Board is responsible for the day-to-day operations of the jQuery project, and has powers delegated to it by our governance plan or a regular vote of the voting membership. The Executive Board is made up of seven members of the voting membership, elected twice annually by the voting membership, in October and April.

[Toggle Animations]

When the user clicks on the button to toggle animations off, subsequent animations such as our growing and shrinking images will occur instantaneously (with a duration of 0 milliseconds), and any callback functions will be called immediately thereafter.

Defining effect durations

Another property of the `$.fx` object is `speeds`. This property is an object itself, consisting of three properties, as evidenced by the jQuery core file:

```
speeds: {
  slow: 600,
  fast: 200,
  // Default speed
  _default: 400
}
```

You've already learned that all of jQuery's animation methods provide an optional speed, or duration, argument. Looking at the `$.fx.speeds` object, we see that the strings `slow` and `fast` map up to 600 milliseconds and 200 milliseconds respectively. Each time an animation method is called, jQuery goes through the following steps to determine the duration of the effect, in this order:

1. It checks if `$.fx.off` is `true`. If so, it sets the duration to `0`.
2. It checks if the duration passed is a number. If so, it sets the duration to that number of milliseconds.
3. It checks if the duration pass matches one of the property keys of the `$.fx.speeds` object. If so, it sets the duration to the value of the property.
4. If the duration is not set by any of the above checks, it sets the duration to the value of `$.fx.speeds._default`.

Given this information, we now know that passing any string duration other than `slow` or `fast` will result in a duration of 400 milliseconds. We can also see that adding our own custom speed is as easy as adding another property to `$.fx.speeds`. If we write `$.fx.speeds.crawl = 1200`, for example, we can use `'crawl'` for any animation method's speed argument to run the animation for 1200 milliseconds, like so:

```
$(someElement).animate({width: '300px'}, 'crawl');
```

Although typing `'crawl'` is no easier than typing `1200`, custom speeds can come in handy in larger projects when a number of animations that share a certain speed need to change. In such cases, we could just change the value of `$.fx.speeds.crawl` rather than searching throughout the project for `1200` and replacing each one only if it represents an animation speed.

While custom speeds can be useful, perhaps even more useful is the ability to change the default speed. We can do this by setting the _default property:

```
$.fx.speeds._default = 250;
```

Listing 11.5

Now that we have defined a new faster default speed, any new animations we add will use it unless we override their durations. To see this at work, we will introduce another interactive element to the page. When the user clicks on one of the portraits, we want to display the details associated with that person. We will create the illusion of the details *unfolding* from the portrait by moving them out from under the portrait into their final positions:

```
$(() => {
  const showDetails = ({ currentTarget }) => {
    $(currentTarget)
      .find('div')
      .css({
        display: 'block',
        left: '-300px',
        top: 0
      })
      .each((i, element) => {
        $(element)
          .animate({
            left: 0,
            top: 25 * i
          });
      });
  };
  $('div.member').click(showDetails);
});
```

Listing 11.6

When a member is clicked, we use the showDetails() function as a handler. This function first sets the detail <div> elements in their starting positions, underneath the member's portrait. Then it animates each of the elements into its final position. By calling .each(), we can calculate a separate final top position for each element.

After the animation, the detail text is visible:

Since the `.animate()` method calls are made on different elements, they happen simultaneously rather than being queued. And, since the calls do not specify a duration, they all use the new default duration of 250 milliseconds.

When another member is clicked, we want to hide the previously displayed one. We can easily track which details are currently on the screen with the use of a class:

```js
const showDetails = ({ currentTarget }) => {
  $(currentTarget)
    .siblings('.active')
    .removeClass('active')
    .children('div')
    .fadeOut()
    .end()
    .end()
    .addClass('active')
    .find('div')
    .css({
      display: 'block',
      left: '-300px',
      top: 0
    })
    .each((i, element) => {
      $(element)
        .animate({
          left: 0,
          top: 25 * i
        });
    });
};
```

Listing 11.7

Ouch! Ten functions chained together? Well hang on a second, this might actually be better than splitting them apart. For one thing, chaining calls together like this means that there's no need for temporary variables to hold intermediary DOM values. Instead, we can just read one line after another to figure out what's happening. Let's walk through these now:

- `.siblings('.active')`: This finds the active `<div>` siblings
- `.removeClass('active')`: This removes the `.active` class
- `.children('div')`: This finds the child `<div>` elements
- `.fadeOut()`: This removes them
- `.end()`: This clears out the `.children('div')` query
- `.end()`: This clears out the `.siblings('.active')` query
- `.addClass('active')`: This adds the `.active` class to the event target, the container `<div>`
- `.find('div')`: This finds all child `<div>` elements to display
- `.css()`: This sets relevant display CSS
- `.each()`: This adds animations to the `top` and `left` CSS properties

Note that our `.fadeOut()` call also uses the faster 250 millisecond duration we've defined. The defaults apply to jQuery's pre-packaged effects just as they do to custom `.animate()` calls.

Multi-property easing

The `showDetails()` function almost accomplishes the unfolding effect we set out to achieve, but because the `top` and `left` properties are animating at the same rate, it looks more like a sliding effect. We can subtly alter the effect by changing the easing equation to `easeInQuart` for the `top` property only, causing the element to follow a curved path rather than a straight one. Remember, however, that using any easing other than `swing` or `linear` requires a plugin, such as the effects core of jQuery UI (`http://jqueryui.com/`).

```
.each((i, element) => {
  $(element)
    .animate({
      left: 0,
      top: 25 * i
    }, {
      duration: 'slow',
      specialEasing: {
        top: 'easeInQuart'
```

```
        }
    });
});
```

Listing 11.8

The `specialEasing` option allows us to set a different acceleration curve for each property that is being animated. Any properties that aren't included in the option will use the `easing` option's equation if it is provided, or the default `swing` equation if not.

We now have an attractive animation presenting most of the details associated with a team member. We aren't yet displaying a member's biography, however. Before we do this, we need to take a small digression to talk about jQuery's deferred object mechanism.

Using deferred objects

At times, we come across situations in which we want to act when a process completes, but we don't necessarily know how long the process will take, or even if it will be successful. To handle these cases, jQuery offers us **deferred objects** (promises). A deferred object encapsulates an operation that takes some time to complete.

A new deferred object can be created at any time by calling the `$.Deferred()` constructor. Once we have such an object, we can perform long-running operations and then call the `.resolve()` or `.reject()` methods on the object to indicate whether the operation was successful or unsuccessful. It is somewhat unusual to do this manually, however. Typically, rather than creating our own deferred objects by hand, jQuery or its plugins will create the object and take care of resolving or rejecting it. We just need to learn how to use the object that is created.

 Rather than detailing how the `$.Deferred()` constructor operates, we will focus here on how jQuery effects take advantage of deferred objects. In `Chapter 13`, *Advanced Ajax*, we will further explore deferred objects in the context of Ajax requests.

Every deferred object makes a promise to provide data to other code. This promise is represented as another object with its own set of methods. From any deferred object, we can obtain its promise object by calling its `.promise()` method. Then, we can call methods of the promise to attach handlers that are executed when the promise is fulfilled:

- The `.then()` method attaches a handler that is called when the deferred object is resolved successfully
- The `.catch()` method attaches a handler that is called when the deferred object is rejected
- The `.always()` method attaches a handler that is called when the deferred object completes its task, either by being resolved or by being rejected

These handlers are much like the callbacks we provide to `.on()`, in that they are the functions called when some event happens. We can also attach multiple handlers to the same promise and all will be called at the appropriate time. There are a few important differences, however. Promise handlers will only ever be called once; the deferred object cannot resolve a second time. A promise handler will also be called immediately if the deferred object is already resolved at the time we attach the handler.

In `Chapter 6`, *Sending Data with Ajax*, we saw a very simple example of how jQuery's Ajax system uses deferred objects. Now we will put this powerful tool to use once again by investigating the deferred objects that jQuery's animation system creates.

Animation promises

Every jQuery collection has a set of deferred objects associated with it tracking the status of queued operations on the elements in the collection. By calling the `.promise()` method on the jQuery object, we get a promise object that is resolved when a queue completes. In particular, we can use this promise to take action upon the completion of all of the animations running on any of the matched elements.

Just as we have a `showDetails()` function to display the member name and location information, we can write a `showBio()` function for bringing the biographical information into view. But first, we'll append a new `<div>` tag to the `<body>` tag and set up two options objects:

```
$(() => {
  const $movable = $('<div/>')
    .attr('id', 'movable')
    .appendTo('body');
```

```
const bioBaseStyles = {
  display: 'none',
  height: '5px',
  width: '25px'
}

const bioEffects = {
  duration: 800,
  easing: 'easeOutQuart',
  specialEasing: {
    opacity: 'linear'
  }
};
});
```

Listing 11.9

This new `movable` `<div>` element is the one that we will actually animate after injecting it with a copy of a biography. Having a wrapper element like this is particularly useful when animating an element's width and height. We can set its `overflow` property to `hidden` and set an explicit width and height for the biographies within it to avoid the continual reflowing of text that would have occurred if we had instead animated the biography `<div>` elements themselves.

We'll use the `showBio()` function to determine what the movable `<div>`'s starting and ending styles should be based on the member image that is clicked. Note that we're using the `$.extend()` method to merge the set of base styles that remain constant with the `top` and `left` properties that vary depending on the member's position. Then, it's just a matter of using `.css()` to set the starting styles and `.animate()` for the ending styles:

```
const showBio = (target) => {
  const $member = $(target).parent();
  const $bio = $member.find('p.bio');
  const startStyles = $.extend(
    {},
    bioBaseStyles,
    $member.offset()
  );
  const endStyles = {
    width: $bio.width(),
    top: $member.offset().top + 5,
    left: $member.width() + $member.offset().left - 5,
    opacity: 'show'
  };

  $movable
```

```
    .html($bio.clone())
    .css(startStyles)
    .animate(endStyles, bioEffects)
    .animate(
      { height: $bio.height() },
      { easing: 'easeOutQuart' }
    );
};
```

Listing 11.10

We're queuing two `.animate()` methods so that the biography first flies from the left as it grows wider and fully opaque, and then slides down to its full height once it is in position.

In Chapter 4, *Styling and Animating*, we saw that callback functions in jQuery's animation methods are called when the animation completes for each element in the collection. We want to show the member's biography after the other <div> elements appear. Before jQuery introduced the `.promise()` method, this would have been an onerous task, requiring us to count down from the total number of elements each time the callback was executed until the last time, at which point we could execute the code to animate the biography.

Now we can simply chain the `.promise()` and `.then()` methods to the `.each()` method inside our `showDetails()` function:

```
const showDetails = ({ currentTarget }) => {
  $(currentTarget)
    .siblings('.active')
    .removeClass('active')
    .children('div')
    .fadeOut()
    .end()
    .end()
    .addClass('active')
    .find('div')
    .css({
      display: 'block',
      left: '-300px',
      top: 0
    })
    .each((i, element) => {
      $(element)
        .animate({
          left: 0,
          top: 25 * i
        }, {
```

```
        duration: 'slow',
        specialEasing: {
          top: 'easeInQuart'
        }
      });
    })
    .promise()
    .then(showBio);
};
```

Listing 11.11

The `.then()` method takes a reference to our `showBio()` function as its argument. Now a click on an image brings all of that member's information into view with an attractive animation sequence:

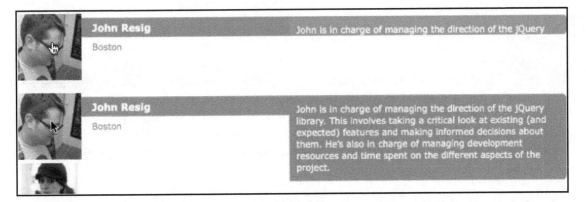

Since jQuery 3.0, the promises returned by the `promise()` method are fully compatible with native ES 2015 promises. This means that where possible, we should use the same API. For example, use `then()` instead of `done()`. They do the same thing, and your asynchronous code will be consistent with other asynchronous code.

Taking fine-grained control of animations

Even though we've looked at a number of advanced features, jQuery's effects module has much more to explore. A rewrite of this module for jQuery 1.8 introduced a number of ways for advanced developers to fine-tune various effects and even change the underlying engine that drives the animations. For example, in addition to offering options such as `duration` and `easing`, the `.animate()` method provides a couple of callback options that let us inspect and modify an animation each step of the way:

```
$('#mydiv').animate({
  height: '200px',
  width: '400px'
}, {
  step(now, tween) {
    // monitor height and width
    // adjust tween properties
  },
  progress(animation, progress, remainingMs) {}
});
```

The `step()` function, which is called roughly once every 13 milliseconds for each animated property during the animation, allows us to adjust properties of the `tween` object such as the end value, the type of easing, or the actual property being animated based on the current value of a property via the passed `now` argument. A complex demonstration might, for example, use the `step()` function to detect a collision between two moving elements and adjust their trajectories on impact.

The `progress()` function is similarly called multiple times throughout the lifecycle of an animation:

- It differs from `step()` in that it is called only once per element at each step, regardless of how many properties are being animated
- It makes available different aspects of the animation, including the animation's promise object, the progress, which is a number between 0 and 1, and the number of milliseconds remaining in the animation

All of jQuery's animations use a JavaScript timer function called `setTimeout()` to repeatedly call functions--every 13 milliseconds by default--and change the style properties during each tick. Some modern browsers, however, provide a new `requestAnimationFrame()` function that has advantages over `setTimeout()`, including increased precision (and therefore perceived smoothness of animations) and improved battery consumption for mobile devices.

At the lowest level of jQuery's animation system lie its $.Animation() and $.Tween() functions. These functions and their corresponding objects can be used to tweak every possible aspect of an animation. For example, we can use $.Animation to create an animation **prefilter**. One such prefilter could take a

particular

action at the end of an animation based on the existence of a property passed to the .animate() method's options object:

```
$.Animation.prefilter(function(element, properties, options) {
  if (options.removeAfter) {
    this.done(function () {
      $(element).remove();
    });
  }
});
```

With this code in place, calling $('#my-div').fadeOut({ removeAfter: true }) would automatically remove <div> from the DOM after it has finished fading out.

Summary

In this chapter, we have further investigated several techniques that can assist us in crafting beautiful animations that are helpful to our users. We can now individually control the acceleration and deceleration of each property we are animating, and halt these animations individually or globally if needed. We learned about the properties that jQuery's effects library defines internally, and how to change some of them to suit our needs. We made our first foray into the jQuery deferred object system, which we will explore further in Chapter 13, *Advanced Ajax*, and we got a taste of the many opportunities to fine-tune jQuery's animation system.

Further reading

A complete list of effect and animation methods is available in *Appendix B* of this book, or in the official jQuery documentation at http://api.jquery.com/.

Exercises

The challenge exercises may require the use of the official jQuery documentation at
`http://api.jquery.com/`.

1. Define a new animation speed constant called `zippy` and apply this to the biography display effect.
2. Change the easing of the horizontal movement of member details so that they bounce into place.
3. Add a second deferred callback function to the promise that adds a `highlight` class to the current member's location `<div>`.
4. **Challenge**: Add a delay of two seconds before animating the biography. Use the jQuery `.delay()` method.
5. **Challenge:** When the active photo is clicked, collapse the bio details. Stop any running animation before doing so.

12
Advanced DOM Manipulation

Throughout this book, we have used jQuery's powerful DOM manipulation methods to alter the content of the document. We have now seen several ways in which we can insert new content, move existing content around, or remove content altogether. We also know how to alter the attributes and properties of elements to suit our needs.

In `Chapter 5`, *Manipulating the DOM*, we were introduced to these important techniques. In this more advanced chapter, we will cover:

- Sorting page elements using `.append()`
- Attaching custom data to elements
- Reading HTML5 data attributes
- Creating elements from JSON data
- Extending the DOM manipulation system using CSS hooks

Sorting table rows

The majority of the topics we're investigating in this chapter can be demonstrated through sorting the rows of a table. This common task is a useful way to assist users in quickly finding the information they need. There are, naturally, a number of ways to do this.

Sorting tables on the server

A common solution for data sorting is to perform it on the server. Data in tables often comes from a database, which means that the code that pulls it out of the database can request it in a given sort order (using, for example, the SQL language's ORDER BY clause). If we have server-side code at our disposal, it is straightforward to begin with a reasonable default sort order.

Sorting is most useful, though, when the user can determine the sort order. A common user interface for this is to make the table headers (<th>) of sortable columns into links. These links can go to the current page, but with a query string appended indicating the column to sort by, as shown in the following code snippet:

```
<table id="my-data">
  <thead>
    <tr>
      <th class="name">
        <a href="index.php?sort=name">Name</a>
      </th>
      <th class="date">
        <a href="index.php?sort=date">Date</a>
      </th>
    </tr>
  </thead>
  <tbody>
    ...
  </tbody>
</table>
```

The server can react to the query string parameter by returning the database contents in a different order.

Sorting tables using Ajax

This setup is simple, but requires a page refresh for each sort operation. As we have seen, jQuery allows us to eliminate such page refreshes by using *Ajax* methods. If we have the column headers set up as links as before, we can add jQuery code that will translate those links into Ajax requests:

```
$(() => {
  $('#my-data th a')
    .click((e) => {
      e.preventDefault();
      $('#my-data tbody')
        .load($(e.target).attr('href'));
    });
});
```

Now when the anchors are clicked, jQuery sends an Ajax request to the server for the same page. When jQuery is used to make a page request using Ajax, it sets the X-Requested-With HTTP header to XMLHttpRequest so that the server can determine that an Ajax request is being made. The server code can be written to send back only the content of the <tbody> element itself, and not the surrounding page, when this parameter is present. This way we can use the response to replace the content of the existing <tbody> element.

This is an example of **progressive enhancement**. The page works perfectly well without any JavaScript at all, as the links for server-side sorting are still present. When JavaScript is available, however, we hijack the page request and allow the sort to occur without a full page load.

Sorting tables within the browser

There are times, though, when we either don't want to wait for server responses when sorting or don't have a server-side scripting language available to us. A viable alternative in this case can be to perform the sorting entirely on the browser using JavaScript and jQuery's DOM manipulation methods.

In order to demonstrate the various techniques in this chapter, we will set up three separate jQuery sorting mechanisms. Each will accomplish the same goal, but in a unique way. Our examples will sort the table using:

- Data extracted from the HTML content
- HTML5 custom data attributes
- A JSON representation of the table data

The tables that we'll be sorting will have different HTML structures to accommodate the varying JavaScript techniques, but each contains columns listing books, their author names, release dates, and prices. The first table has this simple structure:

```html
<table id="t-1" class="sortable">
  <thead>
    <tr>
      <th></th>
      <th class="sort-alpha">Title</th>
      <th class="sort-alpha">Author(s)</th>
      <th class="sort-date">Publish Date</th>
      <th class="sort-numeric">Price</th>
    </tr>
  </thead>
  <tbody>
    <tr>
      <td><img src="images/2862_OS.jpg" alt="Drupal 7"></td>
      <td>Drupal 7</td>
      <td>David <span class="sort-key">Mercer</span></td>
      <td>September 2010</td>
      <td>$44.99</td>
    </tr>
    <!-- code continues -->
  </tbody>
</table>
```

Getting the example code

You can access the example code from the following GitHub repository: ht tps://github.com/PacktPublishing/Learning-jQuery-3.

Before we enhance the table with JavaScript, the first few rows look like this:

	Title	Author(s)	Publish Date	Price
	Drupal 7	David Mercer	September 2010	$44.99
	Amazon SimpleDB: LITE	Prabhakar Chaganti, Rich Helms	May 2011	$9.99
	Object-Oriented JavaScript	Stoyan Stefanov	July 2008	$39.99

Moving and inserting elements revisited

Over the course of the coming examples, we will build a flexible sorting mechanism that works on each of the columns. To do this, we will use the jQuery DOM manipulation methods to insert some new elements and move other existing elements to new positions within the DOM. We will start with the most straightforward piece of the puzzle--linking the table headers.

Adding links around existing text

We'd like to turn the table headers into links that sort the data by their respective columns. We can use jQuery's `.wrapInner()` method to add them; we recall from Chapter 5, *Manipulating the DOM*, that `.wrapInner()` places a new element (in this case an `<a>` element) *inside* the matched element, but *around* child elements:

```
$(() => {
  const $headers = $('#t-1')
    .find('thead th')
    .slice(1);
```

```
$headers
  .wrapInner($('<a/>').attr('href', '#'))
  .addClass('sort');
});
```

Listing 12.1

We skipped the first <th> element of each table (using `.slice()`) because it contains no text other than white space, as there is no need to either label or sort the cover photos. We then added a class of `sort` to the remaining <th> elements so we can distinguish them in our CSS from their non-sortable counterparts. Now the header rows look like so:

	⇕ Title	⇕ Author(s)	⇕ Publish Date	⇕ Price
Drupal 7	Drupal 7	David Mercer	September 2010	$44.99
Amazon SimpleDB: LITE	Amazon SimpleDB: LITE	Prabhakar Chaganti, Rich Helms	May 2011	$9.99
Object-Oriented JavaScript	Object-Oriented JavaScript	Stoyan Stefanov	July 2008	$39.99

This is an example of progressive enhancement's counterpart, **graceful degradation**. Unlike the Ajax solution discussed earlier, this technique cannot function without JavaScript; we are assuming the server has no scripting language available to it for the purposes of this example. Since JavaScript is required for the sort to work, we are adding the `sort` class and the anchors through code only, thereby making sure that the interface indicates that sorting is possible only if the script can run. And since we're actually creating links rather than simply adding visual styles to indicate that the headers can be clicked, we provide the added benefit of accessibility for users who need to navigate to the headers with the keyboard (by pressing the *Tab* key). The page **degrades** into one that is still functional, albeit without sorting available.

Sorting simple JavaScript arrays

To perform the sort, we will be taking advantage of JavaScript's built-in .sort() method. It does an in-place sort on an array, and can take a **comparator function** as an argument. This function compares two items in the array and should return a positive or negative number depending on which item should come first in the sorted array.

For example, take a simple array of numbers:

```
const arr = [52, 97, 3, 62, 10, 63, 64, 1, 9, 3, 4];
```

We can sort this array by calling arr.sort(). After this, the items are in the following order:

```
[1, 10, 3, 3, 4, 52, 62, 63, 64, 9, 97]
```

By default, as we see here, the items are sorted **lexicographically** (in alphabetical order). In this case, it might make more sense to sort the items *numerically*. To do this, we can supply a comparator function to the .sort() method:

```
arr.sort((a, b) => a < b ? -1 : (a > b ? 1 : 0));
```

This function returns a negative number if a should come first in the sorted array, a positive number if b should come first, and zero if the order of the items does not matter. With this information in hand, the .sort() method can sequence the items appropriately:

```
[1, 3, 3, 4, 9, 10, 52, 62, 63, 64, 97]
```

We will next apply this .sort() method to our table rows.

Sorting DOM elements

Let's perform a sort on the Title column of the table. Note that while we added the sort class to it and the others, this column's header cell already has a sort-alpha class provided by the HTML. The other header cells received similar treatment depending on the type of sorting for each, but for now we'll focus on the Title header, which requires a straightforward alphabetical sort:

```
$(() => {
  const comparator = (a, b) => a < b ? -1 : (a > b ? 1 : 0);
  const sortKey = (element, column) => $.trim($(element)
    .children('td')
    .eq(column)
    .text()
```

```
        .toUpperCase()
    );

$('#t-1')
    .find('thead th')
    .slice(1)
    .wrapInner($('<a/>').attr('href', '#'))
    .addClass('sort')
    .on('click', (e) => {
      e.preventDefault();

      const column = $(e.currentTarget).index();

      $('#t-1')
        .find('tbody > tr')
        .get()
        .sort((a, b) => comparator(
          sortKey(a, column),
          sortKey(b, column)
        ))
        .forEach((element) => {
          $(element)
            .parent()
            .append(element);
        });
    });
});
```

Listing 12.2

Once we have found the index of the clicked header cell, we retrieve an array of all the data rows. This is a great example of how `.get()` is useful in transforming a jQuery object into an array of DOM nodes; even though jQuery objects act like arrays in many respects, they don't have all of the native array methods available, such as `.pop()` or `.shift()`.

Internally, jQuery actually does define a few methods that act like native array methods. For example, `.sort()`, `.push()`, and `.splice()` are methods of jQuery objects. However, since these methods are for internal use and not publicly documented, we cannot rely on them behaving in expected ways in our own code, and should thus avoid calling them on jQuery objects.

Now that we have an array of DOM nodes, we can sort them, but to do this, we need to write an appropriate comparator function. We want to sort the rows according to the textual contents of the relevant table cells, so this will be the information the comparator function will examine. We know which cell to look at because we captured the column index with the `.index()` call. We use jQuery's `$.trim()` function to strip out leading and trailing white space, and then we convert the text to uppercase because string comparisons in JavaScript are case-sensitive while our sort should be case-insensitive.

Our array is now sorted, but note that the call to `.sort()` has not changed the DOM itself. To do this, we need to call DOM manipulation methods to move the rows around. We do this one row at a time, reinserting each into the table as we loop through them. Since `.append()` does not clone nodes, this *moves* them rather than copying them. Our table is now sorted:

	⇕ Title	⇕ Author(s)	⇕ Publish Date	⇕ Price
	Amazon SimpleDB: LITE	Prabhakar Chaganti, Rich Helms	May 2011	$9.99
	CakePHP 1.3 Application Development Cookbook	Mariano Iglesias	March 2011	$39.99
	Cocoa and Objective-C Cookbook	Jeff Hawkins	May 2011	$39.99

Storing data alongside DOM elements

Our code works, but it is quite slow. The culprit is the comparator function, which is doing a lot of work. This comparator will be called many times during the course of a sort, which means that it needs to be fast.

Array sorting performance

The actual sort algorithm used by JavaScript is not defined by the standard. It may be a simple sort such as a **bubble sort** (worst case of $\Theta(n^2)$ in computational complexity terms), or a more sophisticated approach such as a **quick sort** (which is $\Theta(n \log n)$ on average). It is safe to say, though, that doubling the number of items in an array will more than double the number of times the comparator function is called.

The remedy for our slow comparator is to **pre-compute** the keys for the comparison. We can do most of the expensive work in an initial loop and store the result with jQuery's `.data()` method, which sets or retrieves arbitrary information associated with page elements. Then we can simply examine the keys within the comparator function, and our sort is markedly faster:

```
$('#t-1')
  .find('thead th')
  .slice(1)
  .wrapInner($('<a/>').attr('href', '#'))
  .addClass('sort')
  .on('click', (e) => {
    e.preventDefault();

    const column = $(e.currentTarget).index();

    $('#t-1')
      .find('tbody > tr')
      .each((i, element) => {
        $(element)
          .data('sortKey', sortKey(element, column));
      })
      .get()
      .sort((a, b) => comparator(
        $(a).data('sortKey'),
        $(b).data('sortKey')
      ))
      .forEach((element) => {
        $(element)
          .parent()
          .append(element);
      });
  });
```

Listing 12.3

The .data() method, paired with its complement .removeData(), provides a data storage mechanism that is a convenient alternative to **expando properties**, or non-standard properties added directly to DOM elements.

Performing additional pre-computation

Now we want to apply the same kind of sorting behavior to the **Author(s)** column of our table. Because its table header cell has the sort-alpha class, the **Author(s)** column can be sorted with our existing code. Ideally, though, authors should be sorted by last name, not first. Since some books have multiple authors, and some authors have middle names or initials listed, we need outside guidance to determine what part of the text to use as our sort key. We can supply this guidance by wrapping the relevant part of the cell in a tag:

```
<td>David <span class="sort-key">Mercer</span></td>
```

Now we have to modify our sorting code to take this tag into account without disturbing the existing behavior for the Title column, which is already working well. By prepending the marked sort key to the key we have previously calculated, we can sort first on the last name if it is called out, but on the whole string as a fallback:

```
const sortKey = (element, column) => {
  const $cell = $(element)
    .children('td')
    .eq(column);
  const sortText = $cell
    .find('span.sort-key')
    .text();
  const cellText = $cell
    .text()
    .toUpperCase();

  return $.trim(`${sortText} ${cellText}`);
};
```

Listing 12.4

Sorting by the **Author(s)** column now uses the provided key, thereby sorting by last name:

⬍ Title	⬍ Author(s)	⬍ Publish Date	⬍ Price
WordPress 3 Plugin Development Essentials	Brian Bondari, Everett Griffiths	March 2011	$39.99
Magento 1.4 Themes Design	Richard Carter	January 2011	$39.99
Amazon SimpleDB: LITE	Prabhakar Chaganti, Rich Helms	May 2011	$9.99

If two last names are identical, the sort uses the entire string as a tiebreaker for positioning.

Storing non-string data

Our user should be able to sort not just by the **Title** and **Author(s)** columns, but the **Publish Date** and **Price** columns as well. Since we streamlined our comparator function, it can handle all kinds of data, but first the computed keys will need to be adjusted for other data types. For example, in the case of prices, we need to strip off the leading $ character and parse the rest so that we can compare them numerically:

```
var key = parseFloat($cell.text().replace(/^[^\d.]*/, ''));
if (isNaN(key)) {
  key = 0;
}
```

The regular expression used here removes any leading characters other than numbers and decimal points, passing the result on to `parseFloat()`. The result of `parseFloat()` then needs to be checked, because if no number can be extracted from the text, NaN (**Not a Number**) is returned. This can wreak havoc on `.sort()`, so we set any non-number to 0.

For the date cells, we can use the JavaScript `Date` object:

```
var key = Date.parse(`1 ${$cell.text()}`);
```

The dates in this table contain a month and year only; `Date.parse()` requires a fully specified date. To accommodate this, we prepend the string with 1, so that September 2010 becomes 1 September 2010. Now that we have a complete date, `Date.parse()` can convert it into a **timestamp**, which can be sorted using our normal comparator.

We can place these expressions into three separate functions, so that later we can call the appropriate one based on the class applied to the table header:

```
const sortKeys = {
  date: $cell => Date.parse(`1 ${$cell.text()}`),
  alpha: $cell => $.trim(
    $cell.find('span.sort-key').text() + ' ' +
    $cell.text().toUpperCase()
  ),
  numeric($cell) {
    const key = parseFloat(
      $cell
        .text()
        .replace(/^[^\d.]*/, '')
    );
    return isNaN(key) ? 0 : key;
  }
};

$('#t-1')
  .find('thead th')
  .slice(1)
  .each((i, element) => {
    $(element).data(
      'keyType',
      element.className.replace(/^sort-/, '')
    );
  })
  // ...
```

Listing 12.5

We've modified the script to store `keyType` data for each column header cell based on its class name. We strip off the `sort-` portion of the class so that we're left with `alpha`, `numeric`, or `date`. By making each sort function a method of the `sortKeys` object, we can use **array notation** and pass in the value of the header cell's `keyType` data to call the appropriate function.

Typically when we call methods, we use **dot notation**. This is, in fact, the way we call methods of the jQuery object throughout this book. For example, to add a class of bar to <div class="foo">, we write $('div.foo').addClass('bar'). Because JavaScript allows properties and methods to be represented in either dot or array notation, we could also write it as $('div.foo')['addClass']('bar'). It doesn't make much sense to do this most of the time, but it can be a great way to conditionally call methods without using a bunch of if statements. For our sortKeys object, we could call the alpha method like sortKeys.alpha($cell) or sortKeys['alpha']($cell) or, if the method name is stored in a keyType constant, sortKeys[keyType]($cell). We'll use this third variation inside the click handler:

```
// ...
.on('click', (e) => {
  e.preventDefault();

  const column = $(e.currentTarget).index();
  const keyType = $(e.currentTarget).data('keyType');

  $('#t-1')
    .find('tbody > tr')
    .each((i, element) => {
      $(element).data(
        'sortKey',
        sortKeys[keyType](
          $(element)
            .children('td')
            .eq(column)
        )
      );
    })
    .get()
    .sort((a, b) => comparator(
      $(a).data('sortKey'),
      $(b).data('sortKey')
    ))
    .forEach((element) => {
      $(element)
        .parent()
        .append(element);
    });
});
```

Listing 12.6

We can now sort by **Publish Date** or **Price** as well:

	⇕ Title	⇕ Author(s)	⇕ Publish Date	⇕ Price
	Object-Oriented JavaScript	Stoyan Stefanov	July 2008	$39.99
	jQuery 1.4 Reference Guide	Karl Swedberg, Jonathan Chaffer	January 2010	$39.99
	Drupal 7	David Mercer	September 2010	$44.99

Alternating sort directions

Our final sorting enhancement is to allow for both **ascending** and **descending** sort orders. When the user clicks on a column that is already sorted, we want to reverse the current sort order.

To reverse a sort, all we have to do is to invert the values returned by our comparator. We can do this with a simple `direction` argument to the sort comparator:

```
const comparator = (a, b, direction = 1) =>
  a < b ?
    -direction :
    (a > b ? direction : 0);
```

If `direction` equals 1, then the sort will be the same as before. If it equals −1, the sort will be reversed. By combining this concept with some classes to keep track of the current sort order of a column, achieving alternating sort directions is simple:

```
// ...
.on('click', (e) => {
  e.preventDefault();

  const $target = $(e.currentTarget);
```

```
    const column = $target.index();
    const keyType = $target.data('keyType');
    const sortDirection = $target.hasClass('sorted-asc') ?
      -1 : 1;

    $('#t-1')
      .find('tbody > tr')
      .each((i, element) => {
        $(element).data(
          'sortKey',
          sortKeys[keyType](
            $(element)
              .children('td')
              .eq(column)
          )
        );
      })
      .get()
      .sort((a, b) => comparator(
        $(a).data('sortKey'),
        $(b).data('sortKey'),
        sortDirection
      ))
      .forEach((element) => {
        $(element)
          .parent()
          .append(element);
      });

    $target
      .siblings()
      .addBack()
      .removeClass('sorted-asc sorted-desc')
      .end()
      .end()
      .addClass(
        sortDirection == 1 ?
          'sorted-asc' : 'sorted-desc'
      );
});
```

Listing 12.7

As a side benefit, since we use classes to store the sort direction, we can style the column headers to indicate the current order:

	⇕ Title	⇕ Author(s)	⇕ Publish Date	⬇ Price
	Amazon SimpleDB: LITE	Prabhakar Chaganti, Rich Helms	May 2011	$9.99
	Object-Oriented JavaScript	Stoyan Stefanov	July 2008	$39.99
	jQuery 1.4 Reference Guide	Karl Swedberg, Jonathan Chaffer	January 2010	$39.99

Using HTML5 custom data attributes

So far, we've been relying on the content within the table cells to determine the sort order. While we've managed to sort the rows correctly by manipulating that content, we can make our code more efficient by outputting more HTML from the server in the form of **HTML5 data attributes**. The second table in our example page includes these attributes:

```
<table id="t-2" class="sortable">
  <thead>
    <tr>
      <th></th>
      <th data-sort='{"key":"title"}'>Title</th>
      <th data-sort='{"key":"authors"}'>Author(s)</th>
      <th data-sort='{"key":"publishedYM"}'>Publish Date</th>
      <th data-sort='{"key":"price"}'>Price</th>
    </tr>
  </thead>
  <tbody>
    <tr data-book='{"img":"2862_OS.jpg",
      "title":"DRUPAL 7","authors":"MERCER DAVID",
      "published":"September 2010","price":44.99,
```

```
        "publishedYM":"2010-09"}'>
        <td><img src="images/2862_OS.jpg" alt="Drupal 7"></td>
        <td>Drupal 7</td>
        <td>David Mercer</td>
        <td>September 2010</td>
        <td>$44.99</td>
      </tr>
      <!-- code continues -->
    </tbody>
  </table>
```

Notice that each `<th>` element (except the first) has a `data-sort` attribute and each `<tr>` element has a `data-book` attribute. We first saw custom data attributes in Chapter 7, *Using Plugins*, where we provided information in attributes for plugin code to use. Here, we will use jQuery to access the attribute values ourselves. To retrieve the value, we pass the part of the attribute's name after `data-` to the `.data()` method. For example, we write `$('th').first().data('sort')` to get the value of the first `<th>` element's `data-sort` attribute.

When we use the `.data()` method to get the value of a data attribute, jQuery converts the value to a number, array, object, Boolean, or null if it determines that it is one of those types. Objects must be denoted using JSON syntax, as we are doing here. Because the JSON format requires double quotes for its keys and string values, we need to use single quotes to surround the attribute value:

```
<th data-sort='{"key":"title"}'>
```

Since jQuery converts this JSON string to an object for us, getting at the values we want is simple. To get the value of the `key` property, for example, we write:

```
$('th').first().data('sort').key
```

Once a custom data attribute is retrieved in this way, the data is stored internally by jQuery and the HTML `data-*` attribute itself is no longer accessed or modified.

One great benefit of using data attributes here is that the stored values can be different from the table cell content. In other words, all of the work that we had to do in the first table to finesse the sorting--converting strings to upper case, changing the date format, converting the price to a number--is already taken care of. This allows us to write much simpler and more efficient sorting code:

```
$(() => {
  const comparator = (a, b, direction = 1) =>
    a < b ?
      -direction :
```

```
      (a > b ? direction : 0);

$('#t-2')
  .find('thead th')
  .slice(1)
  .wrapInner($('<a/>').attr('href', '#'))
  .addClass('sort')
  .on('click', (e) => {
    e.preventDefault();

    const $target = $(e.currentTarget);
    const column = $target.index();
    const sortKey = $target.data('sort').key;
    const sortDirection = $target.hasClass('sorted-asc') ?
      -1 : 1;

    $('#t-2')
      .find('tbody > tr')
      .get()
      .sort((a, b) => comparator(
        $(a).data('book')[sortKey],
        $(b).data('book')[sortKey],
        sortDirection
      ))
      .forEach((element) => {
        $(element)
          .parent()
          .append(element);
      });

    $target
      .siblings()
      .addBack()
      .removeClass('sorted-asc sorted-desc')
      .end()
      .end()
      .addClass(
        sortDirection == 1 ?
          'sorted-asc' : 'sorted-desc'
      );
  });
});
```

Listing 12.8

The simplicity of this approach is clear: the `sortKey` constant is set with `.data('sort').key` and is then used to compare the rows' sort values with `$(a).data('book')[sortKey]` and `$(b).data('book')[sortKey]`. The efficiency is evident in that there is no need to loop through the rows first and call one of the `sortKeys` functions each time before calling the `sort` function. With this combination of simplicity and efficiency, we've also improved the code's performance and made it easier to maintain.

Sorting and building rows with JSON

So far in this chapter, we have been moving in the direction of outputting more and more information from the server into HTML so that our client-side scripts can remain as lean and efficient as possible. Now let's consider a different scenario, one in which a whole new set of information is displayed when JavaScript is available. Increasingly, web applications rely on JavaScript to deliver content as well as manipulate it once it arrives. In our third table sorting example, we'll do the same.

We'll start by writing three functions:

- `buildAuthors()`: This builds a string list of author names
- `buildRow()`: This builds the HTML for a single table row
- `buildRows()`: This builds the HTML for the entire table by mapping the rows built by `buildRow()`

```
const buildAuthors = row =>
  row
    .authors
    .map(a => `${a.first_name} ${a.last_name}`)
    .join(', ');

const buildRow = row =>
  `
    <tr>
      <td><img src="images/${row.img}"></td>
      <td>${row.title}</td>
      <td>${buildAuthors(row)}</td>
      <td>${row.published}</td>
      <td>$${row.price}</td>
    </tr>
  `;

const buildRows = rows =>
  rows
    .map(buildRow)
```

```
.join('');
```

For our purposes, we could get by with a single function to handle both tasks, but by using three separate functions, we leave open the possibility of building and inserting a single row at some other point. These functions will get their data from the response to an Ajax request:

```
Promise.all([$.getJSON('books.json'), $.ready])
  .then(([json]) => {
    $('#t-3')
      .find('tbody')
      .html(buildRows(json));
  })
  .catch((err) => {
    console.error(err);
  });
```

We shouldn't have to wait for the DOM to be ready before making an Ajax call. There's two promises that need to resolve before we can call `buildRows()` with JSON data. First, we need the actual JSON data to come back from the server. Second, we need to ensure that the DOM is ready to be manipulated. So, we simply create a new promise that's resolved when these two things happen, by using `Promise.all()`. The `$.getJSON()` function returns a promise, and `$.ready` is a promise that's resolved when the DOM is ready.

Also worth noting is that we need to treat the `authors` data differently because it comes from the server as an array of objects with `first_name` and `last_name` properties, while everything else arrives as a string or a number. We loop through the array of authors--even though for most rows the array consists of only one--and concatenate the first name and the last. We then join the array values with a comma and a space to end up with a formatted list of names.

The `buildRow()` function assumes that the text we're getting from the JSON file is safe for consumption. Since we're concatenating `<img>`, `<td>`, and `<tr>` tags along with the text content into a single text string, we need to be sure that the text content has no unescaped <, >, or & characters. One way to ensure HTML-safe strings is to process them on the server, converting all instances of < to `&lt;`, > to `&gt;`, and & to `&amp;`.

Modifying the JSON object

The work we're doing with the `authors` array is fine if we only plan to call the `buildRows()` function once. However, since we intend to call it each time the rows are sorted, it's a good idea to have the author information formatted ahead of time. While we're at it, we can format the title and the author information for sorting as well. Unlike the second table, in which each row had sortable data in the `data-book` attribute and display data in the table cells, the JSON data we're retrieving for the third table comes in only one flavor. Still, by writing one more function, we can include modified values for sorting and displaying before we ever get to the table building functions:

```
const buildAuthors = (row, separator = ', ') =>
  row
    .authors
    .map(a => `${a.first_name} ${a.last_name}`)
    .join(separator);

const prepRows = rows =>
  rows
    .map(row => $.extend({}, row, {
      title: row.title.toUpperCase(),
      titleFormatted: row.title,
      authors: buildAuthors(row, ' ').toUpperCase(),
      authorsFormatted: buildAuthors(row)
    }));
```

Listing 12.11

By passing our JSON data through this function, we add two properties to each row's object: `authorsFormatted` and `titleFormatted`. These properties will be used for the displayed table contents, preserving the original `authors` and `title` properties for sorting. The properties used for sorting are also converted to uppercase to make the sort operation case insensitive. We've also added a new separator argument to the `buildAuthors()` function so that we can use it here.

When we call this `prepRows()` function immediately inside the `$.getJSON()` callback function, we store the returned value of the modified JSON object in the `rows` variable and use that one for sorting and building. This means that we also need to change the `buildRow()` function to take advantage of the simplicity that our advance preparation has afforded it:

```
const buildRow = row =>

  <tr>
```

```
   <td><img src="images/${row.img}"></td>
   <td>${row.titleFormatted}</td>
   <td>${row.authorsFormatted}</td>
   <td>${row.published}</td>
   <td>$${row.price}</td>
  </tr>
 `;

Promise.all([$.getJSON('books.json'), $.ready])
  .then(([json]) => {
    $('#t-3')
      .find('tbody')
      .html(buildRows(prepRows(json)));
  })
  .catch((err) => {
    console.error(err);
  });
```

Listing 12.12

Rebuilding content on demand

Now that we've prepared the content for both sorting and displaying, we're ready to once
again implement the column heading modification and the sorting routine:

```
Promise.all([$.getJSON('books.json'), $.ready])
  .then(([json]) => {
    $('#t-3')
      .find('tbody')
      .html(buildRows(prepRows(json)));

    const comparator = (a, b, direction = 1) =>
      a < b ?
        -direction :
        (a > b ? direction : 0);

    $('#t-3')
      .find('thead th')
      .slice(1)
      .wrapInner($('<a/>').attr('href', '#'))
      .addClass('sort')
      .on('click', (e) => {
        e.preventDefault();

        const $target = $(e.currentTarget);
        const column = $target.index();
```

```
              const sortKey = $target.data('sort').key;
              const sortDirection = $target.hasClass('sorted-asc') ?
                -1 : 1;
              const content = buildRows(
                prepRows(json).sort((a, b) => comparator(
                  a[sortKey],
                  b[sortKey],
                  sortDirection
                ))
              );

              $('#t-3')
                .find('tbody')
                .html(content);

              $target
                .siblings()
                .addBack()
                .removeClass('sorted-asc sorted-desc')
                .end()
                .end()
                .addClass(
                  sortDirection == 1 ?
                    'sorted-asc' : 'sorted-desc'
                );
            });
          })
          .catch((err) => {
            console.error(err);
          });
```

Listing 12.13

The code inside the `click` handler is nearly identical to the handler for the second table in *Listing 12.8*. The one notable difference is that here we insert elements into the DOM only once per sort. In tables one and two, even after our other optimizations, we sorted the actual DOM elements and then looped through them one-by-one, appending each one in turn to arrive at the new order. For example, in *Listing 12.8* table rows are reinserted in a loop like so:

```
  .forEach((element) => {
    $(element)
      .parent()
      .append(element);
  });
```

This type of repetitive DOM insertion can be quite costly from a performance perspective, especially with a large number of rows. Compare that with our latest approach in *Listing 12.13*:

```
$('#t-3')
  .find('tbody')
  .html(content);
```

The `buildRows()` function returns a string of HTML representing the rows and inserts it in one fell swoop, replacing the rows instead of moving the existing ones around.

Revisiting attribute manipulation

By now, we are used to getting and setting values that are associated with DOM elements. We have done this with simple methods such as `.attr()`, `.prop()`, and `.css()`, convenient shorthands such as `.addClass()`, `.css()`, and `.val()`, and complex bundles of behavior such as `.animate()`. Even the simple methods, though, do quite a bit of work for us behind the scenes. We can get even more utility out of them if we better understand what they do.

Using shorthand element creation syntax

We often create new elements in our jQuery code by providing an HTML string to the `$()` function or to DOM insertion functions. For example, we create a large HTML fragment in *Listing 12.9* in order to produce many DOM elements. This technique is fast and concise. There are circumstances when it is not ideal. We might, for instance, want to escape special characters from text before it is used, or apply style rules that are browser-dependent. In these cases, we can create the element and then chain on additional jQuery methods to alter it, as we have done many times already. In addition to this standard technique, the `$()` function itself provides an alternative syntax to achieve the same result.

Suppose we want to introduce headings prior to each of the tables in our document. We can use an `.each()` loop to iterate over the tables and create an appropriately-named heading:

```
$(() => {
  $('table')
    .each((i, table) => {
      $('<h3/>', {
        'class': 'table-title',
        id: `table-title-${i}`,
        text: `Table ${i + 1}`,
```

```
        data: { index: i },
        click(e) {
           e.preventDefault();
           $(table).fadeToggle();
        },
        css: { glowColor: '#00ff00', cursor: 'pointer' }
     }).insertBefore(table);
  });
});
```

Listing 12.14

Providing an options object as the second argument to the $() function has the same effect as first creating the element then passing that object to the .attr() method. As we know, this method lets us set DOM attributes such as the id value of the element and its class.

The rest of the options in our example are:

- The text inside the element
- Custom additional data
- A click handler
- An object containing CSS properties

These are not DOM attributes, yet they get set all the same. The shorthand $() syntax is able to handle these because it first checks to see if a jQuery method exists with the given name, and if so, it calls it instead of setting the attribute of that name.

 Because jQuery gives methods precedence over attribute names, we must take care in cases where meaning might be ambiguous; for example, the size attribute of <input> elements, which cannot be set this way because a .size() method also exists.

This shorthand $() syntax, along with the .attr() function, can handle even more features through the use of **hooks**.

DOM manipulation hooks

Many jQuery methods that get and set properties can be extended for special cases by defining the appropriate hooks. These hooks are arrays in the jQuery namespace with names such as $.cssHooks and $.attrHooks. In general, hooks are objects holding a get method that retrieves the requested value, and a set method that provides a new value.

Hook types include:

Hook type	Method altered	Example usage
`$.attrHooks`	`.attr()`	Prevents the `type` attribute of an element from being changed.
`$.cssHooks`	`.css()`	Provides special handling for `opacity` in Internet Explorer.
`$.propHooks`	`.prop()`	Corrects the behavior of the `selected` property in Safari.
`$.valHooks`	`.val()`	Allows radio buttons and checkboxes to report a consistent value across browsers.

Usually the work performed by these hooks is completely hidden to us, and we can benefit from them without thinking much about what is going on. Sometimes, though, we might want to extend the behavior of jQuery's methods by adding hooks of our own.

Writing a CSS hook

The code in *Listing 12.14* injects a CSS property called `glowColor` onto the page. This has no effect on the page at the moment, as such a property does not exist. Instead, we are going to extend `$.cssHooks` to add support for this newly invented property. We will add a soft glow around the text using the CSS3 `text-shadow` property when `glowColor` is set on an element:

```
(($) => {
  $.cssHooks.glowColor = {
    set(elem, value) {
      elem.style.textShadow = value == 'none' ?
        '' : `0 0 2px ${value}`;
    }
  };
})(jQuery);
```

Listing 12.15

A hook consists of a `get` method and a `set` method for an element. To keep our example as brief and simple as possible, we are only defining `set` at this time.

With this hook in place, we now have a 2-pixel soft green glow around the heading text:

> **Table 1**

While the new hook works as advertised, it lacks many features that we might expect. Some of these shortcomings include:

- The size of the glow is not customizable
- The effect is mutually exclusive with other uses of `text-shadow` or `filter`
- The `get` callbacks are unimplemented, so we cannot test for the current value of the property
- The property cannot be animated

With enough work and additional code, we could surmount all of these obstacles. In practice, we rarely have to define our own hooks, however; skilled plugin developers have created hooks for a wide variety of needs, including most CSS3 properties.

Finding hooks

The plugin landscape changes rapidly, so new hooks will crop up all the time, and we cannot hope to list them all here. For a sampling of what is possible, see Brandon Aaron's collection of CSS hooks at `https://github.com/brandonaaron/jquery-cssHooks`.

Summary

In this chapter, we have solved a common problem--sorting a data table--in three different ways, comparing the benefits of each approach. In doing so, we practiced the DOM modification techniques that we have learned earlier and explored the `.data()` method for getting and setting data associated with any DOM element or attached using HTML5 data attributes. We also pulled back the curtain on several DOM modification routines, learning how to extend them for our own purposes.

Further reading

A complete list of DOM manipulation methods is available in *Appendix C* of this book, or in the official jQuery documentation at `http://api.jquery.com/`.

Exercises

The challenge exercise may require the use of the official jQuery documentation at `http://api.jquery.com/`.

1. Modify the key computation for the first table so that titles and authors are sorted by length rather than alphabetically.
2. Use the HTML5 data in the second table to compute the sum of all of the book prices and insert this sum into the heading for that column.
3. Change the comparator used for the third table so that titles containing the word **jQuery** come first when sorted by title.
4. **Challenge**: Implement the `get` callback for the `glowColor` CSS hook.

13
Advanced Ajax

Many web applications require frequent network communication. Using jQuery, our web pages can exchange information with the server without requiring new pages to be loaded in the browser.

In Chapter 6, *Sending Data with Ajax*, you learned simple ways to interact with the server asynchronously. In this more advanced chapter, we will cover:

- Error-handling techniques for dealing with network interruptions
- The interactions between Ajax and the jQuery deferred object system
- Caching and throttling techniques for reducing network traffic
- Ways to extend the inner workings of the Ajax system using transports, prefilters, and data type converters

Implementing progressive enhancement with Ajax

Throughout this book, we encountered the concept of *progressive enhancement*. To reiterate, this philosophy ensures a positive user experience for all users by mandating that a working product be put in place first before additional embellishments are added for users with modern browsers.

As an example, we'll build a form that searches GitHub repositories:

```
<form id="ajax-form" action="https://github.com/search" method="get">
  <fieldset>
    <div class="text">
      <label for="title">Search</label>
      <input type="text" id="title" name="q">
    </div>

    <div class="actions">
      <button type="submit">Request</button>
    </div>
  </fieldset>
</form>
```

Getting the example code

You can access the example code from the following GitHub repository: `ht` `tps://github.com/PacktPublishing/Learning-jQuery-3`.

The search form is a normal form element with a text input and a submit button labeled as **Request**:

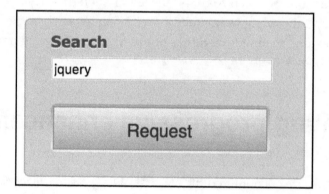

When the **Request** button of this form is clicked on, the form submits as normal; the user's browser is directed to `https://github.com/search` and the results are displayed:

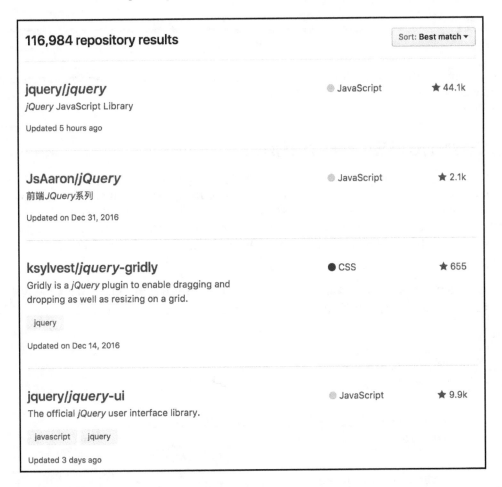

However, we want to load this content into the `#response` container of our search page rather than leaving the page. If the data was stored on the same server as our search form, we could harvest the relevant portion of the page using the `.load()` method:

```
$(() => {
  $('#ajax-form')
    .on('submit', (e) => {
      e.preventDefault();
      $('#response')
        .load(
          'https://github.com/search .container',
```

```
        $(e.target).serialize()
      );
    });
  });
```

Listing 13.1

However, since GitHub is under a different hostname, the default cross-domain policy of the browser will not allow this request to happen.

Harvesting JSONP data

In Chapter 6, *Sending Data with Ajax*, we saw that JSONP is simply JSON with an added layer of server behavior allowing requests to be made from a different site. When a request is made for JSONP data, a special query string parameter is provided that allows the requesting script to process the data. This parameter can be called anything the JSONP server wishes; in the case of the GitHub API, the parameter uses the default name, `callback`.

Because the default `callback` name is used, the only setup required to make a JSONP request is to declare to jQuery that `jsonp` is the data type we are expecting:

```
$(() => {
  $('#ajax-form')
    .on('submit', (e) => {
      e.preventDefault();

      $.ajax({
        url: 'https://api.github.com/search/repositories',
        dataType: 'jsonp',
        data: { q: $('#title').val() },
        success(data) {
          console.log(data);
        }
      });
    });
});
```

Listing 13.2

Now, we can inspect the JSON data in the console. The data in this case is an array of objects, each describing a GitHub repository:

```
{
  "id": 167174,
  "name": "jquery",
  "open_issues": 78,
  "open_issues_count": 78,
  "pulls_url: "https://api.github.com/repos/jquery/jquery/pulls{/number}",
  "pushed_at": "2017-03-27T15:50:12Z",
  "releases_url":
"https://api.github.com/repos/jquery/jquery/releases{/id}",
  "score": 138.81496,
  "size": 27250,
  "ssh_url": "git@github.com:jquery/jquery.git",
  "stargazers_count": 44069,
  "updated_at": "2017-03-27T20:59:42Z",
  "url": "https://api.github.com/repos/jquery/jquery",
  "watchers": 44069,
  // ...
}
```

All of the data we need to display about a repository is included in this object. We simply need to format it appropriately for display. Creating the HTML for an item is somewhat involved, so we'll break that step out into its own helper function:

```
const buildItem = item =>
  `
    <li>
      <h3><a href="${item.html_url}">${item.name}</a></h3>
      <div>★ ${item.stargazers_count}</div>
      <div>${item.description}</div>
    </li>
  `;
```

Listing 13.3

The `buildItem()` function converts the JSON object into an HTML list item. This includes a link to the main GitHub repository page followed by the description.

At this point, we have a function that creates the HTML for a single item. When our Ajax call completes, we'll need to call this function on every returned object and display all of the results:

```
$(() => {
  $('#ajax-form')
    .on('submit', (e) => {
```

```
    e.preventDefault();

    $.ajax({
      url: 'https://api.github.com/search/repositories',
      dataType: 'jsonp',
      data: { q: $('#title').val() },
      success(json) {
        var output = json.data.items.map(buildItem);
        output = output.length ?
        output.join('') : 'no results found';

        $('#response').html(`<ol>${output}</ol>`);
      }
    });
  });
});
```

Listing 13.4

Now that we have a functional `success` handler, performing a search nicely presents the results in a column next to our form:

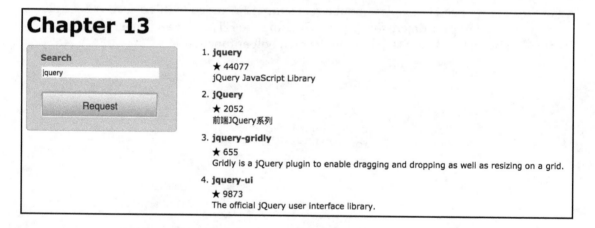

Handling Ajax errors

Introducing any kind of network interaction into an application brings along some degree of uncertainty. The user's connection could drop in the middle of an operation or a temporary server issue could interrupt communications. Because of these reliability concerns, we should always plan for the worst case and prepare for error scenarios.

The $.ajax() function can take a callback function named error to be called in these
situations. In this callback, we should provide some kind of feedback to the user indicating
that an error has occurred:

```
$(() => {
  $('#ajax-form')
    .on('submit', (e) => {
      e.preventDefault();

      $.ajax({
        url: 'https://api.github.com/search/repositories',
        dataType: 'jsonp',
        data: { q: $('#title').val() },
        error() {
          $('#response').html('Oops. Something went wrong...');
        }
      });
    });
});
```

Listing 13.5

The error callback can be triggered for a number of reasons. Among these are:

- The server returned an error status code, such as **403 Forbidden, 404 Not Found,**
  or **500 Internal Server Error.**
- The server returned a redirection status code, such as **301 Moved Permanently.**
  An exception is **304 Not Modified,** which does not trigger an error because the
  browser can handle this condition correctly.
- The data returned by the server could not be parsed as specified (for example, it
  is not valid JSON data when dataType is json).
- The .abort() method is called on the XMLHttpRequest object.

Detecting and responding to these conditions is important in providing the best possible
user experience. We saw in Chapter 6, *Sending Data with Ajax,* that the error code, if any, is
provided to us in the .status property of the jqXHR object that is passed to the error
callback. We can use the value of jqXHR.status to react differently to different kinds of
errors, if that is appropriate.

However, the server errors are only useful when they are actually observed. Some errors
are immediately detected, but other conditions can cause a long delay between the request
and eventual error response.

When a reliable server timeout mechanism is not available, we can enforce our own client-side request timeout. By providing a time in milliseconds to the timeout option, we tell `$.ajax()` to trigger `.abort()` on its own if that amount of time elapses before a response is received:

```
$.ajax({
  url: 'https://api.github.com/search/repositories',
  dataType: 'jsonp',
  data: { q: $('#title').val() },
  timeout: 10000,
  error() {
    $('#response').html('Oops. Something went wrong...');
  }
});
```

Listing 13.6

With the timeout in place, we can be assured that within 10 seconds either the data will be loaded or the user will receive an error message.

Using the jqXHR object

When an Ajax request is made, jQuery determines the best mechanism available for retrieving the data. This transport could be the standard XMLHttpRequest object, the Microsoft ActiveX XMLHTTP object, or a `<script>` tag.

Because the transport used can vary from request to request, we need a common interface in order to interact with the communication. The jqXHR object provides this interface for us. It is a wrapper for the XMLHttpRequest object when that transport is used, and in other cases, it simulates XMLHttpRequest as best it can. Among the properties and methods it exposes are:

- `.responseText` or `.responseXML`, containing the returned data
- `.status` and `.statusText`, containing a status code and description
- `.setRequestHeader()` to manipulate the HTTP headers sent with the request
- `.abort()` to prematurely halt the transaction

This jqXHR object is returned from all of jQuery's Ajax methods, so we can store the result if we need access to any of these properties or methods.

Ajax promises

Perhaps a more important aspect of `jqXHR` than the `XMLHttpRequest` interface, however, is that it also acts as a promise. In `Chapter 11`, *Advanced Effects*, you learned about deferred objects, which allow us to set callbacks to be fired when certain operations are complete. An Ajax call is an example of such operation, and the `jqXHR` object provides the methods we expect from a deferred object's promise.

Using the promise's methods, we can rewrite our `$.ajax()` call to replace the success and error callbacks with an alternate syntax:

```
$.ajax({
  url: 'https://api.github.com/search/repositories',
  dataType: 'jsonp',
  data: { q: $('#title').val() },
  timeout: 10000,
}).then((json) => {
  var output = json.data.items.map(buildItem);
  output = output.length ?
    output.join('') : 'no results found';

  $('#response').html(`<ol>${output}</ol>`);
}).catch(() => {
  $('#response').html('Oops. Something went wrong...');
});
```

Listing 13.7

At first glance, calling `.then()` and `.catch()` doesn't seem any more useful than the callback syntax we used previously. However, the promise methods offer several advantages. First, the methods can be called multiple times to add more than one handler if desired. Second, if we store the result of the `$.ajax()` call in a constant, we can attach the handlers later if that makes our code structure more readable. Third, the handlers will be invoked immediately if the Ajax operation is already complete when they are attached. Finally, we should not discount the readability advantage of using a syntax that is consistent with other parts of the jQuery library, and with native JavaScript promises.

As another example of using the promise methods, we can add a loading indicator when a request is made. Since we want to hide the indicator when the request completes, successfully or otherwise, the `.always()` method will come in handy:

```
$('#ajax-form')
  .on('submit', (e) => {
    e.preventDefault();
```

```
$('#response')
  .addClass('loading')
  .empty();

$.ajax({
  url: 'https://api.github.com/search/repositories',
  dataType: 'jsonp',
  data: { q: $('#title').val() },
  timeout: 10000,
}).then((json) => {
  var output = json.data.items.map(buildItem);
  output = output.length ?
  output.join('') : 'no results found';

  $('#response').html(`<ol>${output}</ol>`);
}).catch(() => {
  $('#response').html('Oops. Something went wrong...');
}).always(() => {
  $('#response').removeClass('loading');
});
});
```

Listing 13.8

Before we issue the $.ajax() call, we add the loading class to the response container. Once the loading is complete, we remove it again. By doing so, we have further enhanced the user experience because there is now a visual indicator that something is happening in the background.

To really get a grasp of how the promise behavior can help us, though, we need to look at what we can do if we store the result of our $.ajax() call for later use.

Caching responses

If we need to use the same piece of data repeatedly, it is wasteful to make an Ajax request each time. To prevent this, we can cache the returned data in a variable. When we need to use some data, we can check to see whether the data is already in the cache. If so, we act on this data. If not, we need to make an Ajax request, and in its .done() handler, we store the data in the cache and act on the returned data.

If we exploit the properties of promises, it can be quite simple:

```
$(() => {
  const cache = new Map();

  $('#ajax-form')
    .on('submit', (e) => {
      e.preventDefault();

      const search = $('#title').val();

      if (search == '') {
        return;
      }

      $('#response')
        .addClass('loading')
        .empty();

      cache.set(search, cache.has(search) ?
        cache.get(search) :
        $.ajax({
          url: 'https://api.github.com/search/repositories',
          dataType: 'jsonp',
          data: { q: search },
          timeout: 10000,
        })
      ).get(search).then((json) => {
        var output = json.data.items.map(buildItem);
        output = output.length ?
          output.join('') : 'no results found';

        $('#response').html(`<ol>${output}</ol>`);
      }).catch(() => {
        $('#response').html('Oops. Something went wrong...');
      }).always(() => {
        $('#response').removeClass('loading');
      });
    });
});
```

Listing 13.9

We've introduced a new Map constant named cache to hold the jqXHR promises that we create. The keys of this map correspond to the searches being performed. When the form is submitted, we look to see whether there is already a jqXHR promise stored for that key. If not, we perform the query as before, storing the resulting object inside api.

The .then(), .catch(), and .always() handlers are then attached to the jqXHR promise. Note that this happens regardless of whether an Ajax request was made. There are two possible situations to consider here.

First, the Ajax request might be sent if it hasn't been before. This is just like the previous behavior: the request is issued and we use the promise methods to attach handlers to the jqXHR object. When a response comes back from the server, the appropriate callbacks are fired and the result is printed to the screen.

On the other hand, if we have performed this search in the past, the jqXHR promise is already stored in cache. In this case, no new search is performed, but we still call the promise methods on the stored object. This attaches new handlers to the object, but since the deferred object has already been resolved, the relevant handlers are fired immediately.

The jQuery deferred object system handles all the hard work for us. With a couple of lines of code, we have eliminated duplicate network requests from the application.

Throttling Ajax requests

A common feature of searches is to display a dynamic list of results as the user is typing. We can emulate this "live search" feature for our jQuery API search by binding a handler to the keyup event:

```
$('#title')
  .on('keyup', (e) => {
    $(e.target.form).triggerHandler('submit');
  });
```

Listing 13.10

Here, we simply trigger the form's submit handler whenever the user types something in the **Search** field. This could have the effect of sending many requests across the network in rapid succession, depending on the speed at which the user types. This behavior could bog down JavaScript's performance; it could clog the network connection, and the server might not be able to handle that kind of demand.

We're already limiting the number of requests with the request caching that we've just put in place. We can further ease the burden on the server, however, by throttling the requests. In Chapter 10, *Advanced Events*, we introduced the concept of throttling when we created a special throttledScroll event to reduce the number of times the native scroll event is fired. In this case, we want to make a similar reduction in activity; this time with the keyup event:

```
const searchDelay = 300;
var searchTimeout;

$('#title')
  .on('keyup', (e) => {
    clearTimeout(searchTimeout);

    searchTimeout = setTimeout(() => {
      $(e.target.form).triggerHandler('submit');
    }, searchDelay);
  });
```

Listing 13.11

Our technique here, sometimes referred to as debouncing, is a bit different from the one we used in Chapter 10, *Advanced Events*. Whereas in that example we needed our scroll handler to take effect multiple times as scrolling continued, here we only need the keyup behavior to happen one time after typing has ceased. To do this, we keep track of a JavaScript timer that starts whenever the user presses a key. Each keystroke resets that timer, so only once the user stops typing for the designated amount of time (300 milliseconds) does the submit handler get triggered and the Ajax request is performed.

Extending Ajax capabilities

The jQuery Ajax framework is powerful, as we've seen, but even so there are times when we might want to change the way it behaves. Unsurprisingly, it offers multiple hooks that can be used by plugins to give the framework brand new capabilities.

Data type converters

In Chapter 6, *Sending Data with Ajax*, we saw that the $.ajaxSetup() function allows us to change the defaults used by $.ajax(), thus potentially affecting many Ajax operations with a single statement. This same function can also be used to add to the range of data types that $.ajax() can request and interpret.

As an example, we can add a converter that understands the YAML data format. YAML (http://www.yaml.org/) is a popular data representation with implementations in many programming languages. If our code needs to interact with an alternative format such as this, jQuery allows us to build compatibility for it into the native Ajax functions.

A simple YAML file containing GitHub repository search criteria:

```
Language:
 - JavaScript
 - HTML
 - CSS
Star Count:
 - 5000+
 - 10000+
 - 20000+
```

We can wrap jQuery around an existing YAML parser such as Diogo Costa's (http://code.google.com/p/javascript-yaml-parser/) to make $.ajax() speak this language as well.

Defining a new Ajax data type involves passing three properties to $.ajaxSetup(): accepts, contents, and converters. The accepts property adds headers to be sent to the server, declaring to the server that particular MIME types are understood by our script. The contents property handles the other side of the transaction, providing a regular expression that is matched against the response MIME type to attempt to autodetect the data type from this metadata. Finally, converters contains the actual functions that parse the returned data:

```
$.ajaxSetup({
  accepts: {
    yaml: 'application/x-yaml, text/yaml'
  },
  contents: {
    yaml: /yaml/
  },
  converters: {
    'text yaml': (textValue) => {
      console.log(textValue);
```

```
        return '';
      }
    }
});

$.ajax({
  url: 'categories.yml',
  dataType: 'yaml'
});
```

Listing 13.12

The partial implementation in *Listing 13.12* uses $.ajax() to read in the YAML file, and declares its data type as yaml. Because the incoming data is parsed as text, jQuery needs a way to convert one data type to the other. The converters key of 'text yaml' tells jQuery that this conversion function will accept data that has been received as text and reinterpret it as yaml.

Inside the conversion function, we are simply logging the contents of the text to ensure that the function is called correctly. To actually perform the conversion, we need to load the third-party YAML parsing library (yaml.js) and call its methods:

```
$.ajaxSetup({
  accepts: {
    yaml: 'application/x-yaml, text/yaml'
  },
  contents: {
    yaml: /yaml/
  },
  converters: {
    'text yaml': (textValue) => YAML.eval(textValue)
  }
});

Promise.all([
  $.getScript('yaml.js')
    .then(() =>
      $.ajax({
        url: 'categories.yml',
        dataType: 'yaml'
      })),
  $.ready
]).then(([[data]]) => {
  const output = Object.keys(data).reduce((result, key) =>
    result.concat(
      `<li><strong>${key}</strong></li>`,
      data[key].map(i => `<li> <a href="#">${i}</a></li>`)
```

```
    ),
    []
  ).join('');

  $('#categories')
    .removeClass('hide')
    .html(`<ul>${output}</ul>`);
});
```

Listing 13.13

The `yaml.js` file includes an object named `YAML` with an `.eval()` method. We use this method to parse the incoming text and return the result, which is a JavaScript object containing all of the `categories.yml` file's data in an easily traversable structure. Since the file we're loading contains GitHub repo search fields, we use the parsed structure to print out the top-level fields and later will allow the user to filter their search results by clicking on them:

The Ajax operations may run immediately, without access to the DOM, but once we have a result from them, we need to wait until the DOM is available before proceeding. Structuring our code to use `Promise.all()` allows the network call to be performed as early as possible, improving the user's perception of the page's loading time.

Next, we need to handle clicks on the category links:

```
$(document)
  .on('click', '#categories a', (e) => {
    e.preventDefault();

    $(e.target)
      .parent()
      .toggleClass('active')
      .siblings('.active')
      .removeClass('active');
    $('#ajax-form')
      .triggerHandler('submit');
  });
```

Listing 13.14

By binding our `click` handler to `document` and relying on event delegation, we avoid some costly repetition and we also can run the code right away, without concerning ourselves with waiting for the Ajax call to complete.
Inside the handler, we make sure the right category is highlighted and then trigger the `submit` handler on the form. We haven't yet made the form understand our category list, but the highlighting works already:

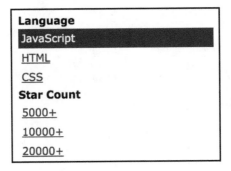

Finally, we need to update the form's `submit` handler to respect the active category if there is one:

```
$('#ajax-form')
  .on('submit', (e) => {
    e.preventDefault();

    const search = [
      $('#title').val(),
      new Map([
        ['JavaScript', 'language:"JavaScript"'],
        ['HTML', 'language:"HTML"'],
        ['CSS', 'language:"CSS"'],
        ['5000+', 'stars:">=5000"'],
        ['10000+', 'stars:">=10000"'],
        ['20000+', 'stars:">=20000"'],
        ['', '']
      ]).get($.trim(
        $('#categories')
          .find('li.active')
          .text()
      ))
    ].join('');

    if (search == '' && category == '') {
      return;
    }

    $('#response')
      .addClass('loading')
      .empty();

    cache.set(search, cache.has(search) ?
      cache.get(search) :
      $.ajax({
        url: 'https://api.github.com/search/repositories',
        dataType: 'jsonp',
        data: { q: search },
        timeout: 10000,
      })).get(search).then((json) => {
        var output = json.data.items.map(buildItem);
        output = output.length ?
          output.join('') : 'no results found';

        $('#response').html(`<ol>${output}</ol>`);
      }).catch(() => {
        $('#response').html('Oops. Something went wrong...');
      }).always(() => {
```

```
        $('#response').removeClass('loading');
    });
});
```

Listing 13.15

Instead of simply fetching the value of the search field, now we retrieve the text of the active language or star count as well, passing both pieces of information on through the Ajax call. We use a `Map` instance to map the link text to the appropriate GitHub API syntax.

We can now view repositories by their primary language, or by their star count. Once we've applied these filters, we can further refine what's displayed by typing in the search box:

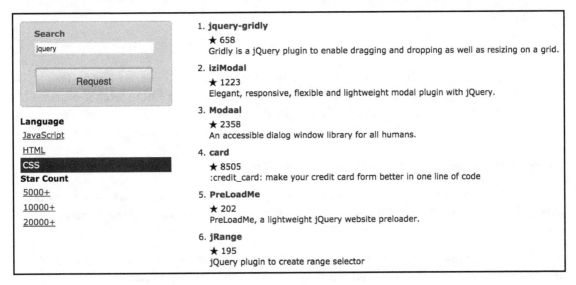

Anytime we have the need to support new data types not already handled by jQuery, we can define them in a similar fashion to this YAML example. We can thus shape jQuery's Ajax library to our specific project's needs.

Adding Ajax prefilters

The `$.ajaxPrefilter()` function can add prefilters, which are callback functions that allow us to manipulate requests before they are sent. Prefilters are invoked before `$.ajax()` changes or uses any of its options, so they are a good place to change the options or act on new custom options.

Prefilters can also manipulate the data type of the request by simply returning the name of the new data type to use. In our YAML example, we specified `yaml` as the data type because we didn't want to rely on the server supplying the correct MIME type for the response. We could, though, provide a prefilter that ensures the data type is `yaml` if the corresponding file extension (`.yml`) is in the URL we request:

```
$.ajaxPrefilter(({ url }) =>
  /.yml$/.test(url) ? 'yaml' : null
);

$.getScript('yaml.js')
  .then(() =>
    $.ajax({ url: 'categories.yml' })
  );
```

Listing 13.16

A short regular expression tests whether `.yml` is at the end of `options.url` and, if so, defines the data type as `yaml`. With this prefilter in place, our Ajax call to fetch the YAML document no longer needs to explicitly define its data type.

Defining alternate transports

We've seen that jQuery uses `XMLHttpRequest`, `ActiveX`, or `<script>` tags as appropriate to handle Ajax transactions. If we wish, we can further extend this arsenal with new transports.

A **transport** is an object that handles the actual transmission of Ajax data. New transports are defined as factory functions that return an object with the `.send()` and `.abort()` methods. The `.send()` method is responsible for issuing the request, handling the response, and sending the data back through a callback function. The `.abort()` method should stop the request immediately.

A custom transport can, for example, use `<img>` elements to fetch external data. This allows image loading to be handled in the same way as other Ajax requests, which can help make our code more internally consistent. The JavaScript required to create such a transport is a little involved, so we will look at the finished product and then discuss its components:

```
$.ajaxTransport('img', ({ url }) => {
  var $img, img, prop;

  return {
    send(headers, complete) {
```

```
    const callback = (success) => {
      if (success) {
        complete(200, 'OK', { img });
      } else {
        $img.remove();
        complete(404, 'Not Found');
      }
    }

    $img = $('<img>', { src: url });
    img = $img[0];
    prop = typeof img.naturalWidth === 'undefined' ?
      'width' : 'naturalWidth';

    if (img.complete) {
      callback(!!img[prop]);
    } else {
      $img.on('load error', ({ type }) => {
        callback(type == 'load');
      });
    }
  },

  abort() {
    if ($img) {
      $img.remove();
    }
  }
};
});
```

Listing 13.17

When defining a transport, we first pass a data type name into $.ajaxTransport(). This tells jQuery when to use our transport rather than the built-in mechanisms. Then, we provide a function that returns the new transport object containing the appropriate .send() and .abort() methods.

For our img transport, the .send() method needs to create a new <img> element, which we give a src attribute. The value of this attribute comes from url, which jQuery passes along from the $.ajax() call. The browser will react to the creation of this <img> element by loading the referenced image file, so we just need to detect when this load has completed and fire the completion callback.

Correctly detecting the completion of an image load is tricky if we want to handle a wide variety of browsers and versions. In some browsers, we can simply attach load and error event handlers to the image element. In others, though, when the image is cached, load and error are not triggered as expected.

Our code in *Listing 13.17* handles these unusual browser behaviors by examining the values of the .complete, .width, and .naturalWidth properties as appropriate for each browser. Once we have detected that the image load has either successfully completed or failed, we call the callback() function, which in turn calls the complete() function that was passed to .send(). This allows $.ajax() to react to the image load.

Handling aborted loads is much simpler. Our .abort() method simply needs to clean up after .send() by removing the <img> element if it has been created.

Next, we need to write the $.ajax() call that uses our new transport:

```
$.ajax({
  url: 'missing.jpg',
  dataType: 'img'
}).then((img) => {
  $('<div/>', {
    id: 'picture',
    html: img
  }).appendTo('body');
}).catch((xhr, textStatus, msg) => {
  $('<div/>', {
    id: 'picture',
    html: `${textStatus}: ${msg}`
  }).appendTo('body');
});
```

Listing 13.18

To use a particular transport, $.ajax() needs to be given a corresponding dataType value. Then, the success and failure handlers need to take into account the kind of data that is passed to them. Our img transport returns an <img> DOM element when it is successful, so our .done() handler uses this element as the HTML contents of a newly created <div> element that is inserted into the document.

However, in this case, the specified image file (`missing.jpg`) does not actually exist. We take into account such a possibility with an appropriate `.catch()` handler, which inserts an error message into the `<div>` where the image would otherwise go:

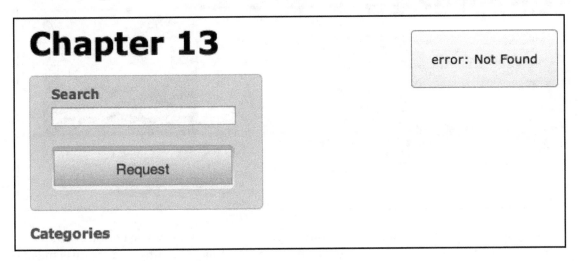

We can correct this error by referencing an image that does exist:

```
$.ajax({
  url: 'sunset.jpg',
  dataType: 'img'
}).then((img) => {
  $('<div/>', {
    id: 'picture',
    html: img
  }).appendTo('body');
}).catch((xhr, textStatus, msg) => {
  $('<div/>', {
    id: 'picture',
    html: `${textStatus}: ${msg}`
  }).appendTo('body');
});
```

Listing 13.19

Now, our transport is able to successfully load the image and we see this result on the page:

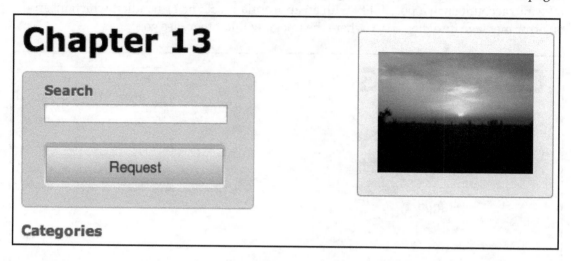

Creating a new transport is uncommon, but even in this case, jQuery's Ajax functionality can be bent to our needs. For example, the ability to treat image loading as a promise means that we could use this Ajax call to synchronize with other asynchronous behavior using `Promise.all()`.

Summary

In this final chapter, we have taken an in-depth look at jQuery's Ajax framework. We can now craft a seamless user experience on a single page, fetching external resources when needed with proper attention to error handling, caching, and throttling. We explored details of the inner operations of the Ajax framework, including promises, transports, prefilters, and converters. You also learned how to extend these mechanisms to serve the needs of our scripts.

Further reading

A complete list of *Ajax methods* is available in `Appendix B`, *Quick Reference*, of this book or in the official jQuery documentation at `http://api.jquery.com/`.

Exercises

The challenge exercises may require the use of the official jQuery documentation at
`http://api.jquery.com/`:

1. Alter the `buildItem()` function so that it includes the long description of each
   jQuery method it displays.
2. Here's a challenge for you. Add a form to the page that points to a Flickr public
   photo search (`http://www.flickr.com/search/`) and make sure it has `<input
   name="q">` and a submit button. Use progressive enhancement to retrieve the
   photos from Flickr's JSONP feed service at
   `http://api.flickr.com/services/feeds/photos_public.gne` instead and insert
   them into the content area of the page. When sending data to this service, use
   `tags` instead of `q` and set `format` to `json`. Also note that rather than `callback`,
   the service expects the JSONP callback name to be `jsoncallback`.
3. Here's another challenge for you. Add error handling for the Flickr request in
   case it results in `parsererror`. Test it by setting the JSONP callback name back
   to `callback`.

A
Testing JavaScript with QUnit

Throughout this book we've written a lot of JavaScript code, and we've seen the many ways in which jQuery helps us write this code with relative ease. Yet whenever we've added a new feature, we've had to take the extra step of manually checking our web page to ensure that everything is working as expected. While this process may work for simple tasks, as projects grow in size and complexity, manual testing can become quite onerous. New requirements can introduce *regression bugs* that break parts of the script that previously worked well. It's far too easy to miss these bugs that don't specifically relate to the latest code changes because we naturally only test for what we've just done.

What we need instead is an automated system that runs our tests for us. The **QUnit** testing framework is just such a system. While there are many other testing frameworks, and they all have their own benefits, we recommend QUnit for most jQuery projects because it is written and maintained by the jQuery project. In fact, jQuery itself uses QUnit. In this appendix, we will cover:

- How to set up the QUnit testing framework within a project
- Unit test organization to aid in code coverage and maintenance
- The various types of tests available with QUnit
- Common practices for ensuring that tests are reliable indicators of successful code
- Suggestions for other types of testing beyond what QUnit offers

Downloading QUnit

The QUnit framework can be downloaded from the official QUnit website at
`http://qunitjs.com/`. There we can find links to the stable version (currently 2.3.0) as well
as a development version (qunit-git). Both versions include a style sheet in addition to the
JavaScript file for formatting the test output.

Setting up the document

Once we have the QUnit files in place, we can set up the test HTML document. In a typical
project, this file would be named `index.html` and placed in the same test subfolder as
`qunit.js` and `qunit.css`. For this demonstration, however, we'll put it in the parent
directory.

The `<head>` element of the document contains a `<link>` tag for the CSS file and `<script>`
tags for jQuery, QUnit, the JavaScript we'll be testing (`A.js`), and the tests themselves
(`listings/A.*.js`). The `<body>` tag consists of two main elements for running and
displaying the results of the tests.

To demonstrate QUnit, we'll use portions of Chapter 2, *Selecting Elements*, and Chapter 6,
Sending Data with Ajax:

```html
<!DOCTYPE html>
<html>
<head>
  <meta charset="utf-8">
  <title>Appendix A Tests</title>
  <link rel="stylesheet" href="qunit.css" media="screen">
  <script src="jquery.js"></script>
  <script src="test/qunit.js"></script>
  <script src="A.js"></script>
  <script src="test/test.js"></script>
</head>
<body>
  <div id="qunit"></div>
  <div id="qunit-fixture">
    <!-- Test Markup Goes Here -->
  </div>
</body>
</html>
```

Since `Chapter 2`, *Selecting Elements*, code that we'll test depends on the DOM; we want the test markup to match what we're using on the actual page. We can simply copy and paste the HTML content that we used in `Chapter 2`, *Selecting Elements*, which should replace the `<!-- Test Markup Goes Here -->` comment.

Organizing tests

QUnit provides two levels of test grouping named after their respective function calls: `QUnit.module()` and `QUnit.test()`. The **module** is like a general category under which the tests will be run; the test is actually a *set* of tests; the function takes a callback in which all of that test's specific **unit tests** are run. We'll group our tests by the chapter topic and place the code in our `test/test.js` file:

```
QUnit.module('Selecting');

QUnit.test('Child Selector', (assert) => {
  assert.expect(0);
});

QUnit.test('Attribute Selectors', (assert) => {
  assert.expect(0);
});

QUnit.module('Ajax');
```

Listing A.1

It's not necessary to set up the file with this test structure, but it's good to have some overall structure in mind. In addition to the `QUnit.module()` and `QUnit.test()` grouping, we have to tell the test how many assertions to expect. Since we're just getting organized, we need to tell the test that there aren't any assertions yet (`assert.expect(0)`) in order for the tests to run.

Notice that our modules and tests do not need to be placed inside a $(() => {}) call because QUnit by default waits until the window has loaded before it begins running the tests. With this very simple setup, loading the test HTML results in a page that looks like this:

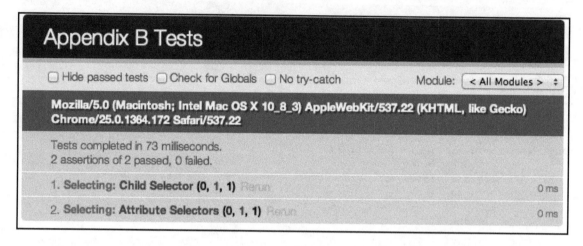

Note that the module name is light blue and the test name is darker blue. Clicking on either one will expand the results of that set of tests, which are collapsed by default when all the tests in the set pass. The Ajax module does not appear yet because we haven't written any tests for it.

Adding and running tests

In **test-driven development**, we write tests before writing code. This way, we can observe when a test fails, add new code, and then see that the test passes, verifying that our change has the intended effect.

Let's start by testing the child selector that we used in Chapter 2, *Selecting Elements*, to add a `horizontal` class to all `<li>` elements that are children of `<ul id="selected-plays">`:

```
QUnit.test('Child Selector', (assert) => {
  assert.expect(1);
  const topLis = $('#selected-plays > li.horizontal');
  assert.equal(topLis.length, 3, 'Top LIs have horizontal class');
});
```

Listing A.2

We're testing our ability to select elements on the page, so we use the assert `assert.equal()` test to compare the number of top-level `<li>` elements against the number 3. If the two are equal, the test is successful and is added to the number of passed tests. If not, the test fails:

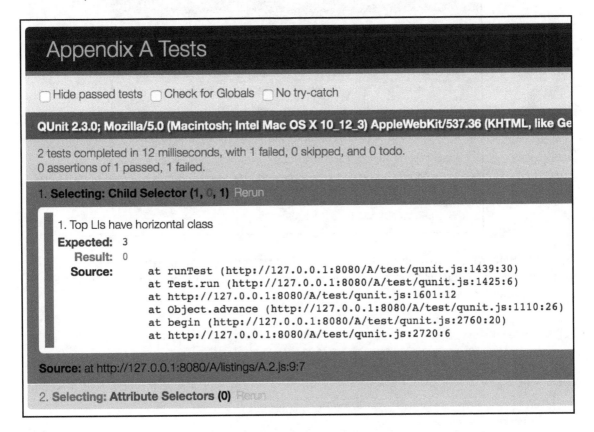

Of course, the test fails because we have not yet written the code to add the `horizontal` class. It is simple to add that code, though. We do so in the main script file for the page, which we called `A.js`:

```
$(() => {
  $('#selected-plays > li').addClass('horizontal');
});
```

Listing A.3

When we run the test now, the test passes as expected:

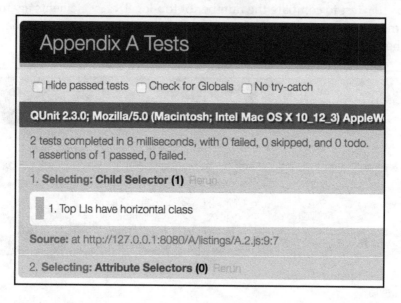

Now the **Selecting: Child Selector** test shows **1** in parentheses, indicating that the total number of tests is one. We can take the testing a step further now by adding a couple of attribute selector tests:

```javascript
QUnit.module('Selecting', {
  beforeEach() {
    this.topLis = $('#selected-plays > li.horizontal');
  }
});

QUnit.test('Child Selector', function(assert) {
  assert.expect(1);
  assert.equal(this.topLis.length, 3,
    'Top LIs have horizontal class');
});

QUnit.test('Attribute Selectors', function(assert) {
  assert.expect(2);
  assert.ok(this.topLis.find('.mailto').length == 1, 'a.mailto');
  assert.equal(this.topLis.find('.pdflink').length, 1, 'a.pdflink');
});
```

Listing A.4

Here we've introduced another type of test: ok(). This one takes two arguments: an expression that should evaluate to true if successful, and a description. Also note that we've moved the local topLis variable out of the **Child Selector** test, where it was in *Listing A.2*, and into the module's beforeEach() callback function. The QUnit.module() function takes an optional second argument, which is a plain object that can include a beforeEach() and an afterEach() function. Within these functions, we can use this as the shared context for all of a module's tests.

Again, the new tests will fail without corresponding working code:

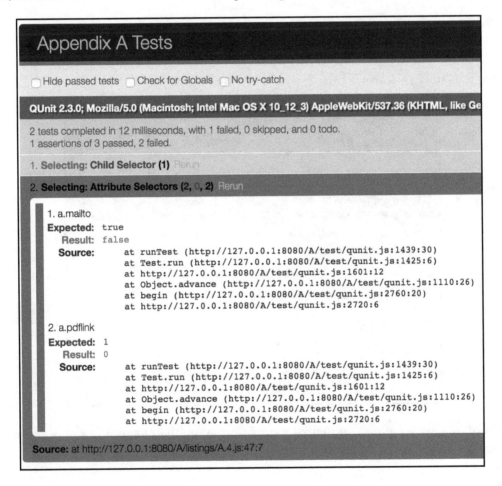

Here we can see the difference in test failure output between the `assert.ok()` test, which only shows the test's label (**a.mailto**) and source, and the `assert.equal()` test, which also details the expected result (instead of always expecting `true`). Because it provides more information for test failures, `assert.equal()` is typically preferred over `assert.ok()`.

Let's include the necessary code:

```
$(() => {
    $('#selected-plays > li').addClass('horizontal');
    $('a[href^="mailto:"]').addClass('mailto');
    $('a[href$=".pdf"]').addClass('pdflink');
});
```

Listing A.5

The two tests now pass, as we can see by expanding the set:

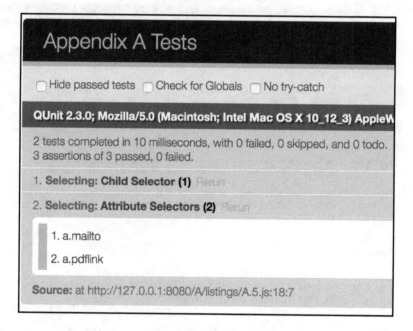

On failure, `assert.equal()` presented more information than `assert.ok()`. On success, both tests simply display the label.

Asynchronous testing

Testing asynchronous code such as Ajax requests presents an additional challenge. The rest of the tests must pause while the asynchronous test occurs, and then they must begin again when it is complete. This type of scenario is by now very familiar; we have seen such asynchronous operations in effects queues, Ajax callback functions, and promise objects. Asynchronous tests in QUnit are just like the regular QUnit.test() function except that it will pause the running of tests until we resume them with a call to a function created by assert.async() function:

```
QUnit.test('JSON', (assert) => {
  assert.expect(0);
  const done = assert.async();

  $.getJSON('A.json', (json, textStatus) => {
    // add tests here
  }).always(done);
});
```

Listing A.6

Here we're simply requesting JSON from a.json and allowing the tests to continue once the request has completed, whether it succeeds or fails, by calling done() inside the .always() callback function. For the actual tests, we're going to check the textStatus value to ensure that the request is successful and check the value of one of the objects within the response JSON array:

```
QUnit.test('JSON', (assert) => {
  const backbite = {
    term: 'BACKBITE',
    part: 'v.t.',
    definition: 'To speak of a man as you find him when he can't find you.'
  };

  assert.expect(2);
  const done = assert.async();

  $.getJSON('A.json', (json, textStatus) => {
    assert.equal(textStatus, 'success', 'Request successful');
    assert.deepEqual(
      json[1],
      backbite,
```

```
            'result array matches "backbite" map'
        );
    }).always(done);
});
```

Listing A.7

For testing the response value, we use yet another test function: `assert.deepEqual()`. Normally when two objects are compared, they are considered not equal unless they actually refer to the same location in memory. If we want to compare the object's contents instead, `assert.deepEqual()` should be used. This function walks through two objects to ensure that they have the same properties and that those properties have the same values.

Other types of tests

QUnit comes with a number of other test functions as well. Some, such as `notEqual()` and `notDeepEqual()`, are simply the inverses of functions we've used, while others, such as `strictEqual()` and `throws()`, have more distinct uses. More information about these functions, as well as details and additional examples regarding QUnit in general, are available on the QUnit website (`http://qunitjs.com/`) as well as the QUnit API site (`http://api.qunitjs.com/`).

Practical considerations

The examples in this appendix have been necessarily simple. In practice, we can write tests that ensure the correct operation of quite complicated behaviors.

Ideally, we keep our tests as brief and simple as possible, even when the behaviors they are testing are intricate. By writing tests for a few specific scenarios, we can be reasonably certain that we are fully testing the behavior, even though we do not have a test for every possible set of inputs.

However, it is possible that an error is observed in our code even though we have written tests for it. When tests pass and yet an error occurs, the correct response is not to immediately fix the problem, but rather to first write a new test for the behavior that fails. This way, we can not only verify that the problem is solved when we correct the code, but also introduce an additional test that will help us avoid regressions in the future.

QUnit can be used for **functional testing** in addition to **unit testing**. While unit tests are designed to confirm the correct operation of code units (methods and functions), functional tests are written to ensure appropriate interface responses to user input. For example, in `Chapter 12`, *Advanced DOM Manipulation*, we implemented a table-sorting behavior. We could write a unit test for a sorting method, verifying that once the method is called the table is sorted. Alternatively, a functional test could simulate a user's click on a table heading and then observe the result to check that the table is indeed sorted.

 Functional testing frameworks that work alongside QUnit, such as dominator.js (`http://mwbrooks.github.io/dominator.js/`) and FuncUnit (`http://funcunit.com/`), can help make writing functional tests and simulating events much easier. To further automate tests in a variety of browsers, the **Selenium** (`http://seleniumhq.org/`) suite can be used in conjunction with these frameworks.

To ensure consistent results for our tests, we need to work with sample data that is reliable and unchanging. When testing jQuery code that is applied to a dynamic site, it can be beneficial to capture and store a static version of the page to run tests against. This approach also isolates your code's components, making it easier to determine whether errors are caused by server-side or browser-side code.

Further reading

These considerations are certainly not an exhaustive list. Test-driven development is a deep topic, and a short appendix is not enough to cover it fully. Some online resources containing more information on the topic include:

- Introduction to unit testing (`http://qunitjs.com/intro/`)
- *QUnit Cookbook* (`http://qunitjs.com/cookbook/`)
- The *jQuery Test-Driven Development* article by Elijah Manor (`http://msdn.microsoft.com/en-us/scriptjunkie/ff452703.aspx`)
- The *Unit Testing Best Practices* article by Bob McCune (`http://www.bobmccune.com/2006/12/09/unit-testing-best-practices/`)

Many books on the topic also exist, such as:

- *Test Driven Development: By Example, Kent Beck*
- *The Addison Wesley Signature Series*
- *Test-Driven JavaScript Development, Christian Johansen, Addison Wesley.*

Summary

Writing tests with QUnit can be an effective aid in keeping our jQuery code clean and maintainable. We've seen just a few ways that we can implement tests in a project to ensure that our code is functioning the way we intend it to. By testing small, discrete units of code, we can mitigate some of the problems that occur when projects become more complex. At the same time, we can more efficiently test for regressions throughout a project, saving us valuable programming time.

B
Quick Reference

This appendix is intended to be a quick reference for the jQuery API, including its selector expressions and methods. A more detailed discussion of each method and selector is available on the jQuery documentation site, `http://api.jquery.com`.

Selector expressions

The jQuery factory function `$()` is used to find elements on the page to work with. This function takes a string composed of CSS-like syntax, called a selector expression. Selector expressions are discussed in detail in Chapter 2, *Selecting Elements*.

Simple CSS

Selector	Matches
`*`	All elements.
`#id`	The element with the given ID.
`element`	All elements of the given type.
`.class`	All elements with the given class.
`a, b`	Elements that are matched by a or b.
`a b`	Elements b that are descendants of a.
`a > b`	Elements b that are children of a.
`a + b`	Elements b that immediately follow a.

| a ~ b | Elements b that are siblings of a and follow a. |

Position among siblings

Selector	Matches
:nth-child(index)	Elements that are the index child of their parent element (1-based).
:nth-child(even)	Elements that are an even child of their parent element (1-based).
:nth-child(odd)	Elements that are an odd child of their parent element (1-based).
:nth-child(formula)	Elements that are the nth child of their parent element (1-based). Formulas are of the form an+b for integers a and b.
:nth-last-child()	The same as :nth-child(), but counting from the last element to the first.
:first-child	Elements that are the first child of their parent.
:last-child	Elements that are the last child of their parent.
:only-child	Elements that are the only child of their parent.
:nth-of-type()	The same as :nth-child(), but only counting elements of the same element name.
:nth-last-of-type()	The same as :nth-last-child(), but only counting elements of the same element name.
:first-of-type	Elements that are the first child of the same element name among their siblings.
:last-of-type	Elements that are the last child of the same element name among their siblings.
:only-of-type()	Elements that are the only child of the same element name among their siblings.

Position among matched elements

Selector	Matches
`:first`	The first element in the result set.
`:last`	The last element in the result set.
`:not(a)`	All elements in the result set that are not matched by a.
`:even`	Even elements in the result set (0-based).
`:odd`	Odd elements in the result set (0-based).
`:eq(index)`	A numbered element in the result set (0-based).
`:gt(index)`	All elements in the result set after (greater than) the given index (0-based).
`:lt(index)`	All elements in the result set before (less than) the given index (0-based).

Attributes

Selector	Matches
`[attr]`	Elements that have the attribute attr.
`[attr="value"]`	Elements whose attr attribute is value.
`[attr!="value"]`	Elements whose attr attribute is not value.
`[attr^="value"]`	Elements whose attr attribute begins with value.
`[attr$="value"]`	Elements whose attr attribute ends with value.
`[attr*="value"]`	Elements whose attr attribute contains the substring value.
`[attr~="value"]`	Elements whose attr attribute is a space-delimited set of strings, one of which is value.
`[attr|="value"]`	Elements whose attr attributes is either equal to value or begins with value followed by a hyphen.

Forms

Selector	Matches
:input	All `<input>`, `<select>`, `<textarea>`, and `<button>` elements.
:text	The `<input>` elements with `type="text"`.
:password	The `<input>` elements with `type="password"`.
:file	The `<input>` elements with `type="file"`.
:radio	The `<input>` elements with `type="radio"`.
:checkbox	The `<input>` elements with `type="checkbox"`.
:submit	The `<input>` elements with `type="submit"`.
:image	The `<input>` elements with `type="image"`.
:reset	The `<input>` elements with `type="reset"`.
:button	The `<input>` elements with `type="button"` and `<button>` elements.
:enabled	Enabled form elements.
:disabled	Disabled form elements.
:checked	Checked checkboxes and radio buttons.
:selected	Selected `<option>` elements.

Miscellaneous selectors

Selector	Matches
:root	The root element of the document.
:header	Header elements (for example, `<h1>`, `<h2>`).
:animated	Elements with an animation in progress.
:contains(text)	Elements containing the given text.
:empty	Elements with no child nodes.
:has(a)	Elements containing a descendant element matching a.
:parent	Elements that have child nodes.

`:hidden`	Elements that are hidden, either through CSS or because they are `<input type="hidden" />`.
`:visible`	The inverse of `:hidden`.
`:focus`	The element that has the keyboard focus.
`:lang(language)`	Elements with the given language code (either due to a `lang` attribute on the element or an ancestor, or a `<meta>` declaration).
`:target`	Whichever element is targeted by the URI's fragment identifier, if any.

DOM traversal methods

After creating a jQuery object using `$()`, we can alter the set of matched elements we are working with by calling one of these DOM traversal methods. DOM traversal methods are discussed in detail in `Chapter 2`, *Selecting Elements*.

Filtering

Traversal method	Returns a jQuery object containing...
`.filter(selector)`	Selected elements that match the given selector.
`.filter(callback)`	Selected elements for which the callback function returns `true`.
`.eq(index)`	The selected element at the given 0-based index.
`.first()`	The first selected element.
`.last()`	The final selected element.
`.slice(start, [end])`	Selected elements in the given range of 0-based indices.
`.not(selector)`	Selected elements that do not match the given selector.
`.has(selector)`	Selected elements that have a descendant matching `selector`.

Descendants

Traversal method	Returns a jQuery object containing...
`.find(selector)`	Descendant elements that match the selector.
`.contents()`	Child nodes (including text nodes).
`.children([selector])`	Child nodes, optionally filtered by a selector.

Siblings

Traversal method	Returns a jQuery object containing...
`.next([selector])`	The sibling immediately following each selected element, optionally filtered by a selector.
`.nextAll([selector])`	All siblings following each selected element, optionally filtered by a selector.
`.nextUntil([selector], [filter])`	All siblings following each selected element up to and not including the first element matching `selector`, optionally filtered by an additional selector.
`.prev([selector])`	The sibling immediately preceding each selected element, optionally filtered by a selector.
`.prevAll([selector])`	All siblings preceding each selected element, optionally filtered by a selector.
`.prevUntil([selector], [filter])`	All siblings preceding each selected element up to and not including the first element matching `selector`, optionally filtered by an additional selector.
`.siblings([selector])`	All siblings, optionally filtered by a selector.

Ancestors

Traversal method	Returns a jQuery object containing...
`.parent([selector])`	The parent of each selected element, optionally filtered by a selector.
`.parents([selector])`	All ancestors, optionally filtered by a selector.
`.parentsUntil([selector], [filter])`	All ancestors of each selected element up to and not including the first element matching `selector`, optionally filtered by an additional selector.
`.closest(selector)`	The first element that matches the selector, starting at the selected element and moving up through its ancestors in the DOM tree.
`.offsetParent()`	The positioned parent, either relative or absolute, of the first selected element.

Collection manipulation

Traversal method	Returns a jQuery object containing...
`.add(selector)`	The selected elements, plus any additional elements that match the given selector.
`.addBack()`	The selected elements, plus the previous set of selected elements on the internal jQuery stack.
`.end()`	The previous set of selected elements on the internal jQuery stack.
`.map(callback)`	The result of the callback function when called on each selected element.
`.pushStack(elements)`	The specified elements.

Working with selected elements

Traversal method	Description
`.is(selector)`	Determines whether any matched element is matched by the given selector expression.
`.index()`	Gets the index of the matched element in relation to its siblings.
`.index(element)`	Gets the index of the given DOM node within the set of matched elements.
`$.contains(a, b)`	Determines whether DOM node b contains DOM node a.
`.each(callback)`	Iterates over the matched elements, executing `callback` for each element.
`.length`	Gets the number of matched elements.
`.get()`	Gets an array of DOM nodes corresponding to the matched elements.
`.get(index)`	Gets the DOM node corresponding to the matched element at the given index.
`.toArray()`	Gets an array of DOM nodes corresponding to the matched elements.

Event methods

To react to user behavior, we need to register our handlers using these event methods. Note that many DOM events only apply to certain element types; these subtleties are not covered here. Event methods are discussed in detail in Chapter 3, *Handling Events*.

Binding

Event method	Description
`.ready(handler)`	Binds `handler` to be called when the DOM and CSS are fully loaded.

Event method	Description
`.on(type, [selector], [data], handler)`	Binds `handler` to be called when the given type of event is sent to the element. If `selector` is provided, performs event delegation.
`.on(events, [selector], [data])`	Binds multiple handlers for events as specified in the `events` object parameter.
`.off(type, [selector], [handler])`	Removes bindings on the element.
`.one(type, [data], handler)`	Binds `handler` to be called when the given type of event is sent to the element. Removes the binding when the handler is called.

Shorthand binding

Event method	Description
`.blur(handler)`	Binds `handler` to be called when the element loses keyboard focus.
`.change(handler)`	Binds `handler` to be called when the element's value changes.
`.click(handler)`	Binds `handler` to be called when the element is clicked.
`.dblclick(handler)`	Binds `handler` to be called when the element is double-clicked.
`.focus(handler)`	Binds `handler` to be called when the element gains keyboard focus.
`.focusin(handler)`	Binds `handler` to be called when the element, or a descendant, gains keyboard focus.
`.focusout(handler)`	Binds `handler` to be called when the element, or a descendant, loses keyboard focus.
`.keydown(handler)`	Binds `handler` to be called when a key is pressed and the element has keyboard focus.
`.keypress(handler)`	Binds `handler` to be called when a keystroke occurs and the element has keyboard focus.

Event method	Description
.keyup(handler)	Binds handler to be called when a key is released and the element has keyboard focus.
.mousedown(handler)	Binds handler to be called when the mouse button is pressed within the element.
.mouseenter(handler)	Binds handler to be called when the mouse pointer enters the element. Not affected by event bubbling.
.mouseleave(handler)	Binds handler to be called when the mouse pointer leaves the element. Not affected by event bubbling.
.mousemove(handler)	Binds handler to be called when the mouse pointer moves within the element.
.mouseout(handler)	Binds handler to be called when the mouse pointer leaves the element.
.mouseover(handler)	Binds handler to be called when the mouse pointer enters the element.
.mouseup(handler)	Binds handler to be called when the mouse button is released within the element.
.resize(handler)	Binds handler to be called when the element is resized.
.scroll(handler)	Binds handler to be called when the element's scroll position changes.
.select(handler)	Binds handler to be called when text in the element is selected.
.submit(handler)	Binds handler to be called when the form element is submitted.
.hover(enter, leave)	Binds enter to be called when the mouse enters the element, and leave to be called when the mouse leaves it.

Triggering

Event method	Description
.trigger(type, [data])	Triggers handlers for the event on the element and executes the default action for the event.
.triggerHandler(type, [data])	Triggers handlers for the event on the element without executing any default actions.

Shorthand triggering

Event method	Description
.blur()	Triggers the blur event.
.change()	Triggers the change event.
.click()	Triggers the click event.
.dblclick()	Triggers the dblclick event.
.error()	Triggers the error event.
.focus()	Triggers the focus event.
.keydown()	Triggers the keydown event.
.keypress()	Triggers the keypress event.
.keyup()	Triggers the keyup event.
.select()	Triggers the select event.
.submit()	Triggers the submit event.

Utility

Event method	Description
$.proxy(fn, context)	Creates a new function that executes with the given context.

Effect methods

These effect methods may be used to perform animations on DOM elements. The effect methods are discussed in detail in `Chapter 4`, *Styling and Animating*.

Predefined effects

Effect method	Description
`.show()`	Displays the matched elements.
`.hide()`	Hides the matched elements.
`.show(speed, [callback])`	Displays the matched elements by animating `height`, `width`, and `opacity`.
`.hide(speed, [callback])`	Hides the matched elements by animating `height`, `width`, and `opacity`.
`.slideDown([speed], [callback])`	Displays the matched elements with a sliding motion.
`.slideUp([speed], [callback])`	Hides the matched elements with a sliding motion.
`.slideToggle([speed], [callback])`	Displays or hides the matched elements with a sliding motion.
`.fadeIn([speed], [callback])`	Displays the matched elements by fading them to opaque.
`.fadeOut([speed], [callback])`	Hides the matched elements by fading them to transparent.
`.fadeToggle([speed], [callback])`	Displays or hides the matched elements with a fading animation.
`.fadeTo(speed, opacity, [callback])`	Adjusts the opacity of the matched elements.

Custom animations

Effect method	Description
.animate(properties, [speed], [easing], [callback])	Performs a custom animation of the specified CSS properties.
.animate(properties, options)	A lower-level interface to .animate(), allowing control over the animation queue.

Queue manipulation

Effect method	Description
.queue([queueName])	Retrieves the queue of functions on the first matched element.
.queue([queueName], callback)	Adds callback to the end of the queue.
.queue([queueName], newQueue)	Replaces the queue with a new one.
.dequeue([queueName])	Executes the next function on the queue.
.clearQueue([queueName])	Empties the queue of all pending functions.
.stop([clearQueue], [jumpToEnd])	Stops the currently running animation, then starts queued animations, if any.
.finish([queueName])	Stops the currently running animation and immediately advances all queued animations to their target values.
.delay(duration, [queueName])	Waits duration milliseconds before executing the next item in the queue.
.promise([queueName], [target])	Returns a promise object to be resolved once all queued actions on the collection have finished.

DOM manipulation methods

The DOM manipulation methods are discussed in detail in Chapter 5, *Manipulating the DOM*.

Attributes and properties

Manipulation method	Description
.attr(key)	Gets the attribute named key.
.attr(key, value)	Sets the attribute named key to value.
.attr(key, fn)	Sets the attribute named key to the result of fn (called separately on each matched element).
.attr(obj)	Sets attribute values given as key-value pairs.
.removeAttr(key)	Removes the attribute named key.
.prop(key)	Gets the property named key.
.prop(key, value)	Sets the property named key to value.
.prop(key, fn)	Sets the property named key to the result of fn (called separately on each matched element).
.prop(obj)	Sets property values given as key-value pairs.
.removeProp(key)	Removes the property named key.
.addClass(class)	Adds the given class to each matched element.
.removeClass(class)	Removes the given class from each matched element.
.toggleClass(class)	Removes the given class if present, and adds it if not, for each matched element.
.hasClass(class)	Returns true if any of the matched elements has the given class.
.val()	Gets the value attribute of the first matched element.
.val(value)	Sets the value attribute of each element to value.

Content

Manipulation method	Description
`.html()`	Gets the HTML content of the first matched element.
`.html(value)`	Sets the HTML content of each matched element to value.
`.text()`	Gets the textual content of all matched elements as a single string.
`.text(value)`	Sets the textual content of each matched element to `value`.

CSS

Manipulation method	Description
`.css(key)`	Gets the CSS attribute named `key`.
`.css(key, value)`	Sets the CSS attribute named `key` to `value`.
`.css(obj)`	Sets CSS attribute values given as key-value pairs.

Dimensions

Manipulation method	Description
`.offset()`	Gets the top and left pixel coordinates of the first matched element, relative to the viewport.
`.position()`	Gets the top and left pixel coordinates of the first matched element, relative to the element returned by `.offsetParent()`.
`.scrollTop()`	Gets the vertical scroll position of the first matched element.
`.scrollTop(value)`	Sets the vertical scroll position of all matched elements to `value`.
`.scrollLeft()`	Gets the horizontal scroll position of the first matched element.
`.scrollLeft(value)`	Sets the horizontal scroll position of all matched elements to `value`.

`.height()`	Gets the height of the first matched element.
`.height(value)`	Sets the height of all matched elements to `value`.
`.width()`	Gets the width of the first matched element.
`.width(value)`	Sets the width of all matched elements to `value`.
`.innerHeight()`	Gets the height of the first matched element, including padding, but not border.
`.innerWidth()`	Gets the width of the first matched element, including padding, but not border.
`.outerHeight(includeMargin)`	Gets the height of the first matched element, including padding, border, and optional margin.
`.outerWidth(includeMargin)`	Gets the width of the first matched element, including padding, border, and optional margin.

Insertion

Manipulation method	Description
`.append(content)`	Inserts `content` at the end of the interior of each matched element.
`.appendTo(selector)`	Inserts the matched elements at the end of the interior of the elements matched by `selector`.
`.prepend(content)`	Inserts `content` at the beginning of the interior of each matched element.
`.prependTo(selector)`	Inserts the matched elements at the beginning of the interior of the elements matched by `selector`.
`.after(content)`	Inserts `content` after each matched element.
`.insertAfter(selector)`	Inserts the matched elements after each of the elements matched by `selector`.
`.before(content)`	Inserts `content` before each matched element.
`.insertBefore(selector)`	Inserts the matched elements before each of the elements matched by `selector`.
`.wrap(content)`	Wraps each of the matched elements within `content`.

Manipulation method	Description
`.wrapAll(content)`	Wraps all of the matched elements as a single unit within `content`.
`.wrapInner(content)`	Wraps the interior contents of each of the matched elements within `content`.

Replacement

Manipulation method	Description
`.replaceWith(content)`	Replaces the matched elements with `content`.
`.replaceAll(selector)`	Replaces the elements matched by `selector` with the matched elements.

Removal

Manipulation method	Description
`.empty()`	Removes the child nodes of each matched element.
`.remove([selector])`	Removes the matched nodes (optionally filtered by `selector`) from the DOM.
`.detach([selector])`	Removes the matched nodes (optionally filtered by `selector`) from the DOM, preserving jQuery data attached to them.
`.unwrap()`	Removes the element's parent.

Copying

Manipulation method	Description
`.clone([withHandlers], [deepWithHandlers])`	Makes a copy of all matched elements, optionally also copying event handlers.

Data

Manipulation method	Description
`.data(key)`	Gets the data item named `key` associated with the first matched element.
`.data(key, value)`	Sets the data item named `key` associated with each matched element to `value`.
`.removeData(key)`	Removes the data item named `key` associated with each matched element.

Ajax methods

We can retrieve information from the server without requiring a page refresh by calling one of these Ajax methods. Ajax methods are discussed in detail in `Chapter 6`, *Sending Data with Ajax*.

Issuing requests

Ajax method	Description
`$.ajax([url], options)`	Makes an Ajax request using the provided set of options. This is a low-level method that is often called via other convenience methods.
`.load(url, [data], [callback])`	Makes an Ajax request to `url` and places the response into the matched elements.
`$.get(url, [data], [callback], [returnType])`	Makes an Ajax request to `url` using the `GET` method.
`$.getJSON(url, [data], [callback])`	Makes an Ajax request to `url`, interpreting the response as a JSON data structure.
`$.getScript(url, [callback])`	Makes an Ajax request to `url`, executing the response as JavaScript.
`$.post(url, [data], [callback], [returnType])`	Makes an Ajax request to `url` using the `POST` method.

Request monitoring

Ajax method	Description
`.ajaxComplete(handler)`	Binds `handler` to be called when any Ajax transaction completes.
`.ajaxError(handler)`	Binds `handler` to be called when any Ajax transaction completes with an error.
`.ajaxSend(handler)`	Binds `handler` to be called when any Ajax transaction begins.
`.ajaxStart(handler)`	Binds `handler` to be called when any Ajax transaction begins, and no others are active.
`.ajaxStop(handler)`	Binds `handler` to be called when any Ajax transaction ends, and no others are still active.
`.ajaxSuccess(handler)`	Binds `handler` to be called when any Ajax transaction completes successfully.

Configuration

Ajax method	Description
`$.ajaxSetup(options)`	Sets default options for all subsequent Ajax transactions.
`$.ajaxPrefilter([dataTypes], handler)`	Modifies the options on each Ajax request before it is processed by `$.ajax()`.
`$.ajaxTransport(transportFunction)`	Defines a new transport mechanism for Ajax transactions.

Utilities

Ajax method	Description
`.serialize()`	Encodes the values of a set of form controls into a query string.
`.serializeArray()`	Encodes the values of a set of form controls into a JavaScript data structure.

`$.param(obj)`	Encodes an arbitrary object of key-value pairs into a query string.
`$.globalEval(code)`	Evaluates the given JavaScript string in the global context.
`$.parseJSON(json)`	Converts the given JSON string into a JavaScript object.
`$.parseXML(xml)`	Converts the given XML string into an XML document.
`$.parseHTML(html)`	Converts the given HTML string into a set of DOM elements.

Deferred objects

Deferred objects and their promises allow us to react to the completion of long-running tasks with a convenient syntax. They are discussed in detail in `Chapter 11`, *Advanced Effects*.

Object creation

Function	Description
`$.Deferred([setupFunction])`	Returns a new deferred object.
`$.when(deferreds)`	Returns a promise object to be resolved when the given deferred objects are resolved.

Methods of deferred objects

Method	Description
`.resolve([args])`	Sets the state of the object to resolved.
`.resolveWith(context, [args])`	Sets the state of the object to resolved while making the keyword `this` refer to `context` within callbacks.
`.reject([args])`	Sets the state of the object to rejected.
`.rejectWith(context, [args])`	Sets the state of the object to rejected while making the keyword `this` refer to `context` within callbacks.
`.notify([args])`	Executes any progress callbacks.

Method	Description
`.notifyWith(context, [args])`	Executes any progress callbacks while making the keyword `this` refer to `context`.
`.promise([target])`	Returns a promise object corresponding to this deferred object.

Methods of promise objects

Method	Description
`.done(callback)`	Executes `callback` when the object is resolved.
`.fail(callback)`	Executes `callback` when the object is rejected.
`.catch(callback)`	Executes `callback` when the object is rejected.
`.always(callback)`	Executes `callback` when the object is resolved or rejected.
`.then(doneCallbacks, failCallbacks)`	Executes `doneCallbacks` when the object is resolved, or `failCallbacks` when the object is rejected.
`.progress(callback)`	Executes `callback` each time the object receives a progress notification.
`.state()`	Returns `'pending'`, `'resolved'`, or `'rejected'` depending on the current state.

Miscellaneous properties and functions

These utility methods do not fit neatly into the previous categories, but are often very useful when writing scripts using jQuery.

Properties of the jQuery object

Property	Description
`$.ready`	A promise instance that's resolved as soon as the DOM is ready.

Arrays and objects

Function	Description
`$.each(collection, callback)`	Iterates over `collection`, executing `callback` for each item.
`$.extend(target, addition, ...)`	Modifies the object `target` by adding properties from the other supplied objects.
`$.grep(array, callback, [invert])`	Filters `array` by using `callback` as a test.
`$.makeArray(object)`	Converts `object` into an array.
`$.map(array, callback)`	Constructs a new array consisting of the result of `callback` being called on each item.
`$.inArray(value, array)`	Determines whether `value` is in `array`.
`$.merge(array1, array2)`	Combines the contents of `array1` and `array2`.
`$.unique(array)`	Removes any duplicate DOM elements from `array`.

Object introspection

Function	Description
`$.isArray(object)`	Determines whether `object` is a true JavaScript array.
`$.isEmptyObject(object)`	Determines whether `object` is empty.
`$.isFunction(object)`	Determines whether `object` is a function.
`$.isPlainObject(object)`	Determines whether `object` was created as an object literal or with `new Object`.
`$.isNumeric(object)`	Determines whether `object` is a numeric scalar value.
`$.isWindow(object)`	Determines whether `object` represents a browser window.
`$.isXMLDoc(object)`	Determines whether `object` is an XML node.
`$.type(object)`	Gets the JavaScript class of `object`.

Other

Function	Description
`$.trim(string)`	Removes whitespace from the ends of `string`.
`$.noConflict([removeAll])`	Reverts $ to its pre-jQuery definition.
`$.noop()`	A function that does nothing.
`$.now()`	The current time in milliseconds since the epoch.
`$.holdReady(hold)`	Stops the `ready` event from being triggered, or releases this hold.

Index

Q

queued effects
  manually applying 116, 117
  overview 123
  queue, bypassing 116
  queuing, with callbacks 121, 122
  single set of elements, working with 114
  versus simultaneous effects 114
quick sort 335
QUnit API site
  reference 392
QUnit
  about 383
  download link 384
  downloading 384
  reference 392, 393

R

refactoring 66
Resizable component 204
response codes
  reference 185

S

Safari Web Development Tools
  reference 21
selector expressions
  about 265, 395
  attributes 397
  forms 398
  miscellaneous selectors 398
  position, among matched elements 397
  position, among siblings 396
  simple CSS 395
selector methods
  about 264
  reference 264
selector specificity 34, 36
selector speed
  testing 269
selectors 256
selectors method
  reference 280
selectors, building blocks

class 30
ID 30
tag name 30
selectors
  customizing 265
  performance 267
Selenium
  reference 393
setter method 149
shorthand events 69
simple events
  handling 59
simple style switcher 59
simultaneous effects
  multiple sets of elements, working with 118, 120
  overview 123
  single set of elements, working with 114
  versus queued effects 114
Sizzle 255
Sizzle selector
  implementation 268
Slider widget 207
sort directions
  alternating 341, 343
  ascending 341
  descending 341
special events 300, 303
synchronous 160

T

table rows
  sorting 327
  striping 260
tables
  data, sorting on server 328
  filtering 257, 259, 262
  sorting, with Ajax 329
  sorting, within browser 329
  striping 262
tasks, performing on page load
  about 55
  argument, passing to document ready callback 58
  multiple scripts, handling on single page 57
  timing, of code execution 56